ARDEN SHAKESPEARES
edited by Kenneth Muir

Macbeth

King Lear

Shakespeare's Sources

I

COMEDIES AND TRAGEDIES

Shakespeare's Sources

{I}

COMEDIES AND
TRAGEDIES

Kenneth Muir

*King Alfred Professor of English Literature
in the University of Liverpool*

METHUEN & CO LTD
36 Essex Street, Strand, London WC2

First published 1957

PR
2952
.m8
v l
c l

38,766
Jan. 1960

CATALOGUE NO 5953/U

PRINTED IN GREAT BRITAIN BY
RICHARD CLAY AND COMPANY, LTD
BUNGAY, SUFFOLK

PREFACE

Professor Allardyce Nicoll in his British Academy Lecture (1952) remarks that although most critics in the present century believe that we cannot profitably continue to explore Shakespeare's sources,

> yet one or two very recently published studies have made it amply apparent that the essential task—the imaginative consideration of Shakespeare's creative genius in the light of these sources—is still largely waiting to be done.

Indeed, in spite of the over-production of books on different aspects of Shakespeare's life and work, there has never been, so far as I can discover, a book devoted to his use of sources. Editors of individual plays have, of course, considered the relevant sources, and even printed some of them; and Professor Geoffrey Bullough is now engaged on the valuable task of editing the main sources. But there would seem to be room for an attempt to survey the subject as a whole, especially as several books and hundreds of articles devoted to major and minor aspects of the subject have been published during the present century. Professor Prouty's book on *Much Ado about Nothing*, Miss Mary Lascelles' on *Measure for Measure*, Professor R. K. Presson's on *Troilus and Cressida*, and Mr H. N. Paul's on *Macbeth* have all shown in different ways that detailed studies of the sources of individual plays may contribute to our understanding of Shakespeare as a dramatist. But until someone has surveyed the whole field our knowledge must remain fragmentary, and our conclusions tentative.

I have waited for some twenty-five years in the hope that some critic with the requisite learning would undertake the task. Great learning is rarely combined with great critical powers, and both the learned and the critics have hung back from so daunting a task. Now, in spite of my 'small Latin and less Greek', I have stepped in to do it myself. I shall be content if the inadequacies of the present attempt act as a spur to some other scholar to replace it with a better.

vii

I hope in a second volume to discuss the Histories and also the influence of particular books and authors on Shakespeare. I shall reserve my conclusions for the second volume, providing in the present one only a brief summary.

I have attempted to discuss here the sources of all the comedies and tragedies, where these are extant. Seven plays, for the plots of which no immediate source has been discovered, are relegated to an appendix. It might have been more logical to have treated *Much Ado about Nothing* and *Hamlet* in the same way, though the reader will appreciate the advantages of dealing with them in the text. *The Comedy of Errors* is discussed in the first chapter as it was necessary to give an example of method. The remaining plays are grouped into chapters, again for convenience, not because the sources are of a similar kind.

I am indebted to many scholars who, hearing that I was engaged on this book, have generously placed unpublished material at my disposal—notably to Professor J. Dover Wilson, Dr Harold Brooks, Mr J. C. Maxwell, Mr J. M. Nosworthy, Mr Ernest Schanzer, Mr Ernst Honigmann, and Mr R. A. Foakes. I am likewise indebted to unpublished theses in the Library of the University of Liverpool, two of which, by Miss Martha Mulligan and Miss Oonah O'Connor, were written under my supervision. It will be apparent that I have profited from the volumes in the new Arden and new Cambridge editions. Finally, I have been able to draw on the patience and learning of many colleagues, especially Mr K. Allott, Mr A. Davenport, Miss I-S. Ekeblad Dr R. G. Faithfull, Mr Frederick May, and Professor F. W. Walbank.

Acknowledgements are due to the editors of *The Review of English Studies*, *Shakespeare Quarterly*, *Notes and Queries*, *English Studies*, and *English Miscellany* for permission to make use of articles and notes which appeared in their pages. I have drawn also on my introductions to *King Lear*, *Macbeth*, and *The Painfull Aduentures of Pericles*. All this material has, however, been revised, and on a number of points I have changed my mind.

KENNETH MUIR

University of Liverpool,
May 1956

CONTENTS

A question arose of what is the difference between active and static thought.

'Static thought', said Whitehead, 'is knowing exactly where Shakespeare bagged all his plots, and identifying all his borrowings from Plutarch and Holinshed.'

Anxious glances swept round toward Professor Livingston Lowes, as Whitehead had humorously intended they should.

LUCIEN PRICE *Dialogues of*
Arthur North Whitehead (1954)

Shakespeare lui-même, tout grossier qu'il était, n'était pas sans lecture et sans connaissance.

JEAN-FRANCOIS DE LA HARPE
Cours de littérature (1799)

{ I }

INTRODUCTION

THE purpose of this book is, first, to ascertain what sources
Shakespeare used for the plots of his plays; secondly, to
analyse the use he made of them; and, thirdly, to give illustrations, necessarily selective, of the way in which his general
reading is woven into the texture of his work. I have not attempted
to provide an up-to-date version of Anders's *Shakespeare's Books*,
though a revision of that work would be extremely useful.

It is necessary at the outset to say something of the amount of
Shakespeare's learning. Professor T. W. Baldwin in his monu-
mental volumes[1] has given us a clear idea of the kind of education
Shakespeare would have followed at a petty school and a grammar
school. There is no real reason to doubt that he attended both, as
he somewhere acquired the equivalent knowledge, but it is possible that because of the financial crisis in his father's fortunes he
did not complete the full curriculum. He acquired a reasonable
knowledge of Latin, and perhaps a slight knowledge of Greek.

The extent of Shakespeare's classical learning is nevertheless
still a matter of dispute. Some believe that Jonson's 'small Latin
and less Greek' should be taken to mean 'hardly any Latin and no
Greek'.[2] Others think that though Shakespeare had little or no
Greek, he understood Latin 'pretty well', and that his knowledge
of the language was small only in comparison with Jonson's.[3]
Those who adhere to the former view point out that many of the
parallels with Latin literature, which have been collected by
numerous critics, may well be fortuitous; that Golding's translation of Ovid is so bad—in spite of Ezra Pound's belief that it is
superior to *Paradise Lost*—that a good Latin scholar would not
have tolerated it;[4] that Shakespeare's actual quotations from Latin

[1] *Shakespere's Petty School; Shakespere's Small Latine and Lesse Greeke; Shakespere's Five-Act Structure; The Literary Genetics of Shakespere's Poems and Sonnets.*
[2] J. A. K. Thomson, *Shakespeare and the Classics* (1952); J. Dover Wilson in a lecture delivered at Stratford-upon-Avon, 1955; F. P. Wilson, *Shakespeare Survey 3* (1950), pp. 14–21.
[3] Edgar I. Fripp, *Shakespeare Man and Artist* (1938), p. 114.
[4] J. Dover Wilson, op. cit.

I

authors are mostly in early plays—*Henry VI* and *Titus Andronicus* —of which he may not have been the sole author, or of passages so familiar that he could have acquired them as general knowledge; that he makes a number of blunders about classical mythology;[1] that his spelling 'triumpherate' suggests that he was ignorant of the derivation of 'triumvir';[2] and that he is guilty of shocking anachronisms. None of these arguments has much substance. It is perfectly true that many of the alleged parallels between Shakespeare's works and classical literature are unconvincing. Mr Percy Simpson's interesting list of parallels contains hardly a single one which is beyond dispute;[3] he does not distinguish between works which were available in translation and those which were not; and in some cases he has ignored sources more easily accessible than those he suggests. For the plot of *Pericles*, for example, it is unnecessary to go to Latin comedy, since it is known that Shakespeare, if indeed he did not rewrite an earlier English play, made use of Gower and Twine. Professor J. A. K. Thomson is probably right in thinking that the parallel between Helena's speech in *A Midsummer-Night's Dream* (I. i. 234 ff.) and Propertius (II. 12. 1–8) is a coincidence.[4] He may also be right to be sceptical of Professor Baldwin's theory that Shakespeare found in the notes to Mantuan a quotation from Persius—

> nunc non e tumulo fortunataque favilla
> nascentur violae?—

and that he echoed it in Laertes' words:

> laye her i' th' earth,
> And from her faire and vnpolluted flesh,
> May Violets spring.

Professor Thomson may even be justified in refusing to believe that Shylock is echoing Horace when he says to Jessica:

> when you heare the drum
> And the vile squealing of the wry-neckte Fife,
> Clamber not you vp to the casements then,
> Nor thrust your head into the publique streete.

Horace similarly instructs a girl:

> prima nocte domum claude neque in vias
> sub cantu querulae despice tibiae.

[1] J. Dover Wilson, op. cit.   [2] ibid.
[3] Percy Simpson, *Studies in Elizabethan Drama* (1955), pp. 13 ff.
[4] J. A. K. Thomson, op. cit., pp. 32–3.

Professor Thomson is perhaps too sceptical of another Horatian echo. The French King in *Henry V* bids his nobles

> Rush on his Hoast, as doth the melted Snow
> Vpon the Valleyes, whose low Vassall Seat,
> The Alpes doth spit, and void his rhewme vpon.

Compare the line from one of Horace's *Satires* (II. 5):

> Furius hibernas cana nive conspuit Alpes.

The parallel is very close; and when we remember that Shakespeare, perhaps unconsciously, alludes to one of Horace's odes and one of his epistles in a single scene of *King Lear*, it seems more than probable that he was echoing Horace in the earlier play.

Golding's translation of Ovid's *Metamorphoses* is read today largely because it is known to have been a favourite of Shakespeare's, but we cannot deduce from its clumsiness that he could read Latin only with difficulty. There are classical scholars today who read translations as well as the originals, and those who use the Loeb edition do not always disdain the use of the right-hand page. Shakespeare read some Ovid in the original at school, and a copy of the *Metamorphoses* bearing his signature is still in existence. Even at the end of his career, when he wrote *The Tempest*, he remembered enough Latin to improve on the accuracy of Golding's translation. The following is part of Medea's invocation:

> Auraeque et venti, montesque, amnesque, lacusque,
> Dique omnes nemorum, dique omnes noctis, adeste.
> Quorum ope, quum volui, ripis mirantibus amnes
> In fontes rediere suos; concussaque sisto,
> Stantia concutio cantu freta; nubila pello
> Nubilaque induco; ventos abigoque, vocoque;
> Vipereas rumpo verbis et carmine fauces;
> Vivaque saxa, sua convulsaque robora terra,
> Et silvas moveo; jubeoque tremiscere montes;
> Et mugire solum, manesque exire sepulchris;
> Te quoque, Luna, traho; quamvis Temesaea labores
> Aera tuos minuant;

This is Golding's translation:

Ye Ayres and Windes; ye Elues of Hills, of Brookes, of Woods alone,
Of standing Lakes, and of the Night approche ye euerychone.

Through helpe of whom (the crooked bankes much wondring at
    the thing)
I haue compelled streames to run cleane backward to their spring.
By charmes I make the calme Seas rough and make the rough Seas
    playne,
And couer all the Skie with Cloudes and chase them thence
    againe.
By charmes I rayse and lay the windes, and burst the Vipers iaw,
And from the bowels of the Earth both stones and trees doe
    drawe.
Whole woods and Forestes I remoue: I make the Mountaines
    shake,
And euen the Earth it selfe to grone and fearfully to quake.
I call vp dead men from their graues: and thee, O lightsome
    Moone
I darken oft, though beaten brasse abate thy perill soone,
Our Sorcerie dimmes the Morning faire, and darkes the Sun at
    Noone.

There is no doubt that Shakespeare made use of Golding in Prospero's farewell to his art. In the opening words,

        Ye Elues of hils, brooks, standing lakes

he borrows Golding's exact words. But it is equally certain that he
knew the original Latin. Ovid uses the phrase 'ventos abigoque,
vocoque'; Golding paraphrases 'I rayse and lay the windes';
Shakespeare has 'call'd forth the mutenous windes'. In the phrase
'at my command' he comes closer than Golding to *jubeo*. Most
striking of all is his version of the lines:

        Vivaque saxa, sua convulsaque robora terra,
        Et silvas moveo.

Shakespeare has 'Ioves stowt Oke' and 'by the spurs pluckt
vp/The Pyne and Cedar'. 'Pluck'd up' conveys, more faithfully
than Golding's version, the sense of *convulsa*; and 'Jove's stout
oak' not merely specifies (as Golding does not) the kind of tree,
but by the epithet *stout* neatly alludes to the alternative meaning of
robora.[1]

    Shakespeare, then, used translations where they were available;
but he did not use them slavishly, and there is plenty of evidence
that he read Latin works of which there was no translation—two
plays by Plautus, Buchanan, Leslie, some of Livy, and (if we are to

[1] Cf. E. I. Fripp, op. cit., pp. 109–10.

believe Mr E. Honigmann) two manuscript chronicles about King John. He knew some Virgil in the original, though he could have read the translations of Douglas, Surrey, Phaer, and Stanyhurst. If the last two of the *Sonnets* are indeed Shakespeare's, he read further afield. There is some evidence that he knew Erasmus's *Colloquies*[1] and *Adagia*.

The absence of Latin quotations in the later plays may merely indicate that Shakespeare had come to recognize that part of his audience would not appreciate them and that they were of dubious dramatic value. The mistakes made by him with regard to classical mythology prove very little. He makes Antony speak of Dido and Æneas in the underworld, though Virgil's Dido scorns her lover when they meet there. It would be dangerous to assume that Shakespeare had not read, or had forgotten, the sixth book of the *Æneid*. His treatment of mythology here and elsewhere was creative, and he used medieval as well as classical sources. He gives a willow to Dido in *The Merchant of Venice* in a picture for which Chaucer's tales of Dido and Ariadne were both drawn upon. In *Troilus and Cressida* he apparently confuses Arachne with Ariadne to form the name Ariachne, but he may have wished to recall Ariadne's thread as well as Arachne's, or varied the name to suit his metre.[2]

---

[1] Cf. p. 108 *post*. It may be added that Rolf Soellner, *N.Q.* (1954), pp. 108–9, suggests that Friar Lawrence's words to Romeo—

> I'll give thee armour to keep off that word;
> Adversity's sweet milk, philosophy,
> To comfort thee, though thou art banished—

were derived from Erasmus's *De Conscribendis Epistolis*, and that Erasmus was recalling Boethius. Erasmus, speaking of banishment, uses the images of armour and milk:

animum armare solet. Hujus ut ita dicam, lacte cum ab ipsis sis incunabulis enutritus . . .

Boethius (Prose I. 2) mentions *lacte* and *arma*, but refers to adversity in general, not specifically to banishment. Chaucer's version runs:

'Art not thou he', quod she, 'that whylom y-norisshed with my milk, and fostered with myne metes, were escaped and comen to corage of a parfit man? Certes, I yaf thee suche armures that, yif thou thy-self ne haddest first cast hem a-wey, they shulden han defended thee in sikernesse that may nat ben overcomen.'

Although Shakespeare's lines appear to be closer to Erasmus than to Boethius, there may have been some intermediate source. See also Rolf Soellner, *J.E.G.P.* (1956) p. 70, for another article on Shakespeare's use of Erasmus.

[2] As Golding uses the name Arachne, and as Shakespeare was perfectly familiar with the stories of Arachne and of Ariadne, the form Ariachne cannot be taken as a proof of ignorance. I. A. Richards, *Speculative Instruments* (1955), p. 210, has the comment: 'The opposites are all before him . . . and yet they come together and are indistinguishable—as Ariadne's clue and Arachne's web are merged in "Ariachne's broken woof".'

Shakespeare frequently takes liberties with the spelling of classical proper names (*Collatium* for *Collatia*, for example), but similar liberties were taken by Elizabethans whose latinity is not in dispute. Golding has some queer versions of Latin names in his translation. Spellings like *triumpherate* do not necessarily prove Shakespeare's ignorance; they may be due to compositors, and this particular case may be a deliberate quibble. Most Elizabethans, including the learned, allowed themselves considerable licence with regard to spelling. Shakespeare himself spelt *silence* as *scilens*, although he must have known its derivation if he had stopped to think. Marston, who could compose in Latin, has the spelling *scilence*.

A similar defence may be made of the anachronisms. Some may be due to ignorance or carelessness. He may have forgotten that Aristotle lived after the fall of Troy; but he must have known that Cato lived after Coriolanus, and most of his anachronisms may be justified on dramatic grounds.[1]

Professor Thomson makes a good deal of the fact that the only witness to Shakespeare's understanding Latin 'pretty well' (because he had been a schoolmaster in the country) is William Beeston, whose anecdotes after the Restoration cannot be regarded as reliable as the evidence of Ben Jonson. Jonson, moreover, is supported by Fletcher, who collaborated with Shakespeare, Hales of Eton, Fuller, and Milton. The support is, perhaps, more apparent than real: Fletcher's remark occurs in a poem addressed to Jonson, and the others were all echoing Jonson. Even Leonard Digges, the stepson of Shakespeare's executor and the translator of Claudian, was probably influenced by Jonson's remarks about 'small Latin and less Greek'.

> Next, Nature only helped him, for look thorough
> This whole Book, thou shalt find he doth not borrow
> One phrase from *Greeks*, nor *Latins* imitate.

He goes on to contrast *Julius Caesar* with Jonson's Roman plays. Yet the lines were prefixed to the 1640 edition of Shakespeare's poems, and these certainly have echoes of Ovid.

The strongest argument in favour of Shakespeare's having had a fluent knowledge of Latin is afforded by his coinages. Occasionally he blunders, as when he uses *orifex* for *orifice*; but his

[1] Cf. K. Muir, 'The Dramatic Function of Anachronism' (*Proceedings of the Leeds Philosophical and Literary Society*, 1951, pp. 529–33).

coinages, or those reputed to be his, generally show both knowledge and tact, and they compare favourably with Chapman's, who
possessed more than small Latin. Indeed, it has been argued that
the excessive latinisms of *Troilus and Cressida* are due to the example of Chapman's Homer.[1]

Of modern languages, Shakespeare acquired some knowledge
of French, Italian, and perhaps a smattering of Spanish. He could
certainly read French, probably even medieval French.[2] He could
write it sufficiently well for his purposes in *Henry V*, and he was a
student of Eliot's *Ortho-Epia Gallica*, a conversation manual.[3]
There is also some evidence that he had read Florio's *First Fruites*
and *Second Frutes*, and this fact would seem to suggest that he had
started to learn Italian.[4] Some of his plots were not available, so
far as we know, in another language. He might have read Boccaccio in a French translation, but he seems to have read parts of
Giraldi's *Hecatommithi* and several Italian plays in the original.[5]

Shakespeare naturally used translations when they were available. In addition to Golding's Ovid and Seneca's *Tenne Tragedies*,
he is known to have read Florio's Montaigne, North's Plutarch,
Holland's Pliny, and Chapman's Homer. It is less certain that he
knew Googe's Palingenius and Holland's translation of Plutarch's
Moralia. He was not, then, a learned man, but he had enough
education for his needs; and he used what he read with a masterly
ease and assurance. He may, of course, have read hundreds of
books which have left no trace on his writings; but the most unlikely books did leave their traces. It is difficult to believe that he
was conscious of echoing Henry Swinburne's *Brief Treatise of
Testaments and Last Willes*[6] in the third scene of *Hamlet*, and we
may suppose that, like Coleridge, he created much of his poetry
from forgotten reading.

The influence of certain books on Shakespeare's work has been
examined in detail. The Bible left its mark on every play in the
canon and, as Mr Richmond Noble has shown,[7] the earlier echoes
are mostly from the Bishops' Bible and the later ones mostly from

---

[1] Fripp, op. cit., p. 114, writes persuasively on Shakespeare's coinages.
[2] The question will be discussed in connection with the sources of *Richard II*.
[3] Cf. F. Yates, *A Study of 'Love's Labour's Lost'* (1936), pp. 50–72, and J. W. Lever,
Shakespeare Survey 6, pp. 79–90.
[4] Cf. R. Warwick Bond, *Studia Otiosa* (1938), pp. 101–2, and K. Muir, *N.Q.*
(1952), pp. 493–5.
[5] Cf. pp. 67 ff., pp. 122 ff. *post*.
[6] See note in *Hamlet* (Var. ed.).
[7] *Shakespeare's Knowledge of the Bible* (1935), *passim*. Cf. Thomas Carter, *Shakespeare and Holy Scripture* (1905).

the Geneva version. We may suspect that neither Noble nor Carter has exhausted the subject, for an earlier critic, Walter Whiter, demonstrated[1] that the story in St Mark's Gospel of the woman who had an issue of blood influenced the phrasing of the Duke's words in the first scene of *Measure for Measure*:

> Heauen doth with vs, as we with Torches doe,
> Not light them for themselues: For if our vertues
> Did not goe forth of vs, 'twere all alike
> As if we had them not: Spirits are not finely touch'd,
> But to fine issues.

St Mark tells how

> a certaine woman, which was diseased with an *issue* of blood . . .
> when shee had heard of Iesus, she came in the presse behind,
> and *touched* his garment. . . . And immediatly when Iesus did
> know in himselfe the *vertue that went out of him*, he turned him
> round about in the preasse, and said, who hath *touched* my
> clothes.

The subject of the Duke's discourse is taken from the previous chapter:

> Cometh the candle in, to bee put vnder a bushell, or vnder the
> bed, and not to be put on a candlestick.

The Ovidian influence is also pervasive, particularly in the earlier plays.[2] Florio's Montaigne affected both thought and vocabulary.[3] *The Mirror for Magistrates* was echoed in the Histories, in *King Lear*, and in *Cymbeline*.[4] The influence of the *Homilies* has been traced in several plays.[5] There are echoes from Harsnet's *Declaration* not only in *King Lear*, but also in *The Tempest*.[6] It would doubtless be possible to trace the influence of many other books on Shakespeare's work, though the majority of these echoes may do little else than exhibit the working of his subconscious mind and the extent of his reading.

It is certain that as an actor he was acquainted with a large num-

---

[1] *A Specimen of a Commentary* (1794), p. 254.
[2] E. I. Fripp, *Shakespeare Studies* (1930), pp. 98–127.
[3] The best discussion of the subject is by G. C. Taylor, *Shakespeare's Debt to Montaigne* (1925).
[4] Mr Harold Brooks has collected some interesting material on this subject.
[5] Cf. A. Hart, *Shakespeare and the Homilies* (1934), pp. 9–77.
[6] Cf. K. Muir, *R.E.S.* (1951), pp. 11–21.

ber of plays in which he performed.[1] He knew many, if not all, of Marlowe's works. He echoes *Tamburlaine*, *Dido*, and *Edward II*; he quotes from *Doctor Faustus*; and he quotes from and echoes *Hero and Leander*.[2] But his debt to Marlowe was more profound: from him he learnt the art of blank verse and developed his own conception of tragedy.

From Greene's *Friar Bacon* and *James IV* Shakespeare may have learnt something about the interweaving of several plots; and there is evidence that he knew *Menaphon*, *Euphues Censure to Philautus*, and the coney-catching pamphlets, as well as *Pandosto*, the source of *The Winter's Tale*.[3] Lodge provided the plot of *As You Like It*, but Shakespeare appears to have been little influenced by his poems or plays.

On the influence of Lyly it will be convenient to quote what I wrote on the subject twenty years ago:[4]

It is not too much to say that every characteristic of Shakespearean comedy, except the skilful blending of prose and verse, is to be found in Lyly. Farcical scenes like those between the Dromios, between Moth, Armado and Costard, between Launce and Speed, and between Launcelot and old Gobbo; wit contests between persons of rank, Boyet and the French ladies, Portia and Nerissa, Beatrice and Benedick, the use of parallel plots, the use of song, the pastoral spirit of *As You Like It* . . . the introduction of fairies, and the disguising of girls as boys, these are a few of the dramatic devices which Shakespeare learned from Lyly. But his indebtedness is more profound, though less tangible, in the creation of atmosphere. The world of Shakespearean comedy is fundamentally the same as Lyly's. The conventions, the style, the very air we breathe is the same. There can be no doubt that Shakespeare's comedies would have been very different had not Lyly preceded him. Not only was Shakespeare generally indebted to his forerunner, but more than fifty specific borrowings have been pointed out. . . . Furthermore, Shakespeare learned from Lyly how to write prose, and though in 1 *Henry IV* he poked fun at the excesses of Euphuism, he remained to the end of his career profoundly affected by it.

[1] Cf. J. Isaacs, *Shakespeare's Earliest Years in the Theatre* (British Academy Lecture 1953).
[2] Cf. 2 *Hen. IV*. II. iv. 174; *Ham*. II. ii.; *R.J*. III. ii. 1–2; *T.C*. II. ii. 82; *A.Y.L.I*. III. v. 82; *Temp*. I. ii. 376 ff., 396 ff.
[3] Cf. Chapter VIII *post*.
[4] K. Muir and S. O'Loughlin, *The Voyage to Illyria* (1937), p. 48.

. . . The civilized prose of the great comedies owes much in its constructions, its rhythms, its balance and its poise to the example of Lyly. It sharpened the edge of Shakespeare's wit, and gave his dialogue more bite and sparkle. Touchstone, Falstaff and Beatrice use a modified form of the style in which its inherent artificiality is toned down.

To this may be added the fact that even as late as *King Lear* Shakespeare bore unconscious witness to his familiarity with *Euphues*. Ferardo in that novel complains of his daughter's ingratitude, declaring as Lear did of Cordelia, that he had hoped to find comfort from her care in his old age.[1] He asks:

Is this the comfort that the parent reapeth for all his care? Is obstinacy payed for obedyence, stubbernenesse, rendred for duetie, malycious desperatnesse, for filiall feare?

In this context Lyly uses words which are echoed by Shakespeare:

But why cast I the effects of this vnnaturalnesse in thy teeth, seeing I my selfe was the cause? I made thee a *wanton*, and thou hast made me a *foole*: I brought thee vp like a *cockney*, and thou hast handled me like a *cockescombe*.

Lear blames his flesh for begetting his Pelican daughters;[2] and the Fool tells him when he is overcome by their unnaturalness:

Cry to it, Nuncle, as the *cockney* did to the eels when she put 'em i' th' paste alive; she knapp'd 'em o' th' *Coxcombs* with a stick, and cried 'Down, *wantons*, down!'

There is some evidence that Shakespeare had read some of the Nashe–Harvey controversy, as it left its traces on *Love's Labour's Lost*;[3] but one of Nashe's pamphlets, *Pierce Penilesse*, seems to have had considerable influence on *Hamlet*.[4] Nashe compares a foppish Dane to a swarm of butterflies,[5] as Hamlet calls Osric a water-fly. He refers several times to the Danish vice of drinking,[6] referring to them as sots and 'this surley swinish Generation' and 'foule drunken swine', as Hamlet said

> They clepe us drunkards and with swinish phrase
> Soil our addition.

[1] Cf. J. C. Maxwell's note in *King Lear*, ed. K. Muir, II. iv. 122.
[2] III. iv. 75.   [3] F. Yates, op. cit., *passim*.
[4] Cf. A. Davenport, *N.Q.* (1953), pp. 371–4, and G. Blakemore Evans, ibid., pp. 377–8.
[5] ed. G. B. Harrison, p. 36.   [6] op. cit., pp. 37, 39, 75, 83.

He points out that this particular vice detracts from their virtues: [1]

> A mightie deformer of mens manners and features, is this vn-
> necessary vice of all other. Let him bee indued with neuer so
> many vertues, and haue as much goodly proportion and fauour
> as nature can bestow vppon a man: yet if hee be thirstie after
> his owne destruction, and hath no ioy nor comfort, but when he
> is drowning his soule in a gallon pot, that one beastly imperfec-
> tion, will vtterlie obscure all that is commendable in him: and
> all his good qualities sinke like lead down to the bottome of his
> carrowsing cups, where they will lie like lees and dregges, dead
> and vnregarded of any man.

Hamlet, after describing how the King 'takes his rouse', goes on
to show how the dram of eale corrupts all the noble substance. In
a later passage, Nashe refers to Rhenish [2] wine and uses the epithet
'heauie headed', [3] both used in the 'dram of eale' context.

Nashe has a long passage in which he attacks cosmetics: [4]

> these aged mothers of iniquitie will haue their deformities
> newe plaistred ouer.

Claudius speaks of the harlot's cheek 'beautied with plastering
art' and Hamlet in the Nunnery scene and in the graveyard complains of painting. Nashe, it may be added, in attacking prostitu-
tion, says, 'Bring me two Virgins that haue vowd Chastitie, and
Ile builde a Nunnerie'. [5]

Nashe tells us [6] that Sloth

> in Nobilitie, Courtiers, Schollers, or any men is the chiefest
> cause that brings them in contempt. . . . The onely enemie to
> Sloth is contention and emulation; as to propose one man to my
> selfe, that is the onely myrrour of our Age.

So Ophelia laments the overthrow of

> The Courtiers, Soldiers, Schollers, Eye, tongue, sword.
> Th' expectansie and Rose of the faire State,
> The glasse of Fashion, and the mould of Forme.

In between these two sentences Nashe inveighs against 'Sloath
and sluggish securitye' [7] and against those who

> sit dallying at home, nor will be awakt by any indignities out of
> his loue-dreame, but suffer euery vpstart groome to defie him,

---

[1] ed. G. B. Harrison, pp. 76–7. [2] ibid., p. 81. [3] ibid., p. 83.
[4] ibid., pp. 40–1. [5] ibid., p. 92. [6] ibid., p. 83. [7] ibid., p. 84.

set him at naught, and shake him by the beard vnreuengde . . .
he shall be suspected of cowardise.

And in the preceding paragraph Nashe speaks of 'the heauie
headed gluttonous house doue'. Hamlet in the soliloquy at the end
of Act II speaks of himself as 'a Rogue and Pesant slaue', 'A dull
and muddy-mettled Rascall', a 'John-a-dreames', and he asks:

> Am I a Coward?
> Who calles me Villaine? breakes my pate a-crosse?
> Pluckes off my Beard, and blowes it in my face?
> Tweakes me by' th' Nose? giues me the Lye i' th' Throate,
> As deepe as to the Lungs?
> 'Swounds I should take it: for it cannot be,
> But I am Pigeon-Liuer'd.

Nashe speaks of the usefulness of war as a safety-valve[1] and of
the people 'for whome there is no vse, but warre' (cf. Fortinbras);
he then defends stage-plays[2] and urges that

they shew the ill successe of treason . . . the wretched end of
vsurpers . . . and how iust God is euermore in punishing of
murther . . . they are sower pils of reprehension wrapt vp in
sweete words.

So Hamlet used a play to catch the conscience of the King, though,
of course, the moral effect of plays was often discussed.

There are a few phrases in *Othello* that recall *Pierce Penilesse*:[3]

What drugs, what sorceries, what oiles, what waters . . .

> What Drugges, what Charmes,
> What Coniuration, and what mighty Magicke . . .

Enuie is a Crocodile that weepes when he kils,
and fights with none but he feeds on . . . this
quick-sighted monster . . .

Oh, beware my Lord, of iealousie,
It is the greene-ey'd Monster, which doth mocke
The meate it feeds on.

The chiefe spur vnto wrath is Drunkennes . . .

It hath pleas'd the diuell drunkennesse, to giue
place to the diuell wrath.

---

[1] ed. G. B. Harrison, p. 85.   [2] ibid., pp. 88–9.   [3] ibid., pp. 40, 45, 53.

Ben Jonson mentioned that Shakespeare surpassed 'sporting Kyd'; and certainly *The Spanish Tragedy* and possibly an earlier version of *Hamlet* were among the most fruitful of the works of the University Wits in their influence on his plays. He also seems to have known *Cornelia* and he alludes to *Soliman and Perseda*.[1]

Shakespeare had read *The Faerie Queene*, but its influence on his own work was surprisingly small.[2] He knew most of Sidney's work—*Astrophel and Stella*, *The Defence of Poesy*,[3] and *Arcadia*[4]—and much of Daniel's, including *Delia*, *Rosamond*,[5] *A Letter from Octavia*,[6] *Cleopatra*,[7] and *The Civil Wars*.[8]

So many books and plays have not survived that even if we read all the extant books published before 1616 we could still be sure that we had not read all the books known to Shakespeare; and, of course, some ideas or phrases apparently echoed from books we know may in fact be echoed from books which are now lost. Even apart from this, some resemblances may be coincidental; or Shakespeare may have derived the word, the phrase, the image, or the idea from a variety of sources—from conversation, from dictionaries, from manuscript, from letters. An interesting example of the kind of pitfall into which the source-hunter is liable to fall is afforded by a discussion on the death of Cleopatra. One critic[9] pointed out a resemblance between Shakespeare's scene and a passage in Peele's *Edward I*, in which an asp is addressed in the words 'Suck on, sweet babe'. Cleopatra speaks of the asp:

> Dost thou not see my Baby at my breast,
> That suckes the Nurse asleepe.

But this striking comparison was a commonplace. Nashe, in *Christ's Tears*, says, 'At thy breasts . . . aspisses should be put out to nurse'; and Cooper, writing of Cleopatra in his *Thesaurus*, speaks of 'two infants sucking at her pappes'. We cannot be sure that Shakespeare derived the idea from any or all of these sources, for it is possible that the sucking image was suggested by Charmian's apostrophe 'O eastern star!' This might have recalled the star in the east, which led the Magi to Bethlehem, where they found the

---

[1] Cf. J. Isaacs, op. cit.
[2] Cf. W. B. C. Watkins, *Shakespeare and Spenser* (1950).
[3] Cf. A. Thaler, *Shakespeare and Sidney* (1947), *passim*.
[4] Cf. K. Muir and John F. Danby, *N.Q.* (1950), pp. 49–51.
[5] Cf. p. 30 *post*.   [6] Cf. p. 209 *post*.   [7] Cf. p. 211 *post*.
[8] Cf. *Richard II*, ed. J. D. Wilson and Michel and Seronsy, *S.P.* lii (1955), pp. 549–77.
[9] Cf. I. Ribner, *N.Q.* (1952), p. 244, and J. D. Reeves, ibid., p. 441.

infant Jesus in his mother's arms.[1] It must therefore be borne in mind that apparently close parallels may be deceptive, and that even when Shakespeare is known to have read the work in question he may rather be echoing a work he is not known to have read. In other cases, as we shall see, a single line in one of his plays may combine echoes of more than one source. When, for example, the Clown tells Autolycus, 'We are but plain fellows, sir', and he replies, 'A lie: you are rough and hairy', he is thinking of the story of Jacob and Esau. In the Geneva version Jacob is 'plain' (i.e. clean-shaven) and Esau is 'rough'. But in the Bishops' Bible Esau is described as 'hairy'.[2] There is a similar conflation in *The Merry Wives of Windsor*.[3] Pistol tells Ford:

> He wooes both high and low, both rich and poor,
> Both yong and old, one with another (*Ford*)

This is based on the prayer-book version of *Psalm* xlix: 'High and low, rich and poor; one with another'. But there is likewise an echo of the metrical version:

> Both hie and low, both rich and poore
> that in the world doe dwell.

Pistol alludes to the same verse in an earlier scene of the play (I. iii):

> And high and low beguiles the rich and poore.

He proceeds to extemporize in doggerel verse:

> And I to *Ford* shall eke vnfold
> How *Falstaffe* (varlet vile)
> His Doue will proue; his gold will hold,
> And his soft couch defile.

The same rhymes and references to illicit gain and adultery are to be found in the metrical version of the next psalm:

> When thou a theefe dost see,
> by theft to liue in wealth,
> With him thou runst and dost agree,
> likewise to thriue by stealth.

---

[1] Cf. E. Holmes, *Aspects of Elizabethan Imagery* (1929), p. 50.
[2] Cf. E. A. Fripp, *Shakespeare: Man and Artist* (1938), pp. 86-7.
[3] *M.W.* II. i. 117. Pointed out by Fripp, op. cit.

> When thou dost them behold,
>   that wiues and maids defile,
> Thou lik'st it well, and waxest bold
>   to vse that life most vile.

Shakespeare thus combined a variety of different sources in the texture of his verse, and the process, in most cases, was unconscious. Just as J. Livingston Lowes was able to demonstrate that 'The Ancient Mariner' and 'Kubla Khan' were a complex tissue of words and phrases borrowed from Coleridge's multifarious reading, so it would be possible, if we had a complete knowledge of Shakespeare's reading, to show that words, phrases, and images coalesce in his poetry. Nor is there reason to doubt that the conditions of such coalescence were the same as with Coleridge. Two or more passages became linked in his mind if they had a common factor, although the resultant phrase might not include that factor. Professor Baldwin again has provided us with many illustrations of the process. One stanza in *Lucrece* may serve as an example:[1]

> The aged man that coffers vp his gold,
> Is plagu'd with cramps, and gouts, and painefull fits;
> And scarce hath eyes his treasure to behold,
> But like still pining *Tantalus* he sits,
> And vselesse barnes the haruest of his wits:
>   Hauing no other pleasure of his gaine,
>   But torment that it cannot cure his paine.

Ovid briefly refers to the story of Tantalus in the *Metamorphoses* (IV. 458–9) and in a note on this passage Regius says: 'hac autem poena avari omnes affici videntur, qui patris pecuniis per avaritiam uti non possunt'. The connexion between the story of Tantalus and avarice is brought out in Horace's first satire, a passage quoted by Erasmus in his *Adagia*, where Shakespeare may have seen it:

> Tantalus a labris sitiens fugientia captat
> flumina. quid rides? mutato nomine de te
> fabula narratur: congestis undique saccis
> indormis inhians, et tamquam parcere sacris
> cogeris aut pictis tamquam gaudere tabellis.

[1] Cf. T. W. Baldwin, *Genetics*, p. 133.

Erasmus goes on to quote (under the same heading) a passage from one of the Odes (III. 16):

> Contemptae dominus splendidior rei,
> quam si quicquid arat impiger Apulus
> occultare meis dicerer horreis,
>   magnas inter opes inops.

This reference to the hoarding of wheat links up with the parable of the covetous man (*Luke* xii. 15–21) who proposed building greater barns, only to be told (in the Geneva version): 'O foole, this night wil they fetche away thy soule from thee'. On this parable the Geneva version has the following note:

> Christ condemneth the arrogancie of the riche worldelings, who as thogh they had God locked vp in their coffres and barnes, set their whole felicitie in their goods, not considering that God gaue them life and also can take it away when he wil.

It will be observed that the coffers and barns of this note are used by Shakespeare as verbs.

Thus in a poem derived mainly from Livy and an annotated edition of Ovid we have in one stanza echoes from two poems of Horace, a Biblical parable and the marginal note on it, and possibly (if we are to believe Professor Baldwin) from Juvenal's description of the miseries of old age. It is probable that Shakespeare consulted Erasmus's *Adagia*, but the echo from the Bible appears to have been unconscious.

We cannot hope to track down more than a small fraction of the passages which Shakespeare made use of, for there is no reason to doubt that he was influenced by conversation as well as by the written word, and often he must have composed lines which resemble those of earlier poets to whom he was not even indirectly indebted. The famous triple image of flatterers-dogs-sweets, for example, may have been a literary commonplace,[1] or (as Caroline Spurgeon thought) it may reflect a personal prepossession of the poet.

We are on surer ground when we attempt to trace the sources of his plots, though even here there are obstacles in the way. In a number of cases—e.g. *Hamlet, The Two Gentlemen of Verona, The Merry Wives of Windsor*—there was probably a lost source-play. The Histories present a special problem, since there is so much

[1] Cf. J. L. Jackson *S.Q.* (1950), pp. 260 ff.

disagreement about the materials on which Shakespeare worked. Ten years ago it appeared to be settled that the second and third parts of *Henry VI* were Shakespeare's unaided work; now it is suggested either that the *Contention* and the *True Tragedy* were used by him as sources, or else that these bad quartos were, like Shakespeare's plays, derived from the work of previous dramatists.[1] It used to be generally accepted that *King John* was based on the *Troublesome Raigne*, but the latest editor assumes that the position of the two plays was reversed, the *Troublesome Raigne* being based on *King John*.[2] There was possibly a source-play behind *Richard II*, so it is unprofitable to discuss whether Shakespeare consulted a number of remoter sources.[3] *Henry IV* and *Henry V* were derived in part from the *Famous Victories*, a play which exists only in a mangled and truncated version, so that we cannot know exactly what Shakespeare borrowed from it. The authenticity of 1 *Henry VI*[4] and *Henry VIII*[5] is still a matter of dispute, and till we can be sure how much Peele and others wrote of the former and how much, if any, Fletcher wrote of the latter the discussion of their sources will be inconclusive. *Richard III* is the only one of the Histories which presents a straightforward problem. It is advisable, therefore, to leave the Histories out of the discussion for the time being.

Shakespeare's method of composition differed from play to play. For one or two no direct source has been discovered, though the poet William Collins claimed to have read the source of *The Tempest*. For several of his plots Shakespeare appears to have used only one source. *As You Like It* is based on Lodge's *Rosalynde*, and *The Winter's Tale* is based largely on Greene's *Pandosto*. Most of the plays, however, have more than one source, and several of them draw on a variety of sources. We may conclude this chapter with an example of Shakespeare's method.

[1] I do not, however, agree with the arguments of Feuillerat and Prouty. See my review of the former, *R.E.S.* (1954), pp. 411–13.

[2] Cf. E. Honigmann's edition; but see J. Isaacs, op. cit.

[3] See editions by J. D. Wilson (Camb.) and Peter Ure (Arden).

[4] L. Kirschbaum, *P.M.L.A.* (1952), pp. 809–22, argues that Shakespeare wrote it all.

[5] G. Wilson Knight (*The Crown of Life*) and Peter Alexander (ed. *Histories*) seem to believe that Shakespeare wrote it all.

(1) The Comedy of Errors

Professor T. W. Baldwin has given an elaborate account of the way in which Shakespeare constructed *The Comedy of Errors* from his materials:[1]

> His grammar-school training had been insistent that he must gather into notebook and mind materials out of which later to compile by imitation his own work. So here he assembles in his mind all accessible plays on mistaken identity; *Amphitruo*, *Menaechmi*, possibly *Miles*, and probably Gascoigne's translation from Ariosto as *Supposes*. . . . *The Comedy* is not merely constructed principally from two plays of Plautus; it also analyses and reconstructs those plays into the *Andria* formula of Terentian structure.

The main plot is taken from the *Menaechmi* of Plautus, in which Menaechmus Surreptus arranges to have lunch with a courtezan. Menaechmus Sosicles is taken for his twin and gets the lunch instead. A friend of Menaechmus Surreptus, who was to have shared the meal, exposes him to his wife. Eventually all is explained. Shakespeare begins his play with a scene, taken from the story of Apollonius of Tyre (in either Gower's version or Twine's), in which Ægeon explains how he lost his wife and sons. His name is probably derived from Ægeus, Theseus's father, who was drowned in the Ægean Sea, which was named after him and which provides the geographical background of the play. Ægeon is condemned to death because of a trade war between Ephesus and Syracuse; and this was suggested by another play of errors, *Supposes*, a play which was later to serve as the main source of *The Taming of the Shrew*. Antipholus of Ephesus says he was brought to the town by Duke Menaphon; and in Greene's *Menaphon* there is a shipwreck which parts the husband from the wife and their infant son, and pirates who separate wife and baby. In *Apollonius of Tyre* the wife is supposed to die in childbirth, the father leaves his daughter in the care of others, and she is stolen by pirates. In *The Comedy of Errors* there is a shipwreck which severs husband and one of the twins from the wife and the other, and rude Corinthian fishermen afterwards rob the wife of

[1] Cf. *Five-Act Structure*, pp. 665 ff.

her son. Shakespeare complicates matters by adding twin servants, separated like their masters, the name Dromio being found in Lyly's *Mother Bombie*.

Shakespeare may have studied the geographer Solinus (in Golding's translation) for details of the journeys of his characters, for he chooses this name for the Duke; but he seems also to have taken hints from the missionary journeys of St Paul. Certain details are taken from *Acts* xix which describes St Paul's visit to Ephesus: Antipholus of Syracuse complains of sorcerers and witches as well as of the cheats mentioned by Plautus, and we are told in this chapter of *Acts* of exorcists, evil spirits, and people who 'used curious arts'. The Ephesus setting may have been suggested by the *Miles*, another play of errors, which immediately follows the *Menaechmi* in editions of Plautus—the first line of the argument mentions the city. Ephesus also figures prominently in *Apollonius of Tyre*, for it is here that the hero is reunited to his wife as in *Pericles*, and as Ægeon is reunited to Æmelia, though the pagan temple of Diana is changed to a Christian priory.

Shakespeare does not directly use the substance of Act I of the *Menaechmi*, and in his second scene he incorporates material from the second act of Plautus's play, and the whole of his second act is developed from *Menaechmi* II. 3. For the first scene of the third act, in which Antipholus of Ephesus is barred from his own house while his twin is inside, Shakespeare took a hint from the fourth act of the *Menaechmi*, where the husband is told by the wife and by Erotium that he will be shut out; but he amplified the hint by a scene in the fourth act of the *Amphitruo*, in which the hero of that play is shut out of his own house while Jupiter is with his wife. The business of the chain in III. 2 and IV. i was suggested by a *spinther* which had formerly belonged to Menaechmus's wife and which the courtezan's maid brings to the other Menaechmus to have repaired. Shakespeare's chain is intended by Antipholus of Ephesus as a present for his wife; when he is shut out of his house he decides to give the chain to the courtezan, though afterwards he apparently promises it in exchange for a diamond ring; when the courtezan is refused the promised chain by Antipholus of Syracuse she decides to tell Adriana that her husband had taken the ring; and Antipholus of Ephesus is arrested at the suit of the goldsmith for refusing to pay for the chain. Adriana, convinced that her husband is mad, goes with Dr Pinch to secure him and exorcise him; and when they afterwards meet the other Antipholus they assume he has escaped. He and Dromio take refuge in the priory. The arrival of Antipholus of Ephesus and the Abbess's recognition of Ægeon, now being led to execution, leads to a resolution of the plot.

Shakespeare's play is much more complicated than Plautus's. The invention of the two Dromios leads to many additional 'errors'. The invention of Luciana provides a bride for Antipholus of Syracuse and a confidante for Adriana. The wife becomes a central figure in the play, instead of a peripheral one, and the courtezan becomes a minor figure, her relationship with Antipholus being comparatively innocent. The invitation to dinner is given by the wife to the wrong Antipholus, not by the courtezan, as in Plautus. The change to a Christian setting enables Adriana to plead for the sanctity of marriage. Although Shakespeare adds more farcical elements to Plautus's plot—Dromio's wife, Dr Pinch and others—he also added elements which are not farcical at all. The doomed Ægeon opens the play on a serious note, and his discovery of his wife is a moving scene. The study of Adriana's jealous love, the lyrical proposal of Antipholus of Syracuse to Luciana, and his sense of bewilderment and horror lift the play above the farcical.

Professor Baldwin has amply demonstrated that in this early comedy Shakespeare combined many different sources—two or three plays by Plautus, *Supposes*, *Menaphon*, a chapter from *Acts*, and *Apollonius of Tyre*—and he has shown that these sources were organized in accordance with the Terentian five-act structure. The art and pains displayed by Shakespeare in this early work are an indication of the kind of craftsmanship we should expect to find in his mature plays.[1]

---

[1] R. Warwick Bond, *Studia Otiosa* (1938), p. 47, suggests that Shakespeare was influenced by Cecchi's *L'Ammalata*.

II

EARLY PLAYS

(2) *Romeo and Juliet*

OF the various versions of the Romeo and Juliet story by Luigi da Porto, Matteo Bandello, Luigi Groto, Boaistuau, William Painter, and Arthur Brooke, there is some slight evidence that Shakespeare knew, besides Brooke, Painter, da Porto, and Groto; but as Brooke asserts that he saw 'the same argument lately set forth on stage', some of the indebtedness to Italian sources may be illusory. It may, nevertheless, be worth while to detail the more significant of them.[1]

In Groto's *La Hadriana* (1578) the Mago comforts the bereaved in these words:[2]

> Non perde il suo colui, che l'altrui rende.
> A la terra doveansi i corpi, l'alme
> A Dio, tutto 'l composto a la natura.
> Non biasmate colui che vi li toglie
> Si tosto.

Friar Lawrence similarly declares:[3]

> Heauen and your selfe
> Had part in this faire Maid; now heauen hath all,
> And all the better is it for the Maid:
> Your part in her, you could not keepe from death,
> But heauen keepes his part in eternall life.

---

[1] In the discussion of *Romeo and Juliet* I am indebted to the following: Mary Martha Mulligan, *The Sources of 'Romeo and Juliet'* (unpublished thesis, Liverpool, 1954); R. A. Law, 'On Shakespeare's Changes of his source material in *Romeo and Juliet*' (*University of Texas Bulletin, Studies in English*, 1929); O. H. Moore, *The Legend of R.J.* (1950).
[2] Cf. J. C. Walker, *Historical Memoir on Italian Tragedy* (1799), p. 61.
[3] IV. v. 66–70.

C

In the parting scene Groto and Shakespeare both introduce the nightingale:[1]

> S'io non erro, è presso il far del giorno.
> Udite il rossignuol, che con noi desto,
> Con noi geme fra i spini, e la rugiada
> Col pianto nostro bagna l'herbe.

> It is not yet neere day:
> It was the Nightingale, and not the Larke,
> That pier'st the fearfull hollow of thine eare.

Neither of these parallels is sufficiently remarkable for us to be sure that Shakespeare had read *La Hadriana*.

Shakespeare is close to da Porto in a number of details. There is no Balcony scene in Brooke's poem, but da Porto tells us that Romeo used to climb Giulietta's balcony and listen to her discourse,[2] and that one night she happens to see him and exclaims:

> Che fate quì a quest 'ora così solo?

So Juliet in the plays asks:

> What man art thou that thus bescreen'd in night
> So stumblest on my counsell?

But some hints for the balcony scene may have come from Brooke. In da Porto and Shakespeare Juliet goes alone to the Friar's cell for her wedding; in all the other versions she is accompanied. But Shakespeare might have departed from his sources in this instance for dramatic reasons. Shakespeare also agrees with da Porto in the scene in which Tybalt is slain. In Bandello's and Brooke's versions Romeo, attacked by Tybalt, is forced to defend himself. In da Porto Romeo at first refrains from fighting, but he attacks Tebaldo when he has seen many of his family wounded.[3] So Shakespeare's Romeo attacks Tybalt only after the death of Mercutio.

The name Romeo must have come either from one of the Italian versions of the story, or, more likely, from Painter—Brooke calls him Romeus. Shakespeare seems to have taken the 'two and forty hours', during which time Juliet would lie entranced, from Pain-

---

[1] J. C. Walker, op. cit., p. 57.

[2] 'E ora sopra la finestra della sua camera per forza tiratosi, ivi, senza ch'ella o altri il sapesse, ad udirla parlare si sedea.'

[3] 'Pure alla fine essendo molti de' suoi feriti, e quasi tutti della strada cacciati, vinto dall'ira, sopra Tebaldo Cappelletti corso, che il più fiero de' suoi nimici pareva, di un sol colpo in terra morto il distese'.

ter's '40 houres at the least', but as Romeo was to be present when Juliet awakened, a dramatist, unlike a writer of narrative, had to be explicit. On the whole, in spite of the lost play, it is reasonable to assume that Shakespeare had read Painter's version, and it is possible, but by no means certain, that he had also read the versions by da Porto and Groto.

Brooke's poem, however, was Shakespeare's main source, and he followed it with reasonable fidelity. Brooke describes the feud between the Montagews and Capulets, and the attempt of Prince Escalus to effect a peace. Romeus, after months of unrequited love for a wise and virtuous maid, is persuaded by a friend to frequent balls and banquets, in order to discover a kinder mistress. At Christmas-tide he and his friends go masked to a ball at the Capulets' house; he and Juliet fall in love, and discover afterwards each other's identity. Romeus for weeks passes by her window and gazes at her, until one night she sees him and insists that unless he intends marriage he must cease his suit. Romeus thereupon goes to consult Friar Lawrence, who eventually consents to the marriage, hoping thereby to effect a reconciliation between the two families. Juliet, using the Nurse as a messenger, is told to go to confession, where she is married to Romeus. A month or two after the marriage a fight breaks out in the course of which Romeus kills Tibalt in self-defence. Romeus is banished, and after a last night together, the lovers are parted. Juliet's mother, seeing her grief but unaware of the cause, gets Capulet to find a husband for her. Juliet refuses to marry Paris, and on the advice of Friar Lawrence she takes a sleeping-potion and, supposed dead, she is placed in the family vault. The messenger sent by Friar Lawrence to Romeus fails to reach him; Romeus hears from his servant of Juliet's death, buys poison of an apothecary, returns to Verona, and takes the poison in the vault. Friar Lawrence arrives just as Romeus dies; Juliet awakens and asks for her lover, and she takes the dagger and kills herself. The watch arrive together with the Prince, and the Friar tells the whole story. The Nurse and the Apothecary are condemned; the Friar is pardoned; and the two families are reconciled.

Shakespeare disposes his material in accordance with the requirements of five-act structure. He begins the play with a brawl between the Montagues and Capulets; the climax of the third act is the fight between Romeo and Tybalt, which results in the hero's banishment; and the conclusion of the play is the reconciliation of the two families. In the first act the lovers meet at the Capulet ball; in the second act they are married; in the third act, after Romeo's banishment the marriage is consummated, and the marriage of Paris and Juliet is arranged; in the fourth act Juliet takes the potion; and in the last act Romeo, hearing that Juliet is dead, takes poison in her tomb, and Juliet, awaking a minute too late, stabs herself with Romeo's dagger. It is difficult to imagine greater technical skill than Shakespeare displays in the plotting of the play; and whereas the action of the poem is spread over nine months, that of the play is condensed into a few days. This not only increases the speed and intensity of the action: it shows the passionate impulsiveness of the two lovers, and it makes them consummate their marriage in the knowledge that they must separate on the morrow.

In some ways, of course, especially when considered in relation to the later tragedies, the play is immature. Shakespeare was writing a tragedy of fortune, the only kind his story allowed, and too much depends on accident: the quarantine of the messenger, and the awakening of Juliet one minute too late. But already Shakespeare was manipulating his source-material with an unerring sense of dramatic possibilities.

Brooke purports to describe

> a coople of vnfortunate louers thralling themselues to vnhonest desire, neglecting the authoritie and aduise of parents and frends, conferring their principall counsels with dronken gossyppes, and superstitious friers (the naturally fitte instrumentes of vnchastitie) attempting all aduentures of peryll for th' attaynyng of their wished lust, vsyng auriculer confession (the kay of whoredome and treason) for furtheraunce of their purpose, abusyng the honourable name of lawefull marriage to cloke the shame of stolne contractes; finallye, by all meanes of vnhonest lyfe, hastyng to most vnhappye death.

Luckily for his poem, however, Brooke does not carry out this moral programme. Sympathy for the lovers keeps breaking in; and Shakespeare goes much further in enlisting the sympathy of his audience. Old Capulet's abominable treatment of Juliet has the effect of retrospectively justifying her secret marriage. Shakespeare nowhere explicitly condemns the Friar, though by realistic standards he behaves foolishly. He convinces us that the love of Romeo and Juliet is more than a lust of the blood; and few critics have agreed with Mr Masefield's severe description of Juliet as 'a deceitful, scheming liar' and of Romeo as 'a frantic madman'. In fact, as Professor Peter Alexander points out,[1] Shakespeare shows Romeo

> behaving with exemplary composure and forbearance, though insulted by a quarrelsome bully in the presence of his friends.

Shakespeare, moreover, convinces us of Juliet's integrity and worth by her delicate avowal of love in the Balcony scene, by her repudiation of the Nurse as 'ancient damnation', and by her courage when she drinks the potion.

The character of Mercutio is developed from a single reference[2] by Brooke to

> one calde *Mercutio*
> A courtier that ech where was highly had in price
> For hee was courteous of his speeche and pleasaunt of deuise.

The character in the play, in life as in death, exemplifies the futility of the blood-feud; he acts as a foil to Romeo and a critic of romantic love; and his death involves Romeo in the act that leads to his banishment.

Tybalt, likewise, appears only once in Brooke's poem[3] as

> A yong man . . . exercisde in feats of armes,
> And noblest of the rowte.

Shakespeare introduces him into several scenes as the most violent of the Capulets—so unreasonable that even without his killing of Mercutio all our sympathies would be with Romeo. The development of the character enabled Shakespeare to emphasize again the futility of the feud and to give every provocation to Romeo. This was the more necessary as by his other alterations the fight took place immediately after the marriage of the lovers, Romeo challenging Tybalt instead of killing him in self-defence.

The other characters are developed from hints given by Brooke. Paris, Capulet, Montague, and the Nurse are not essentially different from the source-characters, but they are made more real and effective. Juliet is made even younger than she is in the source; and Romeo's passion for Rosalind becomes the typical romantic love of the sonneteers for a merciless mistress instead of the sexual

---

[1] P. Alexander, *Shakespeare's Life and Art* (1938), p. 115.
[2] ll. 254–6.   [3] ll. 963–5.

pursuit of a virtuous maid. It is a more effective contrast with Romeo's genuine love of Juliet.

It has been shown[1] that there are many verbal echoes of Brooke's poem in Shakespeare's play. On three occasions the phrasing of the poem is repeated almost word for word. The Nurse's revelation of Romeo's identity:

> His name is *Romeus* (sayd she) a *Montagewe*.

> His name is *Romeo*, and a *Montague*.

Friar Lawrence's words to Romeo:

> Art thou, quoth he, a man; thy shape saith so thou art.

> Art thou a man? thy forme cries out thou art.

Juliet's question on awaking in the tomb:

> Where is my *Romeus*?

> Where is my *Romeo*?

The chorus at the beginning of Act II says that Romeo

> to his foe suppos'd he must complaine,
> And she steale Loues sweet bait from fearfull *hookes*.

This combines two phrases from Brooke's poem. Romeus when he first sees Juliet

Onely seeketh by her sight to feede his hungry eyes;
Through them he swalloweth downe loues *sweet empoysonde baite*.

Juliet, after the feast, exclaims:

> What if with frendly speache the traytor lye in wayte?
> As oft the *poyson'd hook* is hid wrapte in the pleasant *bayte*.

The lines in the balcony scene—

> And the place death, considering who thou art,
> If any of my kinsmen find thee here—

are based on Brooke's line:

> What if your deadly foes, my kinsmen saw you here?

Juliet's interruption of the garrulous nurse—

> What saies he of our marriage? what of that?—

---

[1] Cf. Law, op. cit., Brooke, op. cit., 353, 1353, 2710, 218–9, 387–8, 493, 1031–4, 2370–6, 2585, 920.

is clearly derived from:

But of our marriage say at once, what answere haue you brought?

Benvolio's description of the fight 'Too't they goe like light-ning' was perhaps suggested by Brooke's comparison of the two combatants to 'thunderboltes throwne downe out of the skye'. The scene in which Juliet drinks the potion is closely based on Brooke's account—her fear of being stifled, her fear of waking too soon, her fear of Tybalt's corpse. Romeo asks the Apothecary for 'some soon-speeding gear', and in the poem the Apothecary gives Romeus the poison with the words, 'This is the speeding gere'.

There are many other examples of verbal indebtedness, some of them being in a different context. Brooke tells us that on their wed-ding night the lovers lament its brevity.

> The hastiness of Phoebus steeds in great despyte they blame.

Shakespeare's Juliet, longing for the consummation of her mar-riage, cries:

> Gallop apace you fiery footed steedes,
> Towards *Phoebus* lodging, such a Wagoner
> As *Phaeton* would whip you to the west,
> And bring in Cloudie night immediately.

Brooke's line is here combined with Golding's 'firiefooted horse'[1] and Marlowe's[2]

> Gallop apace bright *Phoebus* through the skie,
> And duskie night, in rustie iron carre,
> Betweene you both, shorten the time I pray.

It has not, I think, been pointed out that one group of images in the play may have been suggested by Brooke's poem.[3]

There is a substantial group of images relating to voyages; and Brooke, who had some experience of voyages and actually met his death by drowning, has many images derived from seafaring. He speaks of the lodestars,[4]

> the weary Pilats marke,
> In stormes to guide to hauen the tossed barke;

[1] Translating Ovid's *iguipedum* (cf. T. W. Baldwin, op. cit., p. 766). Golding speaks of Phaethon as a 'waggoner'.
[2] *Edward II*, 1738–40. But Baldwin thinks Marlowe was the debtor.
[3] Cf. K. Muir, *N.Q.* (1956), pp. 241–3.
[4] Brooke, op. cit. Address to the Reader.

an image used by Shakespeare in one of the grandest of his Sonnets:[1]

> O, no, it is an euer fixed marke
> That lookes on tempests and is neuer shaken;
> It is the star to euery wandring barke,
> Whose worths vnknowne, although his higth be taken.

Brooke, like Shakespeare, speaks of Juliet's bed as the 'long desired port' towards which Romeus's 'steerless ship', his 'Sea-
beaten barke' is driven.[2] Another long simile describes the efforts
made to reach harbour:[3]

As when the winter flawes with dredfull noyse arise,
And heaue the fomy swelling waues vp to the starry skies,
So that the broosed barke in cruell seas betost,
Despayreth of the happie hau'n, in daunger to be lost:
The pylate bold at helme, cries 'Mates, strike now your sayle',
And turnes her stemme into the waues, that strongly her assayle:
Then driuen harde vpon the bare and wrackfull shore,
In greater daunger to be wrackt than he hath been before:
He seeth his ship ful right against the rocke to runne,
But yet he doth what ly'th in him the perilous rocke to shunne:
Some times the beaten boate, by cunning gouernment,
The anchors lost, the cables broke, and all the tackle spent:
The roder smitten off, and ouerboord the maste,
Doth win the long desired port, the stormy daunger past.

Whiter, with his customary acuteness, pointed out[4] the images
relating to voyages. He referred to the scene where the Nurse is
hailed by Mercutio as a sail, and Peter as her convoy, and to
Romeo's two speeches, just before he meets Juliet for the first
time, and just before his suicide. The first of these runs:

> I feare too early, for my mind misgiues,
> Some consequence yet hanging in the starres,
> Shall bitterly begin his fearfull date
> With this nights reuels, and expire the tearme
> Of a despised life clos'd in my brest:
> By some vile forfeit of vntimely death.
> But he that hath the stirrage of my course,
> Direct my sail.

---

[1] No. 116.
[2] Brooke, op. cit., p. 27.
[3] ibid., p. 46. See also pp. 8, 12, 42, 49, 51, 56.
[4] Whiter, op. cit., p. 123.

Here the sequence of words and images—stars, bitterly, date, expire, term, closed, forfeit, death, steerage, course, sail—is close to that of the later speech, where we have stars, seal, dateless, bargain, death, bitter, pilot, and bark:

> Death that hath suckt the honey of thy breath,
> Hath had no power yet vpon thy Beautie. . . .
>   O here
> Will I set vp my euerlasting rest:
> And shake the yoke of inauspicious starres
> From this world-wearied flesh: Eyes looke your last:
> Armes take your last embrace: And lips, O you
> The doores of breath, seale with a righteous kisse
> A datelesse bargaine to ingrossing death:
> Come bitter conduct, come vnsauoury guide,
> Thou desperate Pilot, now at once run on
> The dashing Rocks, thy Sea-sicke wearie Barke.

Whiter did not point out, however, that this last speech is linked not only to the earlier speech in the play, but also to the 85th sonnet in Sidney's *Astrophel and Stella*:

> I see the house, my heart thy selfe containe,
>   Beware full sailes drowne not thy tottring barge:
>   Least joy by Nature apt sprites to enlarge
>   Thee to thy wracke beyond thy limits straine . . .
> But giue apt seruants their due place, let eyes
>   See Beauties totall summe summ'd in her face:
>   Let eares heare speech, which wit to wonder ties.
> Let breath sucke vp those sweetes, let armes embrace
>   The globe of weale, lips *Loues* indentures make;
>   Thou but of all the kingly Tribute take.

In Romeo's speech and in Sidney's sonnet we have the same injunctions to eyes, arms, and lips, and in the same order. Shakespeare's 'sucked', 'honey', and 'breath' may be compared with Sidney's 'breath suck up those sweets'; the legal image of sealing a bargain with a kiss is echoed from Sidney's 'indentures'; and the image of the weary bark shipwrecked on the rocks is echoed from Sidney's 'tottring barge' and 'wrack'. Curiously enough, the piratical First Quarto of *Romeo and Juliet* prints *barge* for *barke*.

It should also be mentioned that Romeo's last speech is

influenced by the concluding stanzas of Daniel's *Complaint of Rosamond*:[1]

> When naught respecting death, the last of paines,
> Plac'd his pale collours, th' ensigne of his might,
> Vpon his new-got spoyle before his right . . .
>
> Pittifull mouth (quoth he) that liuing gauest
> The sweetest comfort that my soule could wish:
> O be it lawful now, that dead thou hauest,
> Thys sorrowing farewell of a dying kisse . . .
>
> Ah how me thinks I see death dallying seekes,
> To entertaine it selfe in loues sweet place:
> Decayed Roses of discoloured cheekes,
> Doe yet retaine deere notes of former grace:
> And ougly death sits faire within her face.

Here we have the idea of the beauty that has not been marred by death, a reference to Death as a lover, the mention of a farewell kiss to a dead woman, and the line about the pale colours, the ensign of Death which suggested the lines:

> Thou art not conquer'd; Beauties ensigne yet
> Is Crymson in thy lips, and in thy cheekes,
> And Deaths pale flag is not aduanced there . . .
>   Shall I beleeue
> That vnsubstantiall Death is amorous,
> And that the leane abhorred Monster keepes
> Thee here in darke to be his Paramour?

Brooke was a feeble poet and he could give Shakespeare little beyond the story and a few phrases and images; but into his play Shakespeare infused the quintessence of Elizabethan love-poetry. In the last scenes he wrote the finest poetry which had yet been heard on the English stage;[2] and in the characters of Mercutio and the Nurse he displayed for the first time his unequalled power of dramatic presentation of character.

---

[1] This is generally recognized by editors.
[2] I assume that the play was written c. 1595 and not before *Doctor Faustus* and *Edward II*.

(3) A Midsummer-Night's Dream

There was probably no comprehensive source of *A Midsummer-Night's Dream*, though Nashe in 1589 mentioned a play about the King of the Fairies.[1] Shakespeare may have owed something to Greene's portrait of Oberon in *James IV*, but most of the fairy matter seems to have been derived from folk-lore. The diminutive fairies were apparently invented by Shakespeare himself when he wrote the Queen Mab speech for Mercutio.[2] Oberon and Titania are more like the conventional fairies in size,[3] but Cobweb and Mustardseed seem to vary in size from that of Mercutio's fairies to that of Titania herself. Titania's name was given by Golding to Diana, and fairies were thought by some to be survivals of Diana's train. That the mother of the Indian Boy was a votaress of Titania's order does not disprove this identification, since Diana, as Lucina, was the goddess of childbirth. It has been suggested that some hints for the play may have come from *Endimion* and other plays by John Lyly.[4] Fripp believed there were ten echoes from Marlowe's *Dido*,[5] though the resemblances may be accidental. It is probable that the magic juice was suggested by Montemayor's *Diana*.[6] The Theseus matter came from North's translation of Plutarch and *The Knightes Tale* of Chaucer: there are verbal echoes of both.[7] It may even be that the rivalry of Demetrius and Lysander for Hermia's love was suggested by the rivalry of Palamon and Arcite; but, if so, Shakespeare added Helena both as a complication and as a means of providing each man with a bride.

Shakespeare, therefore, appears to have taken hints from a number of different sources, but only with the interlude of Pyramus and Thisbe can we be certain what the sources actually were.[8] It has been conjectured that the story of Romeo and Juliet, taken by Shakespeare from Brooke and Painter, was ultimately derived from the story of Pyramus and Thisbe; for in both tales the lovers, because of their parents' opposition, meet in secret, in both the

---

[1] T. Nashe, *Works*, ed. McKerrow, iii. p. 324.   [2] *R.J.* I. iv. 52 ff.
[3] E. Schanzer, *U.T.Q.* (1955), pp. 234 ff.
[4] e.g. J. D. Wilson, *John Lyly* (1905), p. 123; R. W. Bond ed. Lyly, ii. p. 297.
[5] E. I. Fripp, *Shakespeare Man and Artist* (1938), p. 394.
[6] Cf. E. K. Chambers, *William Shakespeare* (1930), p. 363.
[7] Cf. F. Sidgwick, *Sources and Analogues of M.N.D.* (1908).
[8] G. Hart, *Die Pyramus & Thisbe Sage* (1891), may have forestalled me in some of my arguments, but I have not been able to procure a copy.

hero commits suicide in the mistaken belief that the heroine is dead, and in both the man's suicide is followed by that of the woman. The resemblance between the two stories had, indeed, been pointed out by George Pettie, who remarked[1] at the end of one of his tales

> that such pressiness of parents brought Pyramus and Thisbe to a woful end, Romeo and Julietta to untimely death.

Shakespeare seems to have turned to the Pyramus story while he was actually writing *Romeo and Juliet*, for the last scene of the play was influenced by Golding's version of Ovid's tale.[2]

Chaucer, however, provides a link between the interlude and the Oberon–Titania plot. In *The Merchant's Tale* there is a reference to Pyramus and Thisbe:

> By Pyramus and Thisbe may men lere;
> Though they were kept ful long streit ouer all
> They ben accorded, rowning through a wall
> Ther nis no wight couth finde such a sleight.

This occurs between two references to Pluto and Proserpina as the King and Queen of the fairies:

> Ful ofte tyme king Pluto and his quene,
> Proserpina, and all hir fayry
> Disporten hem, and maken melody.

In the other passage Pluto and Proserpina have a long argument about female treachery, Proserpina defending her own sex. Pluto gives January his sight again at the moment when Damian is making love to May. So in *A Midsummer-Night's Dream* we have a quarrel between the King and Queen of the fairies, and the recovery of sight by the enchanted lovers.

Now, parts of Golding's version of the Pyramus story were unintentionally ludicrous, as we shall see. Even Ovid's original account is a trifle absurd. The whispering through the hole in the wall, the lovers' alacrity in suicide, the way Pyramus's blood spurts out to stain the mulberry leaves, like water from a burst pipe, are more likely to evoke a smile than the emotions Ovid intended to arouse. But the various Elizabethan versions were all positively disastrous in different ways. There is, for example, a strip-cartoon version of the story, which appeared as a border on the title-page

---

[1] *The Petite Pallace of Pettie his Pleasure* (ed. 1908), i. 168.
[2] Golding, like Juliet, uses the word 'churl'.

of several books published by Tottel—though not in his best-known book, *Songes and Sonnets*. One book in which it appears is Sir Thomas More's *Dialoge of comfort against tribulacion* (1553). The upper part of the picture shows a not very fierce lion, with Thisbe keeping a discreet distance. To the left is a crude piece of masonry which may be Ninus's tomb, but seems more likely to be the wall that parted the two lovers, for it contains a slit which one is tempted to call a chink or cranny. The lower part of the picture shows Thisbe bending over Pyramus's body. The picture is very crudely drawn; nor does it seem to have any connexion with More's *Dialoge*, unless we assume that Pyramus and Thisbe would not have been so prone to kill themselves if they had had the benefit of More's comfort against tribulation.[1]

Two of the Elizabethan miscellanies had versions of the Pyramus story. The one given in *A Handful of Pleasant Delites* by J. Thomson is a simple and naïve ballad. The one in *The Gorgious Gallery of Gallant Inventions* professes to be 'truly translated', but not apparently from Ovid. According to Professor Bush, it appears to be descended from a twelfth-century French version of the story. At least two other versions of the story appeared in Shakespeare's life-time, one by Dunstan Gale, and one by Thomas Mouffet in his didactic poem, *Of the Silkewormes, and their Flies*. No copies of the first edition of Gale's poem have survived, but it seems from the dedication to have been published in 1596 or 1597. Mouffet's poem appeared in 1599, but it was probably circulating in manuscript for four or five years before that date.

There were four other versions which belong to an earlier date. One, now lost, unless it is that in *The Gorgious Gallery*, was entered in the Stationers' Register as early as 1562. This may have been a play or a poem. Lydgate's *Reson and Sensualyte*[2] contained a version of the story which was designed to point a moral; and, still earlier, Gower had retold it in his *Confessio Amantis*[3] to show that Love's wits are often blind, and that when passion usurps the place of reason the results are apt to be disastrous. But in spite of all these variations on Ovid's theme, Chaucer's tale in *The Legend of Good Women* remained incomparably the best.

The evidence that Shakespeare had read several versions of the Pyramus story is of two kinds, general and particular.

[1] Cf. R. B. McKerrow, *The Library* (1924-5), pp. 17-8, and McKerrow and Ferguson, *Title Page Borders*.
[2] ll. 3960 ff.   [3] III. 1331 ff. Cf. *Anglia*, xii. 16.

Of the first kind there is the knowledge that he had read Ovid and Golding; that he knew some of Chaucer's works and, indeed, made use of the Knight's Tale in the main plot of *A Midsummer-Night's Dream*; and that he had probably read at least one poem in *A Handful of Pleasant Delites*, on the language of flowers, for he remembered some of it when depicting Ophelia's madness:

> Rosemary is for remembrance
>> Between us day and night. . . .
> Fennel is for flatterers,
>> An evil thing it is sure. . . .
> Violet is for faithfulness,
>> Which in me shall abide.

Then, of the second kind of evidence, there are verbal parallels with *A Midsummer-Night's Dream*. When there are several echoes from one version of the Pyramus story, it is reasonable to assume that Shakespeare had read it.

Let us begin, then, with Golding's translation. Here we find the word 'cranny'.

The wall that parted house from house had riuen therein a crannie
Which shroonke at making of the wall.

'Cranny' was also Bottom's word for it (III. i. 62), and it was later incorporated in Snout's speech as Wall:

> And this the cranny is, right and sinister,
> Through which the fearefull Louers are to whisper.

No other version uses this word.

Both Golding and Shakespeare say that Thisbe left her mantle behind, and Thomson also calls it a mantle. In Ovid it is *velamina*, and this becomes a *scarf* (Mouffet), a *kerchief* (*G.G.G.I.*), and a *wimpel* (Chaucer and Gower).

In Ovid the lovers inform the wall that they are not ungrateful to it for enabling them to converse. In Golding this becomes:

And yet thou shalt not find vs churles; we thinke our selues in det
For the same peece of curtesie, in vouching safe to let
Our sayings to our friendly eares thus freely come and go.

We seem to have an echo of *courtesy* in the words:

> Thankes, courteous wall: *Ioue* shield thee well for this!

One characteristic of Golding's translation is the excessive use as padding of the auxiliary *did*, as in these lines:

This neighbrod bred acquaintance first, this neighbrod first did
    stir
The secret sparkes, this neighbrod first an entrance in did show,
For loue to come to that to which it afterward did grow.

So in Quince's Prologue we get four *dids* in three lines:

       This grizly beast (which Lyon hight by name)
       The trusty *Thisby*, comming first by night,
       Did scare away, or rather did affright;
       And as she fled, her mantle she did fall,
       Which Lyon vile with bloody mouth did staine.

Shakespeare does not, however, make use of two of Golding's most ludicrous passages. One of these describes Thisbe's discovery of Pyramus's body:

       Alas, what chance, my *Pyramus*, hath parted thee and mee?
       Make answere, O my *Pyramus*: It is thy *Thisbe*, euen she
       Whome thou doost loue most hartily that speaketh vnto thee,
       Giue eare and raise thy heauie head.

The other describes Thisbe's actual suicide:

This said, she tooke the sword yet warme with slaughter of hir
    loue,
And setting it beneath her brest, did to her heart it shoue.[1]

From Thomson's version in *A Handful of Pleasant Delites* Shakespeare seems to have borrowed the stanza form used in the laments of Pyramus and Thisbe for each other:

       In Babilon
       not long agone,
         a noble Prince did dwell:
       whose daughter bright
       dimd ech ones sight,
         so farre she did excel.

[1] Perhaps the rhyme used by Thisbe, dumbe—tombe, may have been suggested by Golding's 'Tumbe' in the last line of his version of the story.

Now am I dead,
Now am I fled;
 My soule is in the sky:
Tongue, lose thy light;
Moone, take thy flight:
 Now dye, dye, dye, dye, dye.

Like Thomson, Shakespeare refers to Pyramus as a knight (V. i. 282), and the joke is pointed by Flute's earlier question: 'What is *Thisbie*? a wandring Knight?' Thomson likewise refers to the fatal thread of the Fates:

Oh Gods aboue, my faithfull loue
 shal neuer faile this need:
For this my breath by fatall death,
 shal weaue *Atropos* threed.

Professor Douglas Bush thinks these lines 'may have been in Shakespeare's mind when, in providing a tragic vehicle for Bottom, he burlesqued the theatrical heroics of an earlier age'.[1] Certainly the double mixture of metaphor in the idea of a breath weaving Atropos' thread makes the passage memorable; and both Pyramus and Thisbe refer to the Fates in similar terms:

O Fates! come, come:
 Cut thred and thrum,
Quaile, crush, conclude, and quell.

O sisters three,
 Come, come to mee,
With hands as pale as milke
 Lay them in gore,
 Since you haue shore
With sheeres his thred of silke.

It is possible, however, that Shakespeare was also influenced by the story of Cephalus and Procris as told by Howell; for Pyramus and Thisbe both refer to Shafulus and Procrus, and Sephalus in Howell's poem calls on the sisters three:[2]

When Sephalus his Procris founde,
Imbrude with blood on euery side,
The arowe stickinge in the wounde,

---

[1] *Mythology and the Renaissance Tradition*, p. 55. Cf. *C.H.E.L.* iii. 191.
[2] Cf. Bush, op. cit., p. 59.

> That bleedinge sore did gape full wyde,
> He curst the gods that skies possest
> The systers three and all the rest.

Thomson uses an archaic pronunciation for the sake of a rhyme—

> For why he thought the lion had,
>   faire *Thisbie* slaine.
> And then the beast with his bright blade,
>   he slew certaine.—

and Peter Quince does the same thing:

> This beauteous Lady *Thisby* is certaine.

Both Thomson and Shakespeare use the expression 'make moan'.[1]
    Shakespeare seems to have been less indebted to the version of
the Pyramus story given in *A Gorgious Gallery of Gallant Inventions*,
for that is mostly dull rather than ridiculous. But his reading of it
was not entirely barren. He noticed the lines which describe how
Thisbe found the cranny or chink:

> And scarecely then her pearcing looke one blinke therof had got,
> But that firme hope of good successe, within her fancy shot.

This doubtless suggested Pyramus's line:

> Show me thy chink, to blink through with myne eyne!

The anonymous author uses the elegant variation 'name' and
'hight' in successive lines; and Quince speaks of 'Lion hight by
name'. Pyramus is described as 'more fresh then flower in May',
and Shakespeare's is described as

> most Lilly-white of hue,
> Of colour like the red rose on triumphant bryer.

Pyramus revives a moment just before he dies:

> The Gentilman with this, and as the lastest throwes of death,
> Did pearce full fast at that same stroke, to end both life and breath.

So Quince, trying to persuade Bottom to play the part of Pyramus,
assures him that the character is 'a most louely Gentleman-like
man' (I. ii. 90). The last parallel is to be found in the lines describing Thisbe's suicide:

---

[1] Cf. 'Then made he mone' and V. i. 341.

Then Thisbie efte, with shrike so shrill as dynned in the sky,
Swaps down in swoone, shee eft reuiues, & hents the sword
    hereby.
Wherwith beneath her pap (alas) into her brest shee strake,
Saying thus will I die for him, that thus dyed for my sake.

Shakespeare borrows the 'pap' and makes it more ludicrous by
giving it to Pyramus instead of to Thisbe.[1]

    Shakespeare took very little from Chaucer's version of the story,
presumably because it is not naturally ludicrous. But we may suppose that the lines—[2]

> Thus wolde they sayne, alas thou wicked wal
> Through thyn enuye, thou vs lettest al—

suggested Bottom's exclamation:

> O wicked wall, through whom I see no blisse!

And a phrase which occurs in two of Chaucer's lines—

> With blody mouthe, of stranglyng of a beest . . .
> And with her blody mouth it al to rente—

doubtless gave Quince his phrase 'with bloody mouth'.
    Dunstan Gale's *Pyramus and Thisbe* (of which the epistle dedica-
tory is dated 25 November 1596) is both dull and bad. It is written
in heroic couplets divided into 12-line stanzas, the last couplet of
each having a feminine rhyme. These rhymes cause Gale some
difficulty:

e.g.

> Where squint-eyed *Cupid* late vpon his quiuer,
> Viewing his none-eyd body in the riuer.
>   (St. 6)

> Somtimes poor souls, they talkt till they were windles
> And all their talke was of their frends vnkindnes.
>   (St. 11)

> His hand retired still, further backe and further,
> As lothing to enact so vile a murther.
>   (St. 26)

---

[1] This version has also the following words and phrases: 'cursed blade', 'embrude',
and 'wicked cruell wall' (cf. V. i. 147, 351, 181). But 'blade' and 'embrude' are used
by Mouffet, and 'wikked wal' by Chaucer.
[2] Quotations are from the 1545(?) edition.

There are other absurdities, as when he describes how Thisbe escaped from the Lion:

> The Lion came yet meant no harme at all,
> And comming found the mantle she let fall,
> Which now he kist, he would haue kist her too,
> But that her nimble footmanship said no.

But the only passage which has much resemblance to Shakespeare's version is the couplet at the end of the second stanza:

> And this (quoth she) shall be my true loues fauor:
> Her tender nonage did of true loue sauor.

Apparently the resemblance to 'odious savours sweet' is fortuitous, for there is no reason to believe that Shakespeare saw the poem in manuscript, and if Gale was acquainted with *A Midsummer-Night's Dream* it is odd that he should dare to choose the subject of Pyramus and Thisbe, and curious that he nowhere else exhibits knowledge of Shakespeare's version of the story.

There remains to be considered the version from which Shakespeare appears to have taken most, that contained in Thomas Mouffet's poem, *Of the Silkewormes, and their Flies*. Mouffet describes himself as 'a Countrie Farmer, and an apprentice in Physicke'. He was, in fact, a distinguished physician, the author of several medical works, whose reputation brought him many aristocratic patients and led to his appointment to the post of physician to the forces under the Earl of Essex in Normandy in 1591. He was persuaded by the Earl and Countess of Pembroke to settle at Wilton, and he lived there until his death in 1604. His best work, *The Theatre of Insects*, written in Latin, was finished in 1589, but not published until many years later. A translation of it was appended to the 1658 edition of Edward Topsell's *History of Four-Footed Beasts*. I cherish the belief, which the editors of *The Oxford Book of Nursery Rhymes* regard as a delusion, that the heroine of the nursery, Little Miss Muffet, owes her name to the fact that Mouffet wrote at some length about spiders; and some of the illustrations in *The Theatre of Insects* would frighten a stouter heart than that of Miss Muffet, and require a more potent charm than the faeries' song:

> Weauing Spiders, come not heere,
> Hence, you long-leg'd Spinners, hence!

Mouffet's poem on the silkworms was not published until 1599, four years after the staging of *A Midsummer-Night's Dream*, though before it was printed. But there is some evidence that the poem had been written some years before this date. It is dedicated to the Countess of Pembroke, and opens with an address to the Sidneian Muse which would be more appropriate to 1594 than to 1599. There is a reference to 1589 in the poem, and Mouffet mentions that he visited Italy in 1579 when he studied the cultivation of the silkworm. Moreover there is an entry in the Stationers' Register dated 15 January 1589 about a lost book of poems 'by Mr Morfet', who may conceivably be our Thomas Mouffet. It is extremely unlikely that Shakespeare would rewrite the Pyramus and Thisbe interlude just before the publication of his play in 1600 in order to parody Mouffet's verses; and yet there is abundant internal evidence that he must have read them. We may assume, then, that Mouffet wrote the poem between 1590 and 1595, and that Shakespeare read it in manuscript.

The poem was written to advocate the cultivation of the silkworm, and Mouffet introduced the story of Pyramus and Thisbe for the simple reason that silkworms feed on mulberry leaves and, according to Ovid, the fruit of the mulberry, white before the tragedy, was stained for ever with the blood of the lovers. Shakespeare's interlude, as we shall see, was so close to Mouffet's version of the story that it must have been an intentional parody of it. Mouffet was 'a godly and learned phisitian and skilful mathematician', a great naturalist, a future M.P.—but no poet. The art of sinking in poetry has seldom been so superbly exercised. Some of Mouffet's lapses are caused by his blissful unconsciousness of ambiguity. The word *bottom*, for example, is the technical term for the silkworm's cocoon; but when we read at the end of the Pyramus story[1]—

> Leauing their ouall bottoms there behind,
> To shewe the state of eu'ry Louers mind—

we can hardly avoid thinking, though perhaps anachronistically, of the alternative meanings of *bottom* and *behind*. Even more disastrous is the line[2]—

> Where many silken bottoms hangd in piles.

Another kind of absurdity is illustrated by Thisbe's remark about *Pyramus*[3]

[1] p. 18.   [2] p. 8.   [3] p. 17.

One too too hot, for so imports his name—

to which Mouffet obligingly inserts the marginal note:

'Pyramus signifieth as much as fiery'.

It is not surprising, therefore, that Shakespeare should find
Mouffet a fit subject for ridicule, and he read the poem with some
care. The leading actor in the Interlude was christened Bottom,
and as the Silkworm was a spinner, Bottom was made a weaver.
Two of the fairies are also linked with Mouffet's subject by their
names Moth and Cobweb. The orange-tawny beard which he
offers as an alternative, and the orange-tawny bill of the ousel-
cock in the song with which he awakens Titania, were possibly
suggested by Mouffet's lines describing the white moths by mentioning the colours they were not:

> No yellow, where there is no Iealousie . . .
> No orenge colour, where there wants despight,
> No tawny sadde, where none forsaken be.

When Bottom sings his song he feels forsaken and despitefully
used.[1]

Shakespeare did not confine his attention to the section of the
poem devoted to the story of Pyramus and Thisbe. Theseus's first
speech in Act V which begins:

> More strange than true: I neuer may beleeue
> These anticke fables, nor these Fairy toyes . . .

and ends:

> Or in the night, imagining some feare,
> How easie is a bush suppos'd a Beare!

seems to echo three passages from Mouffet's poem:

> As reft our wittes, and made vs al so mad:
> That we resembled melancholique hares,
> Or startling stagges, whom euerie shadow scares.

> Yet some conceiue when *Theban* singer wanne,
> Wood-wandring wights to good and ciuill life,
> (Which erst with beares and wolues in desarts ran).

[1] p. 28. Cf. I. ii. 96–8; III. i. 128.

> I count it but a tale and fable vaine,
> By some olde wife, or cousning friar told:
>> Supposed true, though time and truth descries,
>> That all such workes are but the workes of lies.[1]

Mouffet's reference to the 'Theban singer' may have suggested Shakespeare's reference a few lines later to Thebes and the Thracian singer.

But these casual echoes are less significant than the many echoes of the stanzas in which Mouffet tells the story of Pyramus and Thisbe. Shakespeare copied Mouffet's habit of using words merely to pad out a line. *Eke* and *whereat*, for example, are used over and over again by Mouffet; and Shakespeare uses them with brilliant effect in the lines:

> Whereat, with blade, with bloody blamefull blade . . .
> Most brisky Iuuenall, and eke most louely Iew.

Mouffet uses *Chink* in a later section of his poem, and *Chinkt* in the Pyramus section: [2]

> If also carelessnesse haue left a rift,
> Or chincke vnstopped in thine aged wall;
> When night approacht, they ech bad ech adew,
> Kissing their wal apart where it was chinckt,
> Whence louely blasts and breathings mainely flew:
> But kisses staide on eithers side fast linckt,
> Seal'd to the wal with lips and Louers glue:
>> For though they were both thick and many eake,
>> Yet thicker was the wal that did them breake.

Shakespeare uses the word *Chink* several times, as in the line—

> I see a voyce: now will I to the chinke.

Perhaps, too, this stanza suggested the line:

> I kisse the wals hole, not your lips at all.

Shakespeare and Mouffet both speak of the lion as grisly, and both poets use *fell* in the same context:

> The grisly wife of bruttish monarch strong,
> With new slaine prey, full panched to the chinne,
> Foming out bloud, came ramping there along . . .

---

[1] pp. 2, 4, 44.   [2] pp. 58, 11.

O Lions fierce (or if ought fiercer be)
Among the heards of woody outlawes fell
Rent, rent in twaine this thrise-accursed me:
From out your paunch conuey my soule to hell.[1]

It may even be suggested that Mouffet's curious method of stating
that it was a lioness ('grisly wife') rather than a lion, together with
the fact that the other sources are divided about the sex of the lion,
led Shakespeare to Snug's lines:

> Then know that I, one *Snug* the Ioyner, am
> A Lion fell, nor else no Lions dam.

In the same stanza Mouffet uses the word *quell*, and refers to the
Sisters Three:

> Whose murdring slouth, and not the sisters three,
> Did *Thisbe* sweete, sweete *Thisbe* fowly quell.

Pyramus in the play refers to the fates, and uses the word *quell* in
successive lines; and Thisbe invokes the Sisters Three.

Mouffet speaks of Pyramus's weapon as a *blade*, and he uses the
word *imbrue*; but he is not alone in this. He refers to Thisbe as
'poor soul' and to Pyramus as a paragon. Shakespeare followed
him in all these points. Indeed, it may have been Mouffet's description of the lovers as 'Each of their sex the floure and paragon'
which suggested Shakespeare's comparison of Pyramus to flowers,
as in Thisbe's lines:

> These Lilly Lips,
> This cherry nose,
> These yellow Cowslip cheekes,
> Are gone, are gone,
> Louers, make mone:
> His eyes were greene as Leekes.

But the lines were also suggested by the description of Thisbe's
reactions on encountering the body of her lover:[2]

> Her lips grew then more pale then palest Boxe,
> Her cheekes resembled Ashwood newly feld,
> Graynesse surpriz'd her yellow amber locks,
> Nor any part their liuely lustre held.

Mouffet's similes are somewhat fantastic, and Shakespeare makes

---

[1] pp. 12, 14.   [2] p. 16.

matters worse by confusing them. Instead of yellow amber locks, he gives us yellow cowslip cheeks, and he adds the comparison of the eyes to leeks.

Mouffet's lines—

> Speake loue, O speake, how hapned this to thee?
> Part, halfe, yes all of this my soule and mee.

> Sweete loue, reply, it is thy Thisbe deare,
> She cries, O heare, she speakes, O answere make:
> Rowse vp thy sprights: these heauie lookers cheere.

are parodied by Shakespeare in Thisbe's words 'O Pyramus, arise! Speak, speak' and in Bottom's words when he wants to act the part:

> 'Ah Pyramus, my lover dear! thy Thisbe dear, and lady dear!'[1]

The phrase 'these heauie lookers cheere' may have influenced Bottom's line:

> That liu'd, that lou'd, that lik'd, that look'd with cheere.

Mouffet's stanza on Pyramus's suicide may have combined with Golding's version to suggest the line:

> He brauely broacht his boiling bloudy breast.

The significant word *broached* is paralleled more closely by Mouffet's words:

> Hold earth, receiue a draught eke of my bloud,
> (And therewith lean'd vppon his sword amaine)
> Then falling backward from the crimsin floud,
> Which spowted forth with such a noyse and straine,
> As water doth, when pipes of lead or wood,
> Are goog'd with punch, or cheesil slit in twaine,
>> Whistling in th' ayre, and breaking it with blowes,
>> Whilst heauie moysture vpward forced flowes.

Golding does not have a word suggesting the positive action of breaching. In his version the pipe is merely cracked accidentally:

> The blood did spin on high
> As when a conduit pipe is cracked, the water bursting out
> Doth shoot itself a great way off and pierce the air about.

---

[1] p. 16. Cf. V. i. 333–4 and I. ii. 55. Chaucer's version, however, reads:
> O speke Piramus,
> I am thy Thisbe, that thee calleth thus.

The idea of Bottom's metamorphosis may have been suggested by Mouffet's lines[1] (they occur just before the Pyramus story):

> Transforme thy selfe into a Courser braue,
> (What cannot loue transforme it selfe into?)
> Feede in her walkes; and in a moment haue
> What thou hast woo'd to haue with much adooe:
> Whereto, consent the auncient Suter gaue,
> In courser clothes, learning a maide to wooe,
>   Filling ech wood with neighs and wihyes shrill,
>   Whilst he possest his loue against her will.

This is Venus's advice to Saturn on how to woo the disdainful Phillyra, by means of craft and force. One phrase, 'Feede in her walkes', probably suggested Titania's instructions about Bottom:

> Hop in his walkes and gambole in his eies;
> Feede him with Apricocks.

Moreover, it is possible that Phillyra's refusal of her suitor and her gathering of healing herbs may have given a hint for the 'faire Vestall throned by the West'. In any case the transformation of Bottom was doubtless influenced also by memories of *The Golden Ass*, of a similar transformation mentioned in Scot's *Discouerie of Witchcraft*, and of a recipe, given in the same book, for setting an ass's head on a man's neck and shoulders:[2]

The words used in such case are uncertain, and to be recited at the pleasure of the witch or cozener. But at the conclusion of this, cut off the head of a horse or an ass (before they be dead, otherwise the virtue or strength thereof will be the less effectual), and make an earthen vessel of fit capacity to contain the same, and let it be filled with the oil and fat thereof, cover it close, and daub it over with loam; let it boil over a soft fire three days continually, that the flesh boiled may run into oil, so as the bare bones may be seen; beat the hair into powder, and mingle the same with the oil; and anoint the heads of the standers by, and they shall seem to have horses' or asses' heads.

---

[1] p. 7.
[2] Cited by F. Sidgwick, *The Sources and Analogues of M.N.D.* (1908), p. 139. Most of the parallels with Mouffet's poem have been pointed out by M. L. Farrand (*S.P.* xxvii, pp. 233–43) and A. S. T. Fisher (*N.Q.*, 1949, pp. 376 ff.). D. Bush, however, (*M.L.N.*, xlvi, pp. 144–7) denied Miss Farrand's arguments. He wrote before the more convincing later article.

Even this does not exhaust the probable sources of the Pyramus interlude. It is described as

> A tedious breefe Scene of yong *Piramus*,
> And his loue *Thisby*; very tragicall mirth.

It looks as though Shakespeare was referring to the play of *Cambises*, which is described on the title-page as 'A lamentable tragedy mixed full of pleasant mirth'; and sure enough, if we examine Preston's play, we find that Shakespeare may have delved there too.[1] In the Prologue we read of the fate of Cyrus:

But he, when sisters three had wrought to shear his vital thread.

A mother laments the death of her son in words that have been thought to recall the lament of Thisbe; and the boy's lips, 'silk-soft and pleasant white', may have suggested the lily lips of Pyramus. There is no need to press the last point. It is enough for my purpose if the reader is willing to concede that Shakespeare consulted six or seven versions of the Pyramus story before writing his tedious brief scene. A study of the tragical mirth of Quince's interlude leads one almost to the heart of Shakespeare's craftsmanship and even throws a little light on the workings of the poetic imagination.

It is possible, of course, that all the versions of the Pyramus and Thisbe story Shakespeare had read since childhood coalesced in his mind; but the evidence suggests that he consulted them during the actual composition of *A Midsummer-Night's Dream*. One purpose, no doubt, of the performance by Quince's company was to show by means of a farcical tragedy that lovers cannot rely on the intervention of Oberon or Puck to save them from the consequences of their irrationality. A second purpose was to arouse hearty laughter by exposing the ludicrous inadequacy of some amateur actors. A third purpose was to show intelligent members of the audience that *Romeo and Juliet*, written just before, was an unsatisfactory tragedy because it depended too much on accident.[2] The result had been pitiful, but not tragic. A fourth purpose was akin to that of Nashe in re-telling farcically the story of Marlowe's *Hero and Leander*; the audience would be sophisticatedly amused by the contrast between the burlesque and the original. A fifth purpose—for which any play would have served—was to provide

[1] Cf. M. C. Bradbrook, *Shakespeare and Elizabethan Poetry* (1951), p. 98.
[2] E. Schanzer, *N.Q.* (1955), p. 13, shows that one detail in the interlude was derived from *R.J.*

an occasion for various reflections on the relation of life to art, actors being shadows and life itself being a dream. The masque in *The Tempest* provided a similar opportunity. Lastly, Shakespeare had compiled a kind of anthology of bad poetry, which, like *The Stuffed Owl* in our own day, served as oblique criticism. Quince's play serves to satirize not only the crude mingling of tragedy and comedy still prevalent in the lower levels of popular drama in 1595, but also many of the particular absurdities into which the poetasters of the age were liable to fall. By a beautiful piece of artistic economy Shakespeare was able to cull his choice blooms of absurdity, not from the vast stores of bad poetry available to him, but from all the best-known versions of the Pyramus and Thisbe story.

(4) The Merchant of Venice

Stephen Gosson in his *Schoole of Abuse* (1579) speaks of a play called *The Jew*

> showne at the Bull . . . representing the greedinesse of wordly chusers, and bloody mindes of Usurers.

It has been argued that 'the greedinesse of wordly chusers' refers to the plot of the caskets and the 'bloody mindes of Usurers' to the story of the Pound of Flesh. But it is by no means certain that *The Jew* was the source-play of *The Merchant of Venice*. Dramatists before 1579, so far as we know, did not have the technical skill to combine two plots in this way; both phrases may well refer to a single plot, 'the greedinesse of worldly chusers' referring to those who choose a worldly way of life rather than to suitors like Morocco and Arragon; and 'bloody', a common epithet for Usurers and Jews, does not necessarily imply the pound of flesh story.[1]

Two other lost plays, *The Venésyon Comodye* (acted 1594) and Dekker's *The Jew of Venice* (of unknown date), may have some connexion with Shakespeare's play, but nothing is known about them beyond their titles.[2] Although, therefore, there may have been a dramatic source for *The Merchant of Venice* it is just as likely that Shakespeare himself first dramatized the story given in *Il Pecorone*.

[1] Cf. E. Honigmann, *M.L.R.* (1954), pp. 297–8.
[2] Cf. J. R. Brown, ed. *M.V.*, p. xxx.

Ansaldo's godson, Giannetto, tries on two occasions to win the
lady of Belmonte, a rich widow who agrees to marry the first man
who enjoys her on condition that should he fail he shall forfeit all
his wealth. On both occasions Giannetto is given drugged wine
and, being ashamed to tell Ansaldo what really happened, he pretends he has twice been shipwrecked. Ansaldo borrows 10,000
ducats from a Jew to enable him to equip a third ship for Giannetto on the condition that if the money is not repaid on St John's
Day he will forfeit a pound of flesh. Being warned by a maid not
to drink the wine, Giannetto enjoys the Lady of Belmonte and
marries her. When on St John's Day he recalls Ansaldo's plight,
his wife sends him to Venice with 100,000 ducats, and follows him
there disguised as a lawyer. The Jew refuses the 100,000 ducats
and demands his pound of flesh. The Lady proclaims that she will
settle any dispute and Giannetto persuades the Jew to appear before the lawyer, who tells him to take his pound of flesh without
shedding blood. The Jew tears up the bond and Ansaldo is freed.
Giannetto offers the 100,000 ducats in payment for the lawyer's
services, but the lawyer demands his ring instead. Giannetto returns to Belmonte with Ansaldo, and the Lady accuses him of
giving the ring to one of his former mistresses. Giannetto bursts
into tears and the Lady explains. Ansaldo, somewhat oddly, is
married off to the girl who has warned Giannetto not to drink.
Shakespeare retained the main outlines of the story, but he altered
it in various ways, as we shall see. But the Pound of Flesh story
was a favourite one and Shakespeare knew two or three other
versions of it.

In Alexander Silvayn's *The Orator*, translated by L. Piot (1596),
there are two speeches at the trial by the Jew and the Christian
which seem to have influenced the trial scene in *The Merchant of
Venice*.[1] The Jew begins by saying

> Impossible is it to breake the credite of trafficke amongst men
> without great detriment vnto the commonwealth.

—an idea used three times by Shakespeare. The Jew refers to those
who 'bind al the bodie . . . vnto an intollerable slauerie' as an
example of common cruelty; so Shylock refers to the treatment of
slaves in Venice. Thirdly, the Jew says

> A man may aske why I would not rather take siluer of this man,
> then his flesh.

[1] Cf. J. R. Brown, ed. *M.V.*, p. xxxi.

Shylock has a similar sentence:

> You'l aske me why I rather choose to haue
> A weight of carrion flesh, than to receiue
> Three thousand Ducats.

None of these three points is to be found in *Il Pecorone*.

Another version of the Pound of Flesh story is to be found in Anthony Munday's *Zelauto* (1580), though here the Usurer demands the eyes of his victim. There is strong evidence that Shakespeare knew this version also. Mr J. R. Brown lists[1] a number of parallels of which the most significant are the following:

> In fayth, then fare well frost, more such haue we lost. . . . A colde sute, and a harde penniwoorth haue all they that traffique for such merchandize. . . . I should haue but a colde sute with my wooing. But belyke you are betrothed already: and that makes you so dayntie, if you be tell me, that I loose no more labour.

Although Shakespeare in *The Two Gentlemen of Verona* uses the phrase 'cold suit', the juxtaposition of 'frost' and 'labour lost' with the two uses by Munday of these words makes it certain that these lines in one of the casket scenes (II. vii. 73-5) are echoed from *Zelauto*:

> *Fare you well, your suite is cold* . . .
> Cold indeede, and labour lost,
> Then farewell heate, and welcome frost.

In an earlier scene Portia uses the phrase 'poor pennyworth'. The usurer declares: 'I crave Iustice' and Shylock says, 'I crave the Law'. The Usurer is made to leave all his goods to his son-in-law, as Shylock has to give all of which he dies possessed to Lorenzo.

A third version of the Pound of Flesh story also has two or three significant parallels, but this ballad may have been written after *The Merchant of Venice*. The Jew, Gernutus, in proposing the bond, says 'We will have a merry ieast', as Shylock proposes it 'in a merry sport'. The merchant tells the Jew

> And little good the forfeiture
> will doe you, I dare say.

So, in the play, Solanio tells Shylock:

> Why I am sure if he forfaite, thou wilt not take his flesh,—what's that good for? (III. i. 45-6).

[1] Cf. J. R. Brown, ed. *M.V.*, pp. xxx-xxxi.

49

Finally, the ballad describes the Jew at the trial 'with whetted blade in hand'.

The Caskets plot was apparently derived from R. Robinson's translation of the *Gesta Romanorum* (1595), though the inscription on the leaden casket is quite different from that in the play, and the inscriptions on the other two caskets are interchanged. The word 'insculpt', used by Morocco in the first of the casket-scenes, and used nowhere else by Shakespeare, is to be found in Robinson's translation.[1]

The Jessica story—the elopement of the Usurer's daughter with her lover—was probably suggested by *Zelauto*. As we have seen, the usurer's son-in-law becomes his heir (as in *The Merchant of Venice*) and there are two disguised ladies at the trial, Cornelia and Brisana, and not one as in *Il Pecorone*. Masuccio di Salerno has a story in which a miser's daughter escapes with her father's jewels and joins her lover, which Shakespeare may possibly have read. But it is probable that the Jessica story is influenced by Marlowe's *The Jew of Malta* in which Abigail falls in love with a Christian, turns nun, and betrays her father. When she first goes to the Nunnery it is in order to secure for her father the treasure he has hidden there. She throws down the money-bags, as Jessica throws down a casket to Lorenzo. Barabas, hugging the bags exclaims:

> Oh my girle
> My gold, my fortune, my felicity; . . .
> Oh girle, oh gold, oh beauty, oh my blisse.

Shylock similarly cries out on hearing of his daughter's flight:

> My daughter, O my ducats, O my daughter!

It was, perhaps, the revival of *The Jew of Malta* at the time of the Lopez case, or the later revival in 1596, that suggested to Shakespeare a play with a villainous Jew. Professor J. D. Wilson has even put forward the theory that the play was more or less commissioned by Southampton, since it was Essex who denounced Lopez as a traitor.[2] *Il Pecorone* certainly provided a villainous Jew, but the predatory Lady of Belmonte who drugs her suitors and confiscates the goods of those who failed to sleep with her would not quite do as a heroine, in spite of her adventure at the end of the story. Furthermore, the hero deceives his godfather and shows a

---

[1] Cf. J. R. Brown, ed. *M.V.*, pp. xxxii, 173.
[2] In a lecture at Stratford-upon-Avon.

callous forgetfulness of the latter's danger. Shakespeare removed both blemishes by substituting the casket story for the Lady of Belmonte's method of choosing a husband. The Lady is no longer a widow, but a maiden bound by the will of her father. Bassanio confesses to Antonio the reason for his journey to Belmont, and it is Antonio's ill-fortune, not Bassanio's forgetfulness, that puts Antonio in Shylock's power. Shakespeare, moreover, introduces a close friendship between Antonio and Bassanio. The theme of friendship is an important part of the play, and the nature of true love is a theme naturally developed from the Caskets story. The same story may have suggested the contrast between the values represented by Bassanio and Shylock, the world of Belmont and the world of Venice, while the fact that Shylock was a Jew as well as a usurer enabled Shakespeare to bring in a contrast between the Old and New Testaments, at least in the trial scene. The provision of a daughter to Shylock, suggested by Marlowe or Masuccio—or both—gave the Jew a strong motive for revenge. Indeed, it has been argued that Shylock when he proposes the bond has no intention of enforcing it. Shakespeare added three further motives— hatred of Antonio as a Christian, hatred of him as an opponent of usury, and hatred of him for his ill-usage. Shylock is not the simple villain of the sources: Shakespeare alone stresses the faith and race of the usurer.

Shakespeare made other changes. He provides a more suitable groom for Portia's maid Nerissa than that provided by *Il Pecorone*. Nerissa does not give away her mistress's secrets and she is disguised as a lawyer's clerk at the trial, and this enabled Shakespeare to duplicate the business of the rings. Bassanio gives his ring only at Antonio's request, a request he could not honourably refuse. The trial, moreover, takes place before the Duke. In *Il Pecorone* the constitutional position by which the visiting lawyer is allowed to settle disputes is somewhat odd. Finally, it may be mentioned that Jessica disguises herself as a boy in order to elope with Lorenzo The disguise is Shakespeare's addition.

III

MATURE COMEDIES

(5) Much Ado about Nothing

THERE is little that need be added to Professor Charles T. Prouty's admirable book on the sources of *Much Ado about Nothing*.[1] He discusses eight plays, two of them lost, and the same number of non-dramatic versions of the Hero-Claudio story. Pasqualigo's *Il Fidele* (1579), Fraunce's *Victoria*, and Munday's *Two Italian Gentlemen* (1585)—versions in Latin and English of the Italian original—'all deal with the vengeance of a rejected lover who is denied his former pleasures'. The object of the deception is to cause 'the death of the former mistress'. There is no evidence that Shakespeare knew any of these three plays. There is some resemblance between Della Porta's *Gli duoi fratelli rivali* and Shakespeare's play; but as the former was not published until 1911 the resemblance is probably accidental. A more likely source is a lost play entitled *Ariodante and Genevra* which was performed on 12 February 1583 and from its title may well have been a dramatization of Peter Beverley's *Ariodanto and Genevra* (1566), a poem based on Ariosto's *Orlando Furioso*. Another lost play, also presented at Court, described as 'the matter of Panecia', was probably based on Bandello's tale in which the heroine's name is Fenicia. This play, acted on 1 January 1575, has also been suggested as Shakespeare's main source.

Even if Shakespeare based his comedy on one of the two lost plays, he was also acquainted with two or three other versions of the story. He knew *The Faerie Queene* (II. iv); he knew the *Orlando Furioso*, probably in the original as well as in Harington's translation (1591); and he knew some of Bandello's *Novelle* (1554) and Belleforest's *Histoires Tragiques* (1574) based on them. *Much Ado about Nothing* is based either on Bandello and Ariosto, or on two

[1] C. T. Prouty, *The Sources of 'Much Ado about Nothing'* (1950). Cf. K. Muir, M.L.R. (1952), pp. 219–20.

versions deriving ultimately from those writers, or on a lost version combining the two strains. In all versions of the story the hero is tricked into believing that the heroine is false by a rival who wishes to prevent their marriage. In Ariosto's account, and those derived from it, Genevra's maid, an unwitting accomplice, dresses up as her mistress, and the challenge to a duel is mentioned. In Bandello's version and its derivatives more is made of the friendship of the rivals, the trick does not involve the dressing-up of the maid, Fenicia swoons on being accused of unchastity and does not recover until 'the news of her death has been spread abroad'. When her innocence is established, Timbreo swears that he will marry none but a wife of Lionato's choosing. Here Shakespeare would have found the name of Hero's father. From Whetstone's version in *The Rocke of Regard* (1576) he may have got the idea of Claudio's rejection of Hero in Church. Frizaldo has promised to marry Rosina, Giletta's maid, as a reward for her part in the trick; and when it looks as though he is to marry Giletta after all, he explains to Rosina that he intends to satisfy his desire for vengeance by rejecting Giletta at the altar.

By analysing all the extant versions, Professor Prouty attempts to show what changes were made by Shakespeare. In all the extant versions, except Whetstone's, the 'rival's friendship with the hero is important in varying degrees'. Shakespeare played down the love-versus-friendship theme, perhaps because he had used it in *The Two Gentlemen of Verona*, but more probably because it had become stale. There are two points in the action of *Much Ado about Nothing*, as Professor Prouty points out, where the love-versus-friendship theme is stated, but in neither case is it developed. Claudio soon learns that Pedro has not betrayed him; and although Benedick, at Beatrice's request, challenges Claudio to a duel, the duel never actually takes place. The theme was always somewhat artificial. Although we can be induced to accept Shakespeare's resignation of mistress to friend in the *Sonnets*, there is an element of absurdity at the end of *The Two Gentlemen of Verona*. By the time he wrote *Much Ado about Nothing*, Shakespeare could not make the slanderer of Hero other than a villain: hence the invention of Don John. As the play was to be a comedy, Shakespeare had to inform the audience before the church scene that Don John's villainy would come to light; and for this purpose he created Dogberry, whose character was nicely designed to postpone the unmasking of Don John. If he has been more intelligent and less loquacious,

Hero would never have been accused before the altar; and if he had been even more stupid, Hero's name might never have been cleared.

There is no evidence, except the titles, about the contents of the lost plays; but at the date when they were written sub-plots seem to have been exceptional. It is probable, therefore, that Shakespeare himself was responsible for combining the Hero–Claudio plot with that of Beatrice and Benedick. He may have derived a hint from Castiglione's *Courtier* in which Lord Gaspare and the Lady Emilia carry on a similar kind of merry war.[1] Another possible influence on the character of Beatrice is the Mirabella story in *The Faerie Queene* (VI. 7).[2] On the journey to Cupid's court, Mirabella is guarded by Disdain and Scorn; and Hero, exaggerating for the sake of the listening Beatrice, says that 'Disdain and scorn ride sparkling in her eyes'. But Shakespeare did not have to read Spenser in order to know that some women were disdainful; nor did he have to read Castiglione to find prototypes of quarrelling lovers. There may be some unidentified source of the stratagem by which Beatrice and Benedick are made to avow their love for each other; but it may well have been suggested by the main plot. There Claudio is deceived into falling out of love with Hero by overhearing Borachio; in the other plot Beatrice and Benedick are tricked by a similar device into falling in love. Professor Prouty thinks that Shakespeare obtained a unity of tone by the recurrent device of overhearing, used throughout the play, and Masefield, it will be recalled, believed that the theme of the play was the power of report to alter human destiny.[3] It may be added that the unity is achieved partly by means of the imagery: disguise and counterfeiting are expressed in images and in iteration as well as in the actual plot.[4]

Beatrice and Benedick, by an effective stroke of irony, have been in love all the time. They despise the conventional behaviour of romantic lovers, and both confuse the conventional pattern of behaviour with love itself. They are clearly contrasted with Hero and Claudio, but this does not mean that we need accept Professor Prouty's view that that couple is equally 'unromantic' and that their marriage is one of convenience. Such a change in the original story would, it is true, give Claudio more excuse for his conduct,

[1] Mary A. Scott, *P.M.L.A.* (1901), pp. 475–502.
[2] Abbie Findlay Potts, *S.A.B.*, xvii (1942), pp. 103–11, 126–37.
[3] J. Masefield, *Shakespeare* (1911), p. 134.
[4] F. C. Kolbe, *Shakespeare's Way* (1930), p. 87.

in that if Hero is unchaste both she and her father have been guilty of sharp practice. But Claudio, on the evidence of his speeches, is genuinely in love; and although it is a convenient alliance for both parties, it cannot be regarded merely as a marriage of convenience.

(6) As You Like It

We are on surer ground in discussing the sources of *As You Like It*. Thomas Lodge's *Rosalynde*, published in 1590, has a good claim to be regarded as his masterpiece, and Sir Walter Greg is probably right in thinking that if it had not provided Shakespeare with a plot 'there would have been more chance of its receiving a genuinely critical appreciation'.[1] It is not, of course, great literature; 'but in its own particular style and within the limits of its kind the romance of Arden falls not far short of complete success'.

Lodge's own source was presumably *The Tale of Gamelyn*, and from this he took the story of Sir John of Bordeaux and his three sons, the wrestling match, and the hero's flight to join a band of outlaws. But all the events in the forest and even Rosalynde herself were apparently Lodge's own invention. To his source he added the 'basic ingredients of Elizabethan romance', and Mr J. D. Hurrell is right in thinking that there is no need to suppose that the latter part of the plot was derived from an Italian novel.[2] Lodge adhered to the ordinary conventions of the romance, and the merits of *Rosalynde* are due to his skill in the manipulation of conventional material, to the charming pastoral atmosphere, and to the quality of the interspersed lyrics. The prose, though it sometimes reminds us that the sub-title of the book is 'Euphues' golden Legacy', is less mannered and artificial than Lyly's.

The story begins with Sir John of Bordeaux's legacy to his three sons, Saladyne, Fernandyne, and Rosader, the largest share going to the youngest. It describes how Saladyne begins to ill-treat Rosader, making him his foot-boy for the space of two or three years; and how he bribes a Norman wrestler to put Rosader permanently out of action in a tournament held at the Court of the usurper, Torismond. Rosader, however, defeats the champion in

[1] W. W. Greg, ed. *Rosalynde* (1907), p. 10.
[2] In an unpublished doctoral thesis in the library of the University of Birmingham.

a match which is watched by Alinda, the usurper's daughter, and by Rosalynde, the daughter of the rightful King, the banished Gerismond. Rosader and Rosalynde fall in love with each other. He writes her a sonnet after she has given him a jewel. Rosader quarrels with Saladyne, but they are temporarily reconciled by Adam Spencer, a faithful retainer. Soon afterwards Saladyne chains up Rosader as a madman, but with Adam's help he escapes and, after nearly dying of starvation, they join Gerismond's band of outlaws in the forest of Arden.

Meanwhile, Torismond, afraid that Rosalynde's popularity will make his throne insecure, banishes her; and Alinda, who speaks in her friend's defence, being banished too, they leave the Court, disguised as Ganymede and Aliena, to make their way to the forest of Arden. Ganymede pretends to be Aliena's page. They find poems carved on the bark of trees, written by Montanus to Phoebe; and they overhear 'a pleasant eclogue' between Montanus and Corydon. They buy Corydon's farm from his landlord.

Torismond, coveting Saladyne's estates, has him thrown into prison. There he repents of his misdeeds, and on being banished he sets out in quest of his brother. Rosader meets Ganymede and Aliena, and Rosader plays at wooing Ganymede. Saladyne arrives in the forest, and while he is sleeping a lion waits for him to wake up before attacking him. Rosader kills the lion and saves his brother, who has not recognized him; but, after Saladyne has shown that he has repented, Rosader makes himself known. A few days later Rosader and Saladyne save Ganymede and Aliena from a gang of ruffians, and Aliena and Saladyne fall in love with each other.

When Rosalynde intervenes to help Montanus with his suit, Phoebe falls in love with her. She writes a love-letter to Rosalynde and gets Montanus to deliver it: but Rosalynde, visiting her in her sickness, makes her promise to marry Montanus when her passion for Ganymede has been quenched by reason. At the marriage of Saladyne and Aliena, at which Gerismond is a guest, Rosalynde reveals her identity. She marries Rosader, and Phoebe marries Montanus. Then Fernandyne arrives on the scene to announce that the twelve peers of France are up in arms to recover Gerismond's right, and that Torismond is at the edge of the forest, ready to give battle. The brothers distinguish themselves in the battle, Torismond is killed, and Gerismond is restored to his throne. Rosader is made heir-apparent, Saladyne recovers his father's lands, Fernandyne obtains the post of principal secretary to the King, Montanus is made lord of the forest of Arden, Adam Spencer Captain of the King's guard, and even Coridon is rewarded by being made Master of Alinda's flocks.

Shakespeare retained the main outlines of the story, but he made a number of changes. Some are of no particular significance. He altered many of the names. The brothers become Oliver, Jaques, and Orlando; Alinda becomes Celia, a name less likely to be confused with the one she takes with her disguise; King Torismond becomes Duke Frederick; Montanus becomes Silvius, and Corydon Corin. More significant are the additional characters— Le Beau, who adds a satirical touch to Duke Frederick's Court; Touchstone,[1] who provides a companion for the ladies on their journey to Arden and a satirical commentor on the other characters; Amiens and Jaques (unfortunately given the same name as one of the sons of Sir Rowland de Boys), who lend variety to the outlaws; and Audrey and William, whose function is discussed below. Another change is of considerable importance: he makes the usurper brother to the rightful Duke, Celia and Rosalind being cousins; and this provides a parallelism in the two plots, since Orlando, too, is cheated of his rights by a villainous brother, and both villains repent before the end of the play.

Shakespeare constructed his play with practised, if careless, skill. In his first act he introduces us to Orlando, Oliver, Adam, Duke Frederick's Court, Rosalind, Celia, and Touchstone; and before the end of the act he has shown the wrestling-match, made Orlando and Rosalind fall in love, and ended with the decision of Rosalind and Celia to seek the outlaws in the Forest of Arden. But the exposition is apparently clumsy, for in the first scene we have Orlando telling Adam a number of facts with which he must be well acquainted. Presumably Shakespeare regarded the opening speech as a kind of prologue in which he was not concerned with verisimilitude, but solely with acquainting the audience with the situation.

Rosader is persuaded by his brother to challenge the Norman wrestler. In the play Oliver has heard that Orlando has decided to wrestle with the champion, and Charles too warns him of his brother's purpose. The alteration has the effect of raising our opinion of Orlando.

In the wrestling-scene there is a long conversation between

---

[1] The name the Clown assumes when he leaves for Arden.

Celia and Rosalind which exhibits their love for each other, and Rosalind's grief for her banished father. There is nothing of this in the source. Then Touchstone and Le Beau are introduced in turn; and instead of exhibiting on the stage the killing of the Franklin's three sons by the wrestler, Shakespeare makes Le Beau describe it. The ladies in the story have no hesitation in watching the wrestling; Rosalind and Celia's reactions to the 'good sport' described by Le Beau show them as humane and sensitive, even though they agree to watch the remainder of the wrestling. Shakespeare inserts the incident of Rosalind and Celia, at the Duke's suggestion, trying to dissuade Orlando from the match, though the incident may be based on Lodge's words:

> but seeing it were to his dishonour to hinder him from his enterprise, they wisht him to bee graced with the palme of victorie.

The Norman is slain by Rosader; Charles, in accordance with the Shakespearian convention of avoiding deaths in comedy, is only put out of action.

When the King learns that Rosader is the son of Sir John of Bourdeaux he embraces him; when Duke Frederick hears of Orlando's parentage he is displeased. The alteration has the function of showing that Frederick has been opposed by the good people and reminds us that the rightful Duke is an outlaw; it prepares the way for Orlando's decision to go to the Forest of Arden; and it gives Celia and Rosalind an excuse for speaking kindly to Orlando. Lodge's Rosalynde 'accounted loue a toye, and fancie a momentary passion . . . and therefore feared not to dally in the flame'. To let Rosader know she affected him, she takes a jewel from her neck and sends it to Rosader by a page. Shakespeare's Rosalind takes a chain from her neck and gives it directly to Orlando, and it is apparent from her words and behaviour, even without her confession to Celia in the next scene, that she has fallen in love. Rosader sends a 'sonnet' to Rosalynde; Orlando is allowed a single exclamation at the end of the scene, 'But heavenly Rosalind!' The direct expression of love is deliberately curtailed, but Shakespeare convinces us that if the lovers talk less about their passion they feel more.

Shakespeare omits Lodge's account of Rosader's return to his brother's house with his friends to find the door barred against him, of his breaking into the house and giving a party, and of

Adam Spencer's reconciliation of the two brothers. Saladyne had earlier promised Rosader the restitution of his lands, and after this incident he pretended friendship with his brother. Oliver grudgingly consents to give Orlando part of his will, but he makes no pretence of reconciliation.

Lodge gives a long soliloquy to Rosalynde on the banishment of her father and on her love for Rosader. At the end she sings the most famous of Lodge's lyrics, beginning:

> Loue in my bosome like a bee
> Doth sucke his sweete.

Immediately after this song, Torismond enters and banishes Rosalynde, Alinda makes a set oration in defence of her friend, Torismond thereupon banishes both girls, Alinda comforts Rosalynde, and they decide to disguise themselves and seek out the banished King. Shakespeare condenses all this material into the third scene of the play. In place of Rosalynde's soliloquy and song there is a dialogue with Celia. In place of Alinda's long defence of her friend, Celia is given a short speech of eight lines; and, as the Duke does not banish her, but tells her she is put in the shade by her cousin, her decision to accompany Rosalind appears as a positive act of affection.

In the second act Shakespeare depicts the life of the outlaws and the arrival of Rosalind, Celia, Touchstone, and Orlando in Arden. In the first scene we are introduced to the rightful Duke; in the second scene the usurping Duke hears of his daughter's flight; in the third scene Adam informs Orlando of his brother's plot to kill him and arranges to fly with him; in the fourth scene we witness the arrival of Rosalind and her companions in Arden; the fifth scene of the act is merely a setting for Amiens' first song; in the sixth scene Orlando and Adam arrive in Arden, and in the last scene of the act they are succoured by the outlaws, Jacques discourses on the world as a stage, and Amiens sings his second song. The main purpose of the act is to bring the fugitives to Arden; but there is a continual contrast of the world of the Court with the world of the forest.

It will be noticed that in this act Shakespeare re-arranges his source-material. Lodge, after describing the arrival of Ganymede and Aliena in Arden and their discovery of Montanus's verses on the bark of a pine-tree, gives us an eclogue in verse between Montanus and Coridon, and goes on to describe the purchase of a farm. This, much condensed, is the substance of Shakespeare's fourth scene. Lodge then describes how Rosader is chained as a lunatic, his escape with Adam's assistance, his killing of some of his brother's guests, and his escape with Adam to Arden. For this Shakespeare substitutes the simpler version of his third scene. Lodge continues with the collapse of Adam through exhaustion—there is a long moralizing speech on Fortune, which may have suggested Touchstone's railing in II. 7—and Orlando's succour by the outlaws. The banished King asks for tidings of Rosalynde. This material, except the last item, Shakespeare utilized in the last two scenes of the act. Shakespeare's additions to this act include the presentation and defence of the outlaws' life, the two songs, the matter relating to Jaques' melancholy humour, and the rumour that Celia and Rosalind have gone off in Orlando's company. This last provides a link with Frederick's anger with Oliver in the third act. Oliver is thus not allowed to fade out of the play, for he appears in Arden in Act IV. In the source there is no connexion between Rosader's flight and Torismond's seizure of Saladyne's estates; in the play the Duke seizes Oliver's property as a revenge for Orlando's disappearance. In the source Saladyne repents in prison and is banished, ostensibly, for the wrongs he has done his brother. Shakespeare makes use of this motive incidentally in the Duke's reply to Oliver's statement that he never loved his brother, 'More villaine thou'.[1]

In the second scene of Act III we have Orlando hanging poems on the trees of the forest. In the source, having obtained the job of forester from Gerismond, he carves his poems on the bark of trees. After a dialogue between Touchstone and Corin, the function of which is discussed below, Rosalind and Celia discover two of Orlando's poems, and Celia reveals that she has seen him in the forest. In the novel Aliena and Ganymede see him at the same time. Orlando enters with Jaques and after the latter's departure Rosalind addresses Orlando as 'forester', as in the novel. Before the end of the scene Rosalind offers to play the part of his Rosalind, ostensibly to cure him of his love. In the novel the wooing eclogue between Rosalynde and Rosader (in verse) takes place at their second meeting, and there is no suggestion that it will cure him of his love. Both Orlando and Rosalind retain their wit and humour; and although they are deeply in love they are able to joke about it. Rosalind satirises the behaviour of her own sex and

[1] III. i. 15.

is witty at Orlando's expense. In the novel, the love-making is carried on in a pastoral vein, so that there is no real contrast between the Montanus–Phoebe scenes and the Rosader–Rosalynde ones.

The third scene is devoted to Touchstone's wooing of Audrey, for which there is no corresponding scene in the source. In the fourth scene, inserted mainly to prepare the way for Orlando's later unpunctuality, Rosalind mentions casually that she had met her father without being recognized. In the fifth scene Rosalind intervenes on Silvius's behalf, and Phoebe falls in love with her. This complication occurs much later in the novel, after Saladyne's arrival. Shakespeare wished to complicate the plot in this way by the end of the third act, Silvius being in love with Phoebe, who is in love with Ganymede, who is in love with Orlando, who is in love with Rosalind.

In the first scene of the fourth act we have the mock wooing and the mock marriage, suggested by Rosalind herself and not, as with Lodge, by Aliena. The second scene is an excuse for the third song 'What shall he have that kill'd the deer?' In the third scene Silvius delivers Phoebe's poem to Rosalind—in the novel Phoebe sends a letter and a poem—and Shakespeare adds Rosalind's pretence that the poem is full of chiding. Oliver enters to recount his rescue from the snake and the lioness. The snake is Shakespeare's supererogatory addition. The account of Orlando's hesitation before rescuing his brother is based on a long soliloquy in the novel, but Shakespeare omits Saladyne's failure to recognize Rosader and his long confession to him of his evil conduct. In the novel Rosader takes his brother to Gerismond; in the play Oliver is sent with the bloody napkin to excuse his broken promise to Ganymede. The scene thus ends with Rosalind nearly betraying her sex by her swoon. In the novel Rosader is occupied in showing his brother the forest, and Rosalynde's impatience at not seeing her lover had been used by Shakespeare earlier in the play.

For Loue measures euery minute, and thinkes houres to bee dayes, and dayes to bee moneths, till they feede theyr eyes with the sight of theyr desired object.

Shakespeare omits the incident of the attack on Ganymede and Aliena and makes Celia fall in love with Oliver without this occasion for gratitude. He omits the tedious love-making of Saladyne and Aliena, Phoebe's sickness, and Ganymede's visit to her. He complicates the matter of Touchstone's wooing by the introduction of the easily intimidated rival, William. He adds the quartet of the four lovers—Silvius, Phoebe, Orlando, and Rosalind—and he makes Rosalind boast that she is a magician, not that she has a friend who is one. He inserts another scene for the sake of the song 'It was a lover and his lass'. In place of the wedding in church he has the masque of Hymen; and the play concludes with the arrival of Jaques de Boys to announce the conversion and abdication of Duke Frederick. There is no battle, as there is in the novel.

There is a forest of Arden near Stratford, and it has been surmised that Shakespeare was depicting that rather than the Ardennes of the source; but the pastoral world of the play owes more to literature than it does to the countryside of England. *As You Like It* is not a straight dramatization of Lodge's pastoral novel. Shakespeare uses it in such a way as to produce a satire on pastoralism, and hence a comedy on love: for the pastoral, amongst other things, was a mode of love poetry. This satire is obtained by the use of several different levels of artificiality.[1] There is, first of all, the noble outlaw, the Robin Hood, convention, which is expressed through the portrait of the exiled Duke and his followers. The satire is double-edged. It is a criticism of Court life, which the exiles sour-grapishly disdain; and it is a criticism of the exiles themselves. This double-edged satire is illustrated by the song, 'Under the Greenwood Tree', the first stanzas of which profess to prefer life in the forest to life at court:

> Vnder the greenewood tree
> Who loues to lye with mee,
> And tune his merrie Note
> Vnto the sweet Birds throte:
> Come hither, come hither, come hither:
> Heere shall he see
> No enemie
> But Winter and rough Weather.

But the stanza sung by Jaques turns the tables on the exiles:

> If it do come to passe,
> That any man turne Asse,

---

[1] Cf. James Smith, *Scrutiny*, ix (1940); E. C. Pettet, *Shakespeare and the Romance Tradition* (1949), pp. 128 ff.; J. C. Maxwell, *Pelican Guide to Literature*, ii. pp. 201 ff.; Harold Jenkins, *Shakespeare Survey 8*, pp. 40–51. I am indebted also to another essay, written about twenty years ago, on the different levels of pastoral; but I cannot trace the authorship, or find more than a few notes from it.

> Leauing his wealth and ease,
> A stubborne will to please,
> Ducdame, ducdame, ducdame:
> Heere shall he see
> Grosse fooles as he,
> And if he will come to me.

But it should be remembered that Jaques is also satirized. His name was an unsavoury pun. He is attacked by the exiled Duke because his satirical humour is a reaction against youthful excesses. He boasts that he will

> through and through
> Cleanse the foule bodie of th' infected world,
> If they will patiently receiue my medicine.

The Duke retorts:

> Most mischeeuous foule sin, in chiding sin:
> For thou thy selfe hast been a Libertine,
> As sensuall as the brutish sting it selfe,
> And all th' imbossed sores, and headed euils,
> That thou with license of free foot hast caught,
> Would'st thou disgorge into the generall world.

Rosalind always gets the better of him in their arguments. Jaques gives an affected analysis of his melancholy, but Rosalind forthwith pricks the bubble:

> I haue neither the Schollers melancholy, which is emulation: nor the Musitians, which is fantasticall; nor the Courtiers, which is proud: nor the Souldiers, which is ambitious: nor the Lawiers, which is politick: nor the Ladies, which is nice: nor the Louers, which is all these: but it is a melancholy of mine owne, compounded of many simples, extracted from many obiects, and indeed the sundrie contemplation of my trauells, in which my often rumination wraps me in a most humorous sadnesse.
>
> *Ros.:* A Traueller: by my faith, you haue great reason to be sad: I feare you haue sold your owne Lands, to see other mens; then to haue seene much, and to haue nothing, is to haue rich eyes and poore hands.

Travel was a recognized cause of melancholy. Nashe speaks of

> some that haue continued there by the space of halfe a dozen yeares, and when they haue come home, they haue hid a litle weerish face vnder a broad French hat, kept a terrible coyle with the dust in the streete in their longe cloakes of gray paper, and spoke English strangely . . . yea and peraduenture this also . . . to weare a veluet patch on their face, and walke melancholy with their Armes folded.

G. B. Harrison suggests[1] that Jaques' melancholy arises from the decline of belief in Christianity, from an unwilling agnosticism and from a morbid fear of death. Shakespeare, however, gives no hint of this explanation, for the famous speech on the Seven Ages of Man is a variation on the motto of the new theatre to which Shakespeare's company had recently moved. Oscar Campbell argues[2] with more plausibility that Jaques is a portrait of satirists whose works had been banned just before.

The second form of pastoralism to be found in the play is in the tradition of eclogues, and to be found in Theocritus, Vergil, Spenser, and Sidney's *Arcadia*. One of the most commonly used conventions was that of the love-sick swain enamoured of the hard-hearted shepherdess. Rosalind makes short work of this when she attacks the scornful Phoebe:

> And why, I pray you? Who might be your mother,
> That you insult, exult, and all at once,
> Ouer the wretched? What though you haue no beauty—
> As, by my faith, I see no more in you
> Than without Candle may goe darke to bed:
> Must you be therefore prowd and pittilesse? . . .
> I see no more in you than in the ordinary
> Of Natures sale-worke. 'Ods my little life,
> I think she meanes to tangle my eies too!
> No, faith, proud Mistresse, hope not after it:
> 'Tis not your inkie browes, your blacke silke haire,
> Your bugle eye-balls, nor your cheeke of creame,
> That can entame my spirits to your worship.
> You foolish Shepheard, wherefore do you follow her,
> Like foggy South, puffing with winde and raine?
> You are a thousand times a properer man

---

[1] G. B. Harrison ed. Breton, *Melancholike Humours* (1929), pp. 49 ff.
[2] *Shakespeare's Satire* (1943), pp. 48 ff.

Than she a woman: 'Tis such fooles as you
That makes the world full of ill-fauour'd children:
. . . But, Mistris, know your selfe: downe on your knees,
And thank heauen, fasting, for a good mans loue:
For I must tell you friendly in your eare,
Sell when you can: you are not for all markets.

Then, thirdly, Rosalind and Celia play at being a shepherd and
shepherdess much as the lords and ladies of the reign of Louis XV,
and we have in some scenes something of the effect of Watteau's
paintings; though here again, a satirical touch is never far away.

Fourthly, we have a picture of shepherds as imagined by the
town; characters like William and Audrey, typical country bump-
kins, who are satirized by Touchstone. And, lastly, we get a portrait of shepherds as they are. Touchstone does not get it all his
own way with Corin:

Touch.: Wast euer in Court, Shepheard?

Cor.: No, truly.

Touch.: Then thou art damn'd.

Cor.: Nay, I hope.

Touch.: Truly, thou art damn'd like an ill-roasted Egge, all on
one side.

Cor.: For not being at Court? Your reason?

Touch.: Why, if thou neuer wast at Court, thou neuer saw'st
good manners; if thou neuer saw'st good manners,
then thy manners must be wicked; and wickednes is
sin, and sinne is damnation. Thou art in a parlous state,
shepheard.

Cor.: Not a whit, *Touchstone*: those that are good manners at
the Court are as ridiculous in the Countrey as the behauiour of the Countrie is most mockeable at the Court.
You told me, you salute not at the Court, but you kisse
your hands: that courtesie would be vncleanlie, if
Courtiers were shepheards.

Later on Corin replies to Touchstone's gibes with an almost
Wordsworthian dignity:

Sir, I am a true Labourer: I earne that I eate, get that I weare,
owe no man hate, enuie no mans happinesse, glad of other
mens good, content with my harme: and the greatest of my
pride, is to see my Ewes graze and my Lambes sucke.

There is, in fact, an extraordinary complexity of cross-satire in the play. Jaques satirizes the Duke, Orlando, and Touchstone. Touchstone, as his name indicates,[1] satirizes everyone. Rosalind satirizes not only Jaques and Phoebe, but the whole conception of romantic love. In answer to Orlando's declaration that he will die if his mistress refuses him, Rosalind mocks at the convention that rejected lovers pine away and die:

> No faith, die by Attorney: the poore world is almost six thousand yeeres old, and in all this time there was not anie man died in his owne person (*videlicet*) in a loue cause: *Troilus* had his braines dash'd out with a Grecian club, yet he did what hee could to die before, and he is one of the patternes of loue. *Leander*, he would have liu'd manie a faire yeere, though *Hero* had turn'd Nun; if it had not bin for a hot Midsommer-night; for (good youth) he went but forth to wash him in the Hellespont, and being taken with the crampe, was droun'd; and the foolish coroners of that age found it was *Hero* of Sestos. But these are all lies: men haue died from time to time and wormes have eaten them, but not for loue.

It is important to remember, of course, that in spite of this mockery Rosalind herself is deeply in love. To mock the illusions and the conventions of love, to believe that most loving is mere folly, is not necessarily a denial of love. In fact, Shakespeare is rescuing the reality of love from the fashionable counterfeits and distortions of his age. 'True love undergoes the refining process of satire, and survives in a less questionable and ambiguous form.'[2]

(7) Twelfth Night

Twelfth Night, it has been said, is a masterpiece of recapitulation.[3] Shakespeare had already used the device of mistaken identity of twins in *The Comedy of Errors*; in *Twelfth Night*, as in many Italian plays, the twins were made of opposite sex. In *The Two Gentlemen of Verona* a girl, disguised as a page, had acted as emissary from the man she loves to the woman he loves. In *Love's Labour's Lost* we hear of a woman who died of unrequited

---

[1] Cf. Leslie Hotson, *Shakespeare's Motley* (1952), p. 89.
[2] I cannot trace this quotation, if, indeed, it is a quotation.
[3] Barrett Wendell, *William Shakespeare* (1898), p. 209.

love, and her fate may have suggested the Patience on a monument speech. In *The Merchant of Venice* we have the deep affection of Antonio for Bassanio, which is paralleled by the love of the later Antonio for Sebastian. In *As You Like It* we have a fool and a singer; in *Twelfth Night* we have a singing Fool. In *Much Ado about Nothing* Beatrice and Benedick are tricked into loving each other; Malvolio is tricked into believing that Olivia is in love with him. Sir Toby is a reduced version of Falstaff, and Slender was developed into Sir Andrew Aguecheek.

But there were sources apart from Shakespeare's own work. John Manningham in his diary (unless the passage is a Collier forgery[1]) mentions that he saw the play at the Middle Temple and says that it is 'much like the *Commedy of Errores*, or *Menechmi* in Plautus, but most like and neere to that in Italian called *Inganni*'. There are at least three plays of that title, one of them later than *Twelfth Night*. *Gl'Inganni* of Curzio Gonzaga (1592) has some links with Shakespeare. The disguised woman takes the name of Cesare, and the author's name reminds us of *The Murder of Gonzago*, the play 'written in very choice Italian' performed before Claudius. Secchi's play (published 1562) has a woman, Ginevra, disguised as a man, in love with Gostanzo. Gostanzo is told by the disguised Ginevra that a woman is secretly in love with him, and that she is the same age as Ginevra. In a later scene, as Miss Helen A. Kaufman points out,[2] Gostanzo asks his supposed page why he is so upset by the girl's suffering, and Ginevra replies that she loves the girl as much as she does herself. Similarly Viola admits that she is in love. Given the situation of the girl disguised as a page in love with her master, repeated in other plays and stories, I do not find the resemblance in actual dialogue very striking.

Another play by Secchi, *L'Interesse*, also has some resemblances to *Twelfth Night*, though the plot itself is totally different. To win a wager, Pandolfo disguises his daughter as a boy and names her Lelio. Her elder sister, Virginia, is wooed by two men, Fabio and Flaminio. Lelio falls in love with Fabio, disguises herself as her sister, and becomes pregnant by him. As Miss Kaufman points out, we have here, in a different form, the situation of a girl disguised as a man, in love with a man who loves another woman. There is a comic duel in the play, Fabio fighting his own wife, Lelio, whom he thinks to be Virginia's brother. Although

[1] Cf. S. Race, *N.Q.* (1954), p. 380.   [2] *S.Q.* (1954), pp. 271–80.

the scene in *Twelfth Night* is totally different, Secchi's may have suggested to Shakespeare the comic possibilities of involving his heroine in a duel. A scrap of dialogue in which Fabio asks Lelio about her love is very close to a similar passage in *Twelfth Night*:

Fabio: Is she young?
Lelio: About your age.
Fabio: Is she beautiful?
Lelio: A sweet face, and comely like yours.

There is also in the same scene an account by Lelio of an unknown girl who is pining away for love, which has a slight resemblance to Cesario's account of her sister. Miss Kaufman claims that Lelio resembles Viola in her wit, her gaiety, and her freedom from sentimentality.

Two other plays, sometimes bound up with *Gl'Inganni*, are of varying importance. In one there is a character called *Orsino innamorato*, but it should be said that Orsino was also the name of the Duke of Bracciano, before whom, on Twelfth Night, 1601, the play was perhaps first performed.[1] The other play, the anonymous *Gl'Ingannati*, resembles *Twelfth Night* so closely that it is usually assumed that Manningham was referring to this when he spoke of *Inganni*. In the introduction to this play mention is made of 'Messer Agnol Malevolti', though Malvolio's name may be derived rather from the phrase *mala voglia*, which occurs seven times in Bandello's version of the story. The comedy is in prose. Lelia, the heroine, with the help of the nuns in the convent where she has been living, disguises herself as a man and takes the name of Fabio, for love of Flaminio, in whose household she becomes a page. Flaminio sends her on love embassies to Isabella, who falls in love with her as Olivia falls in love with Viola. Lelia tells Isabella, 'Perhaps I may love you, if you dismiss Flaminio.' Fabrizio, Lelia's lost brother, comes to Modena with his tutor, who shows him the 'remarkable places of the town'.[2] Virginio, Lelia's father, learns of her disguise from a nun, and he and Gherardo—her father's choice for her husband and Isabella's father—meet Fabrizio and take him for Lelia. Thinking him mad, they lock him up in Isabella's room. Then Gherardo meets Lelia, and thinking she must have escaped, he returns to his house and finds that Fabrizio and Isabella are betrothed. The play ends with a recogni-

[1] Cf. L. Hotson, *The First Night of 'Twelfth Night'* (1954), *passim*.
[2] *T.N.* III. iii. 41.

tion scene and the marriages of Fabrizio to Isabella and Flaminio to Lelia.

There is no shipwreck in this play. Fabrizio had been separated from his family at the sack of Rome. There is a farcical element which Luce thought had affinities with *Twelfth Night*.[1] But it is difficult to see any resemblance between the dealings of Stragualcia with Piero and those of Sir Toby with Malvolio, or between the tricking of an old Spaniard, Giglio, by the housekeeper, Pasquella, and the gulling of Malvolio by Maria. Nor is it likely that Malvolio was a combination of Gherardo, Giglio, and Piero.

A Latin version of this play was revived at Queen's College, Cambridge, in 1595 under the title *Laelia*; Shakespeare may have heard of it, but the evidence that he had read it consists of vague and doubtful parallels. On the other hand, a phrase in the prologue of *Gl'Ingannati*, 'la notte di Beffana' (i.e. the night of Epiphany) presumably gave Shakespeare his title, even though it is usually assumed that the play was first performed on Twelfth Night.[2]

The same story of Lelia was told by Bandello[3] and in Belleforest's translation. Shakespeare probably read one of these versions, as he had used one or the other author for *Much Ado about Nothing*. The closest parallel with *Twelfth Night* is the following. Nicuola speaks to Lattanzio of the girl he once loved—herself:[4]

> Who knoweth but this fair damsel yet loveth you and liveth in sore affliction for your sake? More by token that I have many a time heard say that girls, in their first loves, love far more tenderly and with greater fervour than do men. My heart forebodeth me this hapless lass must needs languish for you, and live a life of anguish and misery.

This resembles Orsino's confession that men's fancies are more giddy and unfirm than women's, and Viola's declaration that she knows 'Too well what love women to men may owe' and her story of her father's daughter. Bandello's phrase—

> l'amoroso verme veracemente con grandissimo cordoglio le rodena il core—

[1] M. Luce, *Rich's 'Apolonius and Silla'* (1912), p. 11.
[2] Cf. L. Hotson, op. cit., pp. 173 ff.   [3] *Novelle* (1554), ii. 36.
[4] *Histoires Tragiques*, iv. (1571), 59. Belleforest's version of the Bandello quotation runs as follows: 'Et que sçavez vous si ceste fille languist encore pour l'amour de vous, et vist en destresse? Car i'ay ouy dire que les filles en leurs premieres apprehensions aiment d'vne vehemence tout autre, et plus grande qui ne font les hommes, et que malaisement on estaint ceste flamme ainsi viuement esprise, ayant trouvé suiet non occupé en autre chose'.

may have suggested:

> She neuer told her loue,
> But let concealment, like a worme i' th' bud,
> Feede on her damaske cheeke.

The story of Lelia is to be found also in Giraldi's *Hecatommithi*, the source of *Othello* and one of the probable sources of *Measure for Measure*.[1] This version, like *Twelfth Night*, contains a shipwreck; but there is a shipwreck in the version of the story given in *Riche his Farewell to Militarie profession* (1581), which is generally regarded as the main source of Shakespeare's play. It may be mentioned that Riche in other parts of his book uses four words —*coisterell*, *garragascoynes* (gaskins), *pavion* (pavin), and *galliarde*— which are to be found in *Twelfth Night* and in no other of Shakespeare's plays. In Riche's fifth story a man tries to reform his shrewish wife by treating her as a lunatic:

> he tied her in a darke house that was on his backside, and then callyng his neibours about her, he would seeme with greate sorrowe to lament his wiues distresse, telling them that she was sodainly become Lunatique.

Luce points out that this incident bears some resemblance to the treatment of Malvolio in Act IV, Scene 2. It should be said, however, that the scene may owe something to the story of the exorcisms of Nicholas Starkey's children by John Darrell, who in his *True Narration* (1600) described the behaviour of the children in these words:

> Theis 4, especially 3 of them, vsed much light behauiour and vayn gestures, sundry also filthy scurrilous speaches, but whispering them for the most part among themselues, so as they were no let to that holy exercise we there had in hand. Sometimes also they spake blasphemy calling the word preached, bible bable, he will neuer haue done prating, prittle prattle.

Samuel Harsnett exposed the bogus exorcisms in his *Discovery of the Fraudulent Practises of John Darrell*, though I have not found in this pamphlet the word 'bible-bable'.[2] Feste as Sir Topas, it will be remembered, urges Malvolio to leave his vain bibble-babble.

Riche in his epistle dedicatory to gentlewomen tells us that he is not a good dancer:

---

[1] V. 8.   [2] Hunter and Luce say the word is used in this pamphlet.

At firste for Dauncyng, although I like the Measures verie well, yet I could neuer treade them a right, nor to vse measure in any thyng that I went aboute, although I desired to performe all thynges by line and by leauell, what so euer I tooke in hande.

Our Galliardes are so curious, that thei are not for my daunsyng, for thei are so full of trickes and tournes, that he whiche hath no more but the plaine Sinquepace, is no better accoumpted of then a verie bongler, and for my part, thei might assone teache me to make a Capricornus, as a Capre in the right kinde that it should bee.

For a Ieigge my heeles are too heauie: And these braules are so busie, that I loue not to beate my braines about them.

A Rounde is too giddie a daunce for my diet, for let the daun-cers runne about with as much speede as thei maie: yet are thei neuer a whit the nier to the ende of their course, vnlesse with often tourning thei hap to catch a fall. And so thei ende the daunce with shame, that was begonne but in sport.

This passage seems to have contributed to the picture we get of Sir Andrew in I. 3. Sir Andrew has 'the back-trick as strong as any man in Illyria', he can 'cut a caper', and Sir Toby asks:

Why dost thou not goe to Church in a Galliarde and come home in a Carranto? My verie walke should be a Iigge; I would not so much as make water but in a Sink-a-pace.

His later question, 'Were we not borne vnder Taurus?' may like-wise have been suggested by Riche's reference to Capricorn.

Even without the evidence that Shakespeare had read Riche's tale of *Apolonius and Silla*, it therefore appears that he had read the book in which that tale occurs. The following is a summary of the story.

Duke Apolonius, after having spent a year's service in the Turkish wars, was driven by a storm to the island of Cyprus, where he was well received by Duke Pontus, the Governor. His daughter, Silla, fell in love with Apolonius, but he sailed away to Constantinople ignorant of her feelings. Silla thereupon asked her servant Pedro to accompany her to Constantinople, and she dis-guised herself as his sister. The Captain of the ship tried to seduce her, and she was saved from suicide by a providential shipwreck in which Pedro and the Captain were both drowned. Silla was saved by clinging to a chest containing money and apparel belonging to the Captain. For better safety she disguised herself as a man, calling herself Silvio, the name of her twin brother. She travelled to Constantinople and took service with Apolonius, who employed her to carry love-tokens and letters to a wealthy widow called Julina with whom he had fallen in love. Julina fell in love with Silla and told her: 'It is enough that you have saied for your maister; from henceforthe either speake for your self, or saie nothyng at all.'

Meanwhile Silvio, returning from the wars, heard of his sister's flight; and, assuming that she had been carried off by Pedro, he went in search of the couple, in due course arriving at Constantinople. Here, 'walkyng in an euenyng for his owne recreation, on a pleasaunte greene yarde, without the walles of the citie' he encountered Julina, who invited him to supper on the following night. Surprised at being addressed by his own name by a complete stranger, and attracted by Julina's beauty, he consented. After supper Julina came to share his bed, and in the morning, 'for feare of further euilles', Silvio went off to seek for his sister 'in the parts of *Grecia*'.

After a while Apolonius asked Julina for a direct answer to his suit, and she replied that she was pledged to another, 'whose wife I now remaine by faithfull vowe and promise'. Soon afterwards Apolonius heard that his page was his successful rival, and he cast Silla into a dungeon. Julina, finding herself with child, and hearing that the supposed Silvio was imprisoned, hastened to the Duke's palace, confessed her love, and asked Apolonius to impute to her charge the fault of which her lover was accused. Apolonius sent for Silla and reproached her for her abuse of his trust and for her perjuries. Silla urged Julina to confess that she had faithfully undertaken her master's behests. Julina replied that it was at her own suggestion that they had been betrothed, and she urged Silla not to be afraid to acknowledge the truth:

Now is the tyme to manifest the same vnto the worlde, whiche hath been done before God, and betwene our selues.

Silla said she did not understand; and Julina then declared she was with child. Apolonius drew his rapier and threatened to kill Silla if she did not give Julina satisfaction by marrying her. Silla asked permission to speak with Julina alone, and revealed that she was a woman. Julina informed Apolonius, and he forthwith agreed to marry Silla. Hearing of the marriage, Silvio hastened back to Constantinople and was told the whole story by Apolonius. Silvio, ashamed of his desertion of Julina, at once agreed to marry her.

There appear to be no verbal echoes of Riche's story in *Twelfth Night*, with one possible exception. Julina's words:

Ah, vnhappie, and, aboue all other, most vnhappie, that haue so charely preserued myne honour, and now am made a praie to satisfie a yong mans lust.

may have suggested Olivia's words to Viola:[1]

I have said too much vnto a hart of stone,
And laid mine honour too vnchary out.[2]

But although there are few or no verbal echoes of Riche's story, there is good reason to believe that Shakespeare had read it. Riche's version and Giraldi's are the only ones that introduce a shipwreck; and Silvio's acceptance of Julina's invitation, Julina's revelation of her betrothal, her criticism of Silvio's fearful refusal to acknowledge it, and the Duke's anger with Silla are sufficiently close to the corresponding scenes of *Twelfth Night* to make it certain that Shakespeare knew Riche's version.

Manningham refers to Olivia as a widow; and some critics think that the play he witnessed must have differed in this respect from the one we know. It is possible that the original play followed Riche in this detail, but it is more likely that Manningham's recollection was at fault. He may have remembered the mourning but forgotten the reason; or, indeed, his memory may well have been confused by his knowledge of Riche as Forman's was by his knowledge of Holinshed. In any case the advantages of having Olivia young and inexperienced are obvious; and it would not have suited the atmosphere of the play to have Olivia and Sebastian sharing a bed with the celerity displayed by Julina and Silvio. Shakespeare's lovers are united by a religious ceremony, and Olivia is not deserted as Julina is.

Riche's story has no underplot, nor have the Bandello and Belleforest versions. In complicating his play by the introduction of Sir Andrew's wooing of Olivia, his challenge to Cesario, and the gulling of Malvolio, Shakespeare may have taken a hint from the two absurd suitors in *Gl'Ingannati*—Gherardo and Giglio—but the hint was very small. The Malvolio plot is more likely to have been suggested by the topical story of the Comptroller of the

---

[1] But F. reads *on't* for *out*.   [2] Perhaps we should read *uncharely*.

Household, Sir William Knollys, who demonstrated against a noisy party in the small hours of the morning by walking amongst the revellers dressed only in his shirt, with a copy of Aretine in his hand.[1] Like Malvolio he complained of bear-baiting; he was connected with Banbury, a place noted for its cakes and ale as well as its puritans; and his father is known to have defended the puritans. Malvolio speaks of his 'austere regard of *control*'. Dr Hotson suggests, less plausibly, that the name Malvolio is a pun on *Mallvoglio* (I want Mall) and is an allusion to the fact that Knollys at the age of fifty-three had fallen in love with his charge, Mary Fitton, who became pregnant by another man. Dr Hotson shows that Viola was the flower of faithfulness, and that the *viola da braccia* was Apollo's instrument and the symbol of passion and chastity. He does not, however, suggest that there was a pun on *braccia* and Virginio Orsino, Count of *Bracciano*, before whom the play was probably performed. It should be mentioned that in Emmanuel Forde's *Parismus* (1598) there is a Violetta who is shipwrecked while following her lover in the disguise of a page, and also an Olivia.

Whether because the play was performed on Twelfth Night, or because of the reference to the Epiphany in *Gl'Ingannati*, or for both reasons, Shakespeare introduces references to the message of the Epiphany as expressed in the words 'Today we are liberated from darkness and illuminated by the light of divine knowledge'. Feste, for example, tells Malvolio that 'there is no darkness but ignorance', and the phrases 'rain odours' and 'sweet south' (if that is the true reading) recall the Epiphany ceremony.[2]

It has been suggested by Mr F. Pyle[3] and others that Shakespeare drew on Sidney's *Arcadia* for certain details, but the resemblances are slight. Women disguised as men and men who are tricked by forged letters are too common to be significant. Nor is there any evidence that Shakespeare was influenced by the play, formerly ascribed to Peele, entitled *Sir Clyomon and Sir Clamydes*, or by another crude play entitled *Common Conditions*.

These were the materials on which Shakespeare set to work. I find it difficult to accept Dr Hotson's theory that the play was written, acted, and rehearsed within a fortnight, though it is possible that the poet adapted a play already written, or partly written,

[1] Cf. E. K. Chambers, *William Shakespeare*, i. 407, and L. Hotson, op. cit., pp. 93 ff.
[2] Hotson, op. cit., pp. 145 ff.
[3] Cf. F. Pyle, *M.L.R.* (1948), p. 449, and the Variorum *T.N.*

to suit the topical occasion of Orsino's visit. Shakespeare was not enormously prolific, like the Spanish dramatists with whom Dr Hotson compares him. If he could have written a masterpiece in ten days his company would have expected him to write more than two plays a year.

Shakespeare adopts a new setting for the plot, abandoning both the Italian town of Modena and the city of Constantinople in favour of Illyria. The social *milieu* of his characters is closest to that of Riche's novel, but Olivia's Illyrian household is essentially Elizabethan. From Riche, too, Shakespeare borrowed the shipwreck as a convenient beginning to his play, but he rejected the episode of the lecherous Captain. Viola's Captain has a fair behaviour in him. Silla is disguised first as Pedro's sister and then in the Captain's clothes; Viola disguises herself as much like her brother as possible, and this makes it more plausible that she should be mistaken for him. Silla is journeying to Constantinople for love of Apolonius when she is shipwrecked. Although Viola decides to take service with Orsino—as a eunuch[1]—she does so only after she has been told that she has no chance of serving Olivia. Shakespeare also avoids the situation of *Gl'Ingannati* in which Lelia has been jilted by Flaminio. Viola and Sebastian—we are not told the purpose of their voyage—are separated by shipwreck, as the twins had been separated in *The Comedy of Errors*. This brings them both to Illyria, each thinking the other drowned. It is dramatically important that Sebastian should think Viola dead, as he would otherwise jump to the conclusion that he had been mistaken for her. Silvio, although he is looking for Silla, never puts two and two together.

Shakespeare wisely dispenses with the parents of Lelia and Isabella and with Lelia's unwelcome suitor, Isabella's father. Sebastian and Viola are orphans, and Olivia is alone in the world. The courage and self-reliance of Viola are thus increased and Olivia's isolation allows both Sir Andrew and Malvolio to aspire to her hand.

In the first act of *Gl'Ingannati* we have the situation presented to us of Isabella falling in love with Lelia, who is in love with Flaminio, who loves Isabella, and Isabella's father wishes to marry Lelia. By cutting out Gherardo, Shakespeare, by the end of his first act, is able to reach the same point in his plot, with Olivia in love

---

[1] But presumably she changes her mind when it comes to the point, for Orsino assumes that Cesario will eventually marry.

with Viola, Viola in love with Orsino, and Orsino in love with
Olivia—too hard a knot for Viola to untie; but in the first act we
have also been introduced to the characters of the underplot; Sir
Andrew's pretensions to Olivia's hand prepare the way for his duel
with Viola, and Malvolio's scorn for Feste makes an enemy of
him.

Lelia's brother does not appear till the third act of Gl'Ingannati;
Shakespeare introduces Sebastian at the beginning of Act II, and
in the same act we have the interruption of the revellers, the hatch-
ing of the plot against Malvolio, and a scene in which Viola is able
indirectly to express her love for Orsino. In the second act of
Gl'Ingannati Flaminio hears of the favours granted to his page, and
he wishes to kill both Isabella and Lelia. In Riche's version Apolonius does not become jealous until after Silvio has been enter-
tained by Julina. Shakespeare does not allow Orsino to hear of
Olivia's love for Cesario until just before the end of the play, and
he then proposes to sacrifice the lamb he loves (Cesario) to spite
Olivia. It is obvious that he is unconsciously fonder of Cesario
than of Olivia; and this, together with Viola's willingness to die
for love, prepares the way for the sudden transfer of Orsino's
affections. To make possible the postponement of Orsino's knowledge of Olivia's love of Cesario it was necessary to postpone her
declaration of love until the third act and Sebastian's meeting with
her until the fourth. The intervening scenes, which prevent the
action from seeming slow, are filled with plenty of matter for a
May morning—Malvolio's appearance in yellow stockings and his
treatment as a lunatic, Sir Andrew's challenge, the intervention
and arrest of Antonio, and Viola's realization that Sebastian is
alive. In the second half of the play Shakespeare owes nothing to
the complicated intrigue of Gl'Ingannati, which, indeed, more resembles the farce of The Comedy of Errors; but by having Sir Andrew, Sir Toby, and the Fool all mistake Sebastian for Cesario he
makes a similar use of mistaken identity. In Gl'Ingannati Lelia and
Fabrizio are never on the stage together and they could be played
by one actor or actress. In Apolonius and Silla Silvio does not discover his lost sister until after her marriage. Shakespeare has the
more dramatic confrontation of brother and sister and the revelation of Cesario's sex in the last act of the play.

Professor T. W. Baldwin has shown with what skill Twelfth
Night was constructed 'on the Andria variety of the Terentian
formula'; and he suggests that the interest of Gl'Ingannati falls off

after the second act when we reach the epitasis of the more interesting story and have to wait for the catastrophe for more than two acts. Shakespeare, on the other hand, delays the epitasis both of the Viola–Olivia situation and of Malvolio's suit to Olivia until the third act.[1] But although we may well admire the art with which Shakespeare has constructed his play, its superiority to all its sources is displayed more obviously in the characterization, in the humour of the prose scenes, and above all in the poetic texture of the play as a whole.

[1] Cf. T. W. Baldwin, *Five-Act Structure*, p. 715.

IV

PROBLEM PLAYS

(8) Troilus and Cressida

THE main source of *Troilus and Cressida*, as we might expect, was Chaucer's great poem, *Troilus and Criseyde*.[1] But, like all Elizabethans, Shakespeare was also acquainted with Henryson's sequel, *The Testament of Cresseid*, in which the heroine suffers as a leper for her unfaithfulness. For the other incidents of the play, relating to the siege of Troy, Shakespeare consulted the first instalment of Chapman's translation of Homer, published in 1598, though he may have used Hall's translation as well. He also knew part (at least) of Virgil's *Æneid*. He had read Caxton's *Recuyell of the Historyes of Troy*, translated from the French, and Lydgate's *Troy Book*, and, as we have seen, he knew Golding's translation of Ovid's *Metamorphoses*, which deals with some incidents in the tale of Troy.

The main outlines of the love-plot are to be found in Chaucer's poem. In Book I Troilus falls in love with Criseyde and enlists Pandarus's help to woo her. In Book II Pandarus carries out this plan. In Act I of the play Troilus is already in love with Cressida, and Pandarus is engaged in furthering his suit. In Book III of the poem the lovers meet at the house of Deiphebus, and their love is consummated in Pandarus's house. In Act III of the play the lovers are united at the house of Pandarus. In Book IV of the poem the Trojans decide to exchange Criseyde for Antenor, Pandarus contrives another meeting, and the lovers part. In Act IV of the play news is brought that Cressida is to be exchanged for Antenor. On the morning after the lovers have been united,

---

[1] The best book on the sources of the play is R. K. Presson's *Shakespeare's 'Troilus and Cressida' and the Legends of Troy* (1953); but he tends, perhaps, to overestimate the Homeric influence. There is a wider survey in the Variorum edition (ed. Hillebrand and Baldwin) with references to previous work on the subject. I am also indebted to an unpublished Liverpool thesis by Mary F. Bruce, *The Middle English Versions of the Troy Legend and Shakespeare's 'Troilus and Cressida'* (1948).

Diomed arrives to conduct Cressida to the Greek camp. In Book V Criseyde is wooed by Diomed, and eventually she yields. She writes to Troilus, and he seeks to drown his grief in fighting and in revenging himself on Diomed. In the last act of the play Troilus is a witness to Cressida's unfaithfulness. Cressida writes to him. He fights desperately, seeking to avenge himself on Diomed, and also to avenge the murder of Hector by Achilles.

The action of the poem, as becomes a narrative, is leisurely. Shakespeare makes it more dramatic by beginning his play just before Cressida capitulates to Troilus, and he ends it only three days later, after Cressida has exchanged Troilus for Diomed. The effect of this telescoping is to intensify Cressida's unfaithfulness. Chaucer treats his heroine with gentleness and sympathy, and depicts her as a young widow, charming, pliable, and timid. He avoids any direct explanation of her unfaithfulness, and he excuses her as much as he can. She turns to Diomed, not out of lust, but because she feels lonely and isolated in the Greek camp, and because she always takes the line of least resistance. Shakespeare's Cressida is unmarried and she is a coquette by temperament. She is less innocent than Chaucer's heroine, and her unfaithfulness is caused apparently by sexual desire. Chaucer's poem is written in the tradition of courtly love, which laid down an elaborate code of behaviour for the lover. The two chief rules were secrecy and faithfulness. The code had nothing to do with the love of husband and wife, and the aim of the man was not marriage but faithful service, and, if the lady consented, a love affair—which was only frowned upon if it became public. The basis of courtly love was adultery, because marriages were all of convenience, and there was often a complete separation of love on the one hand and the duties of a wife and mother on the other. Shakespeare wrote his play more than two centuries later. By this time the code of society had changed. The Elizabethan writer usually assumed that the right, true end of love was marriage. The dramatists all frowned on adultery, except occasionally in farcical comedy, and Shakespeare was placed in something of a difficulty in dramatizing the story of Troilus and Cressida. On the one hand, Troilus was the pattern of a faithful lover; on the other hand, he did not in any of the sources marry Cressida. Shakespeare retains the secrecy demanded by the code of courtly love, and he never raises the question of marriage at all. One critic has argued that the meeting of the lovers before a witness constituted a common-law marriage, but this appears to contradict the impression one gets not only from this scene but from the whole play. But there is some ambiguity in the situation. An honest and devoted lover, as Troilus undoubtedly is, one who gives and demands eternal faithfulness, might be expected to marry the object of his love. But the clandestine nature of the affair and his use of Pandarus as a go-between have an element of incongruity. Shakespeare, I think, was deliberately ambiguous; and he was conveniently vague about the Trojan customs relating to love and marriage. They are clearly different from those depicted by Chaucer; but they are also different from the customs of Elizabethan drama.

It is important to remember that editions of Chaucer in the sixteenth century contained Henryson's sequel, *The Testament of Cresseid*. In this poem Chaucer's heroine is smitten with leprosy and reduced to beggary after she has been thrown over by Diomed and become the mistress of a succession of Greek warriors. Under the influence of this sequel Cressid had become a synonym not merely for an unfaithful woman, but for a harlot. Pistol calls Doll Tearsheet 'the lazar kite of Cressid's kind', and Feste mentions that Cressida was a beggar.[1] There is another small indication that Shakespeare had read Henryson's poem. There Cynthia speaks of Cresseid's 'voice so cleir'; and Cresseid herself speaks of 'my cleir voice'. So in Shakespeare's play, Cressida, on being told that she must leave Troy, says[2]:

> I will goe in and weepe . . .
> Teare my bright haire, and scratch my praised cheekes
> Cracke my cleere voyce with sobs . . .

The character of Troilus in Chaucer's poem is very similar to that of Shakespeare's hero. His prowess as a warrior, second only to Hector, is mentioned by both poets, and so, too, are his faithfulness in love, and his attempt to forget his love in fighting. Both hope to die in battle; Chaucer's Troilus cries:

> My owen deth in armes wol I seche,
> I recche nat how soone be the day!

And Shakespeare's uses similar language:

> I reck not though I end my life today.

Chaucer's Pandarus is younger and pleasanter than Shake-

[1] Cf. *Henry V*, II. i. 80; *T.N.* III. i. 62. Pistol's phrase, however, had been used elsewhere (e.g. Pettie's *Petite Palace*).   [2] *T.C.* IV. ii. 112.

speare's. He is the chief vehicle for Chaucer's own irony and humour, and he brings Troilus and Criseyde together because he is fond of them both and wants them to be happy. Shakespeare's Pandarus also acts without hope of reward, but he gets a vicarious pleasure from the affair, he is sentimental and silly, and he is continually indulging in leers and innuendoes. He serves as a bawdy chorus to the love-scenes of the play, and, though he is not so vile as some critics have painted him, his conception of sex is contrasted with the idealism of the hero. The coarsening of Pandarus was necessary to Shakespeare's purpose. He is depicted in such a way as to exemplify the pandar, the word derived from his name, and also to fit in with the less sympathetic portrayal of Cressida. In the scene where Pandarus brings the lovers together, the three characters are presented for a moment as types of faithful lover, wanton, and pandar. The primitive 'morality' technique is used by Shakespeare with extreme sophistication, to exhibit, as it were, the birth of a legend.

Shakespeare's Diomed is also a coarsened version of Chaucer's. Whereas in Chaucer he is a noble warrior who wins Criseyde by his long and eloquent wooing, in Shakespeare's play he hardly bothers to woo Cressida, except by the crudest methods. He never pretends to love her and obviously despises her. This degrading of Diomed's character is a corollary to the alteration in Cressida's. She has to fall to the first man who bothers to seduce her—and the cruder his advances the more violent the contrast between her vows and her actions.

The general outline of the love-plot is therefore to be found in Chaucer's poem, but of the four main characters only Troilus is left more or less unchanged, and the atmosphere of the play is totally different from that of the poem. This is partly due to Henryson's sequel, but it is due much more to the change of customs and ideas in the intervening centuries, to the Inns of Court audience for which Shakespeare probably wrote, and to the dramatic purpose of the whole play.

For his other plot Shakespeare used at least three sources— Lydgate's *Troy Book*, Caxton's *Recuyell*, and Chapman's translation of Homer. Lydgate's poem is very long and it never rises above mediocrity. Shakespeare would have found in it character-sketches of all his chief personages. Hector, for example, is not only an outstanding warrior, but he is also wise and temperate—

Sadde and discret and prudent neuer-the-les.

He was magnanimous in battle and wise in counsel:

> For he was ay so iust and so prudent,
> So wel avised and so pacient,
> And so demenyed in his gouernaunce,
> That hym was loth for to do vengance,
> Wher-as he myght in esy wyse trete
> For to reforme thinges smale and grete;
> For lothe he was, this noble worthi knyght,
> For any haste to execute ryght,
> Or causeles by rigour to condempne.

> (II. 1129–1137)

Shakespeare mentions that Hector spares his fallen enemies, he refers to his patience 'as a virtue, fix'd', and in the council-scene he makes him advise the surrender of Helen because their cause is bad. Caxton does not mention these characteristics, though he states that 'ther yssued neuer oute of his mouth a vyllaynous word' and 'ther was neuer knyght better belouyd of his peple than he was'. He also mentions that Hector lisped—a peculiarity Shakespeare had used in his portrayal of Hotspur.

Caxton says that Helenus was 'a man of grete scyence and knewe all the artes lyberall'. Lydgate adds that he

> toke but litel hede
> Of alle the werre, knyghthod, nor manhede.

> (II. 4859–4860)

Shakespeare also mentions that Helenus is a priest with a dislike of war.

Lydgate and Caxton both refer to Troilus as a second Hector:

> And called was Hector the secounde . . .
> Excepte Ector, ther was nat swiche another . . .

> (II. 288, 4895)

In strength and merinesse hee resembled and was much like vnto Hector, and was the second after him in prowesse.

Lydgate also emphasizes that Troilus

> was alwey feithful, iust and stable,
> Perseueraunt, and of wil immutable . . .
> In his dedis he was so hool and pleyn;

> (II. 4880 ff.)

and that in battle—

> He was so fers thei myght him nat withstonde
> Whan that he hilde his bloodly swerde on hond.

So Ulysses, in his portrait of Troilus, mentions that he is 'firm of word' and more dangerous than Hector in battle; and Troilus himself remonstrates with his brother for his 'vice of mercy' and urges his fellow Trojans to 'leaue the Hermit Pitty with our Mothers'.

Both Lydgate and Caxton mention two characters of the name of Ajax. Ajax Telamonius has no resemblance to Shakespeare's character; but Oileus Ajax is large in size,[1]

> And of his speche rude and rekkeles:
> Ful many worde in ydel hym asterte,
> And but a coward was he of his herte.
>
> (II. 4578–4580)

There is no suggestion that Shakespeare's Ajax is cowardly, and it is probable that the main source for his portrait was the *Iliad* in which Ajax Telamon is compared to a mill-ass.[2] Shakespeare refers to him as a blockish, brainless, scurvy-valiant ass, sodden-witted, and slow as the elephant.

Lydgate and Caxton both refer to Ulysses's cunning and eloquence, and Lydgate also mentions his discretion and prudence; but his subtlety and wisdom were proverbial. Both Lydgate and Caxton, unlike Chaucer, speak of Diomed's lecherous disposition.

There are a number of similarities[3] between the incidents in Shakespeare's play and those in the *Troy Book*:

Lydgate mentions an encounter between Hector and Ajax which Hector breaks off when he discovers that he is fighting his cousin, and in the play Hector has only one bout with Ajax for the same reason. Caxton has the same incident, and like Shakespeare uses the term 'cousin-german'. Both Lydgate and Caxton mention Andromache's dream in which she has a premonition of Hector's death, and the fruitless attempt of Priam, Cassandra, Hecuba, and Helen to dissuade him from the battle. Both Lydgate and Caxton describe the incidents leading up to Hector's death— the fight between Hector and Achilles, in which Achilles is worsted, the fight between Hector and the Greek in sumptuous

---

[1] *Troy Book*, ii. 4571 ff.   [2] *Seven Bookes*, xi. 485.
[3] Cf. Presson, op. cit., *passim*.

armour—in Lydgate Hector kills him, in Caxton he takes him prisoner—and the killing of Hector by Achilles, while he is unprepared. Lydgate inserts a sermon on the sin of covetousness which led to Hector's death. Shakespeare increases Achilles's guilt and the horror of Hector's murder by making Hector disarm Achilles and spare his life in the first encounter, and by making Achilles and his myrmidons murder Hector. This incident both in Lydgate and Caxton belongs to the death of Troilus:

> And afore that Achilles entered into the battaile, he assembled his Mirmidones, and praied them that they would intend to none other thing, but to inclose Troylus, and to hold him without flying till hee came, and that he would not be farre from them. And they promised him that they so would. And he thronged into the battell. . . . Then the Mirmidones . . . thrusted in among the Troyans, and recouered the field . . . and sought no man but Troylus, they found him, that hee fought strongly, and was inclosed on all partes, but he slew and wounded many. And he was all alone among them, and had no man to succour him, they slew his horse, and hurt him in many places, and plucked off his head his helme, and his coife of yron, and he defended him in the best manner he could. Then came on Achilles, when he sawe Troylus all naked, and ran vpon him in a rage, and smote off his head and cast it vnder the feete of his horse, and tooke the body and bound it to the taile of his horse, and so drew it after him throughout the host.

Lydgate and Caxton both describe Hector's visit to the Greek camp, and 'Achilles behelde him gladly, forasmuch as hee had neuer seen him vnarmed'. So in the play Achilles wishes 'to see the great Hector unarmed'. Lydgate mentions the wounding of Paris by Menelaus, and in the play the incident is referred to by Aeneas. Caxton describes how Diomed fought with Troilus and took his horse, and sent it as a present to Cressida. This incident also appears in the play. Caxton, but not Lydgate, mentions that Achilles had refused to go to battle one day because he was in love with Polyxena and had promised Priam and Hecuba 'that he sholde helpe no more the Grekes'. Achilles, in the play, mentions his love of Polyxena and his vow, but it is apparently not his main motive for keeping to his tent.

The debate in Troy about the restoration of Helen is to be found in Caxton, and the arguments used by Hector, Paris, Helenus, and

Troilus correspond to those used in the play. But in Caxton the debate takes place before the outbreak of the war. Its position in the play is determined by the position of a similar debate in Book VII of the *Iliad*.[1]

Dr Tillyard adds a few more parallels[2] with Caxton and Lydgate. The speech on Time seems to be based on Ulysses's appeal to Achilles in Lydgate's poem:

> By youre manhood, that is spoke of so ferre
> That your renoun to the worldis ende
> Reported be, wherso that men wende,
> Perpetually, by freshnes of hewe
> Day by day to encrese newe,
> That the triumphe of this highe victorie
> Be put in story and eke in memorie,
> And so enprented that foryetilnes
> No power have by malis to oppresse
> Your fame in knyghthod, dirken or difface,
> That shyneth yit so clere in many place
> Withoute eclipsynge, sothly this no les;
> Which to conserve ye be now rekeles
> Of wilfulnes to cloude so the lyght
> Of youre renoun that whilom shon so bright . . .
>
> (IV. 1770 ff.)

As Tillyard points out, Lydgate condemns the Trojan war because of its trivial cause:

> We trewly may adverten in oure thought
> That for the valu of a thing of nought
> Mortal causes and werris first by-gonne;
> Strif and debate here under the sonne
> Wer meved first of smal occasioun
> That caused after gret confusioun,
> That no man can the harmys half endite.
>
> (II. 123 ff.)

Caxton blames Hector for yielding to a request to call off the day's battle when victory was in his power:

> There is no mercy in battaile. A man ought not to be too mercifull, but take the victory who may get it.

So Troilus in the play blames his brother for his mistaken chivalry.

---

[1] Cf. Presson, op. cit., pp. 91 ff., and the Variorum.
[2] *Shakespeare's Problem Plays* (1950), pp. 33 ff., 149 ff.

These parallels are sufficient proof that Shakespeare made use both of Lydgate and Caxton. But for many of the incidents and characters Shakespeare must have gone to Chapman's translation of Homer.[1] Thersites is to be found in Homer, but not in Chaucer, Lydgate, or Caxton. He is thus described in the 1598 edition— there are considerable differences in later editions:

> A man of tonge, whose rauen like voice, a tuneless iarring kept,
> Who in his ranke minde coppy had of vnregarded wordes,
> That rashly and beyond al rule, vsde to oppugne the Lords,
> But what soeuer came from him, was laught at mightilie:
> The filthiest Greek that came to Troy: he had a goggle eye,
> Starcke-lame he was of eyther foote, his shoulders were contract
> Into his brest and crookt withall: his head was sharpe compact,
> And here and there it had a hayre.

He is not only a filthy deformed railer, but also a coward who weeps when he is chid by Ulysses. Shakespeare keeps these characteristics and even uses the same epithet 'rank'. Later Thersites says he will croak like a raven—words suggested by the opening lines of the above quotation.

The passage about dissension in the Greek army is based on the Homeric account. Shakespeare follows Homer in making Achilles withdraw from the battle through excessive pride, though he omits the reason for his resentment of Agamemnon, and adds the motive of love of Patroclus (derived partly from Homer) and love of Polyxena (derived from Caxton). Shakespeare can be vague about the cause of the quarrel since, as he declares in the prologue, he begins in the middle of the story. But in the first act he shows us the results of the feud, and then passes on to the matter of Book VII, the challenge of Hector to Ajax and the debate in Troy about the restoration of Helen. In Book VII Shakespeare would have found the device of the lottery, although it is there Nestor's suggestion. Shakespeare invents the idea of the manipulation of the lottery by Ulysses and his use of the challenge to arouse Achilles. In all the sources the embassy to Achilles is merely a suit: in the play it is part of Ulysses's plot, and it is linked with Hector's challenge. Shakespeare treated the combat between Hector and Ajax differently from any of his predecessors, though the incident itself is a combination of elements derived from his

---

[1] I can find no internal evidence that Shakespeare had read Arthur Hall's translation.

sources. In Book IX Ulysses and Phoenix give advice to Achilles; Shakespeare again strengthens the importance of Ulysses's part by omitting Phoenix. The death of Patroclus was derived from *Achilles Shield* (*Iliad* XVIII): in Caxton the death of Patroclus takes place much earlier and is not related to the death of Achilles. In motivating Achilles's return to battle Shakespeare is indebted to Homer alone.

In depicting Nestor Shakespeare relied on Homer rather than on Caxton. In his portrait of Menelaus Shakespeare follows Homer's conception. In his complete translation (though not in 1598) Chapman describes Menelaus as 'short-spoken, after the country, the laconical manner, yet speaking thick and fast'. Shakespeare's Menelaus is also laconical. He utters only two words on his first appearance and six on his second.

Certain Homeric details Shakespeare took from parts of the *Iliad* not yet translated. He may have read the poem in a French or Latin translation, but the treatment of Hector's dead body by Achilles he could have found in the *Æneid* or in a classical dictionary.[1] Achilles surveys Hector in order to find the best place to kill him, very much as Achilles chooses the death stroke in the *Iliad* (Book XXII).

Hector's visit to the Greek camp is derived from Caxton, but it seems to have been amplified from Greene's collection of stories and debates entitled *Euphues his Censure to Philautus* (1587).[2] In a description of a similar visit to the Greek camp during a truce, Greene mentions that Hector walked with Achilles and Troilus with Ulysses, as in the play. The same book contains a discussion on the quality most necessary for a soldier—wisdom, fortitude, or liberality. Helenus, in arguing for the necessity of wisdom in a soldier uses language similar to Ulysses's, when he speaks of the way the Greeks scorn the work of the staff officer.

For suppose the captaine hath courage enough to braue the enemy in the face, yet if hee knew not by a wise and deepe insight into his enemies thoughts, how with aduantage to preuent such ambushes as may be layd to preiudice his army, had hee as great courage as the stowtest champion in the worlde, yet might the defect of wisdome in the preuention of such perills, ruinate both him selfe, his honor, and his Souldiours.

[1] The story was, of course, well known.
[2] Cf. C. H. Herford (*N.S.S. Trans.*, 1888, p. 186) and K. Muir, *N.Q.* (1955), p. 141.

There is another discussion on the question of whether Helen should be restored, in the course of which she is referred to as a gem, a pearl, and as a piece.[1] In Shakespeare's play Troilus speaks of her as a pearl, and Diomed speaks of her as a piece. Hector's argument that[2] 'Nature . . . hath taught vs . . . to mayntayne my Brothers deede with the Swoorde, not to allow such a fact honorable but as holding it princely, with death to requite an iniury' is not unlike Hector's attitude in the play. He condemns the rape of Helen, but agrees to continuing the war because it 'hath no mean dependence upon [their] joint and several dignities'.

Greene mentions[3] Hecuba's dream that she has given birth to a firebrand; one of his characters criticizes the Trojans for being ignorant of moral philosophy,[4] as Hector accuses his brothers of being unfit to hear it; he mentions the definition of virtue as a mean between two extremes (which is usually thought to be the point of the line 'Betweene whose endless iarre Iustice recides'); he refers to the palace of Ilium (though this is also in Caxton); and he makes Ulysses critical of women:[5] 'An ounce of giue in a Ladies ballaunce, weygheth downe a pound of loue mee'. Finally it may be mentioned that one character speaks of beauty as metaphysical,[6] much as Troilus claimed that beauty was an absolute value; Cressida is described as[7] 'tickled a little with a selfe conceipt of hir owne wit'; and a lustful woman in one of the illustrative tales mislikes[8] 'hir olde choyce, through the tickling desire of a new chaunge'. Ulysses, speaking of Cressida, uses the epithet *tickling*[9] or *ticklish*. Shakespeare appears to have taken a good deal of atmospheric detail from Greene's book.

In Ulysses's famous speech on degree Shakespeare was influenced by[10] a number of different sources. From Homer he took the general idea of the speech:

> wretch keepe thy place and heare
> Others besides thy Generall that place aboue thee beare:
> Thou art vnfit to rule and base without a name in war
> Or state of counsaile: nor must Greekes be so irregular:
> To liue as euery man may take the scepter from the king:
> The rule of many is absurd, one Lord must leade the ring.

[1] ed. A. Grosart, p. 165.
[2] op. cit., p. 167.
[3] op. cit., p. 155.
[4] op. cit., p. 169.
[5] op. cit., p. 263.
[6] op. cit., p. 160.
[7] op. cit., p. 166.
[8] op. cit., p. 195.
[9] These are the readings of Q and F.
[10] There is a full discussion in the Variorum edition, and a short one, to which I contributed, in Bonamy Dobrée's.

Agamemnon says that the Greeks would have conquered Troy if they had not quarrelled amongst themselves, and Homer also uses the image of bees. The Greeks hastening to the council are compared to tribes of thronging bees.[1] So Ulysses in the play asks

> When that the Generall is not like the Hiue,
> To whom the Forragers shall all repaire,
> What Hony is expected?

Virgil[2] also uses the image of the bees, repairing to their hive, and Shakespeare had used this in *Henry V*. He was also acquainted with Elyot's *The Governour*, where the bee image is explicitly related to the question of order[3] and to Ulysses's speech on the need for order.

A publike weale is a body lyuyng, compacte or made of sondry astates and degrees of men, whiche is disposed by the ordre of equite and gouerned by the rule and moderation of reason. . . . For as moche as *Plebs* in latin, and comminers in englisshe, be wordes only made for the discrepance of degrees, wherof procedeth ordre: whiche in thinges as wel naturall as supernaturall hath euer had suche a preeminence, that therby the incomprehensible maiestie of god, as it were by a bright leme of a torche or candel, is declared to the blynde inhabitantes of this worlde. More ouer take away ordre from all thynges what shulde then remayne? Certes nothynge finally, except some man wolde imagine eftsones *Chaos*: whiche of some is expounde a confuse mixture. Also where there is any lacke of ordre nedes must be perpetuall conflicte: and in thynges subiecte to Nature nothynge of hym selfe onely may be norisshed; but whan he hath distroyed that where with he dothe participate by the ordre of his creation, he hym selfe of necessite muste than perisshe, wherof ensuethe uniuersall dissolution. But nowe to proue, by example of those thynges that be within the compasse of mannes knowledge, of what estimation ordre is, nat onely amonge men but also with god, all be it his wisedome, bounte, and magnificence can be with no tonge or penne sufficiently expressed. Hath nat he set degrees and astates in all his glorious warkes? . . .

Beholde also the ordre that god hath put generally in al his creatures, begynnyng at the most inferiour or base, and assend-

---

[1] Cf. *Seven Bookes*, ii. 71 ff.   [2] *Æneid*, I. 430.   [3] Chaps. I, II.

ynge upwarde: he made not only herbes to garnisshe the erthe, but also trees of a more eminent stature than herbes, and yet in the one and the other be degrees of qualitees; some pleasant to beholde, some delicate or good in taste, other holsome and medicinable, some commodious and necessary . . . so that in euery thyng is ordre, and without ordre may be nothing stable or permanent; and it may nat be called ordre, excepte it do contayne in it degrees, high and base, accordynge to the merite or estimation of the thyng that is ordred. Nowe to retourne to the astate of man kynde . . . it is therfore congruent, and accordynge that as one excelleth an other in that influence, as therby beinge next to the similitude of his maker, so shulde the astate of his persone be auanced in degree or place where understandynge may profite: whiche is also distributed in to sondry uses, faculties, and offices, necessary for the lyuing and gouernance of mankynde. . . .

The populare astate, if it any thing do varie from equalitie of substance or estimation, or that the multitude of people haue ouer moche liberte, of necessite one of these inconueniences muste happen: either tiranny, where he that is to moche in fauour wolde be elevate and suffre none equalite, orels in to the rage of a communaltie, whiche of all rules is moste to be feared. For lyke as the communes, if they fele some seueritie, they do humbly serue and obaye, so where they imbracinge a licence refuse to be brydled, they flynge and plunge: and if they ones throwe downe theyr gouernour, they ordre euery thynge without iustice, only with vengeance and crueltie: and with incomparable difficultie and unneth by any wysedome be pacified and brought agayne in to ordre. Wherfore undoubtedly the best and most sure gouernaunce is by one kynge or prince. . . . For who can denie but that all thynge in heuen and erthe is gouerned by one god, by one perpetuall ordre, by one prouidence? One Sonne ruleth ouer the day, and one Moone ouer the nyghte; and to descende downe to the erthe, in a litell beest, which of all other is moste to be maruayled at, I meane the Bee, is lefte to man by nature, as it semeth, a perpetuall figure of a iuste gouernaunce or rule: who hath amonge them one principall Bee for theyr gouernour, who excelleth all other in greatnes, yet hath he no pricke or stinge, but in hym is more knowledge than in the residue. . . . The capitayne hym selfe laboureth nat for his sustinance, but all the other for hym; he onely seeth that if any drane or other unprofitable bee entreth in to the hyue, and consumethe the hony, gathered by other, that he be immediately expelled from that company. . . .

The Grekes, which were assembled to reuenge the reproche of Menelaus . . . dyd nat they by one assent electe Agamemnon to be their emperour or capitain: obeinge him as theyr soueraine duryng the siege of Troy? . . . They rather were contented to be under one mannes obedience, then seuerally to use theyr authorities or to ioyne in one power and dignite: wherby at the last shuld haue sourded discention amonge the people, they beinge seperately enclined towarde theyr naturall soue-rayne lorde, as it appered in the particuler contention that was betwene Achilles and Agamemnon for theyr concubines, where Achilles, renouncynge the obedience that he with all other princes had before promised, at the bataile fyrst enterprised agaynst the Troians. For at that tyme no litell murmur and sedi-tion was meued in the hoste of the grekes, whiche nat with-standyng was wonderfully pacified, and the armie unscatered by the maiestie of Agamemnon, ioynynge to hym counsailours Nestor and the witty Ulisses.

The importance of order is stressed by many authors Shake-speare is known to have read. In *Troilus and Criseyde*, for example, Chaucer celebrates the power of Love[1] to hold all things together, even to restrain the greedy sea from overflowing—

To drenchen erthe and al for ever-mo.

In the Homily on obedience, appointed to be read in churches, Shakespeare would have heard order in the state connected with order in the universe, and the dangers of chaos there set forth are similar to those stressed in Ulysses's speech:[2]

Almightie God hath created and appointed al things in heauen, earth, and waters, in a moste excellent and perfect ordre. In heauen he hath appointed distinct and seuerall orders and states of Archangells and Angels. In earth he hath assigned and ap-pointed kynges, princes and other gouernors vnder them, all in good and necessary ordre. The water aboue is kept, and raineth doune in due time and season. The sunne, moone, sterres, rain-bow, thunder, lightnyng, cloudes, and al birdes of the aire, do kepe their ordre. The earth, trees, seedes, plantes, herbes, corne,

---

[1] III. 250-2.   [2] Cf. A. Hart, *Shakespeare and the Homilies* (1934), p. 34.

grasse, and al maner of beastes, kepe them in their ordre. All
the partes of the whole yere, as winter, somer, monethes,
nightes, and daies continue in their ordre. All kindes of fishes in
the sea, riuers, and waters; with all fountaines, and sprynges;
yea, the seas themselfes, kepe their comely course and ordre.
And man himself also, hath al his partes both within and without, as soule, harte, mynd, memory, vnderstandyng, reason,
speache, withall and synguler corporall members of his body, in
a profitable, necessary and pleasaunt ordre. Euery degre of
people in their vocacion, callyng and office, hath appointed to
them their duetie and ordre. Some are in high degre, some in
lowe, some kynges and princes, some inferiors and subiects,
priestes and laimen, masters and seruantes, fathers and children,
husbandes and wifes, rich and poore, and euery one haue nede
of other, so that in al thinges is to be lauded and praised the
goodly ordre of God, without the whiche, no house, no cite, no
common wealth, can continue and endure. For wher there is no
right ordre, there reigneth all abuse, carnall libertie, enormitie,
syn, and babilonicall confusion. Take awaye kynges, princes,
rulers, magistrates, iudges, and such states of Gods ordre, no
man shall ride or go by the high waie vnrobbed, no man shall
slepe in his owne house or bed vnkilled, no man shall kepe his
wife, children, and possessions in quietnes, all thynges shalbe
common, and there must nedes folow all mischief and vtter
destruction both of soules, bodies, goodes, and common
wealthes.

Shakespeare had also read Hooker's *Ecclesiastical Polity* (1597)—
there is an echo of it in *The Merry Wives of Windsor*—and in the first
book of that treatise, in a context which uses the image of the
untuned string and the phrase 'degrees in schools' (both used by
Shakespeare) Hooker has an eloquent passage[1] on the necessity of
order:

[God's] commanding those things to be which are, and to be in
such sort as they are, to keep that tenure and course which
they do, importeth the establishment of natures law. . . . And
as it commeth to passe in a kingdom rightly ordered, that after
a law is once published, it presently takes effect far and wide,
all states framing themselues thereunto; euen so let vs thinke
it fareth in the naturall course of the world: since the time

[1] I. iii. 2.

that God did first proclaime the edicts of his law vpon it, heauen and earth haue hearkned vnto his voice, and their labour hath bene to do his wil: He made a law for the raine. He gaue his decree vnto the sea, that the waters should not passe his commandement. Now if nature should intermit her course, and leaue altogether, though it were but for a while, the obseruation of her own lawes: if those principall and mother elements of the world, wherof all things in this lower world are made, should loose the qualities which now they haue, if the frame of that heauenly arch erected ouer our heads should loosen and dissolue it self: if celestiall spheres should forget their wonted motions and by irregular volubilitie, turne themselues any way as it might happen; if the prince of the lightes of heauen which now as a Giant doth runne his vnwearied course, should as it were through a languishing faintnes begin to stand and to rest himselfe: if the Moone should wander from her beaten way, the times and Seasons of the yeare blend themselues by disordered and confused mixture, the winds breath out their last gaspe, the cloudes yeeld no rayne, the earth be defeated of heauenly influence, the fruites of the earth pine away as children at the withered breasts of their mother no longer able to yeeld them reliefe, what would become of man himselfe, whom these things now do all serue? See we not plainly that obedience of creatures vnto the lawe of nature is the stay of the whole world?

There have been many other suggested sources for this speech. Florio in his translation of Montaigne's essays[1] uses the word *imbecility* and refers to cannibalism in a passage about the necessity of obedience—but it is not certain that Shakespeare read this translation in manuscript, or that it was published before he wrote the play. One critic argues that Shakespeare may have remembered the introductory stanzas to Book V of the *Faerie Queene* on the subject of justice,[2] but there is only one, not very striking, verbal parallel. Hanford argued that Shakespeare was influenced by Plato's analysis of the evils of democracy in the eighth book of *The Republic*, though not necessarily directly.[3] Professor T. W. Baldwin claims that Shakespeare was influenced by Cicero's *Tusculans*,[4] which discusses the origin and foundation of society and uses the analogy of the planets. Shakespeare may have read it

---

[1] Cf. Temple ed. ii. 275; iv. 1.   [2] Cf. Steevens ed. (1793).
[3] Cf. *S.P.*, xiii (1916), pp. 100–9. I. A Richards, op. cit., has an interesting essay on Platonic ideas in the play.   [4] Cf. Var. ed., p. 412.

in the original, since he uses the unique word *insisture*, which was apparently derived from a note on the word *institiones*, 'cum insistere videntur'. *Course* in the same line is derived from *cursus*. Neither word is used in Dolman's translation.

Green suggested that Shakespeare was influenced by one of Whitney's *Emblems*,[1] representing chaos, with the winds, waters, and stars all in confusion mingling. Henderson[2] pointed out that Lydgate uses the word *degree* three or four times, and his Agamemnon delivers a speech of some two hundred lines against the indiscipline of the Greeks. Lydgate comments on the mischief of

> variaunce
> Among lordis, whan thei nat accorde . . .
> Envie is cause of swiche divisioun,
> And couetyse of dominacioun . . .
> That everyche wolde surmounte his felaw.

So Shakespeare speaks of the envious fever of Emulation.

It is not necessary to believe that Shakespeare deliberately, or even unconsciously, combined material from all the books I have mentioned. He was writing within a tradition, and the speech was a collection of commonplaces. Elsewhere he follows Chaucer in arguing that it is love that prevents chaos. But the nature of the situation in *Troilus and Cressida* and the example of Lydgate would make him stress degree as a concomitant of order. Few will accept Professor Baldwin's arguments that the speech is un-Shakespearian. The conclusion of it—with disorder leading to Cannibalism—can be paralleled in *Coriolanus*, *King Lear*, and the Shakespearian scenes in *Sir Thomas More*.

> Troy yet vpon his basis had bene downe,
> And the great *Hectors* sword had lack'd a Master
> But for these instances.
> The specialty of Rule hath beene neglected;
> And looke how many Grecian Tents do stand
> Hollow vpon this Plaine, so many hollow Factions.
> When that the Generall is not like the Hiue,
> To whom the Forragers shall all repaire,
> What Hony is expected? Degree being vizarded,
> Th' vnworthiest shewes as fairely in the Maske.

[1] Cf. H. Green, *Shakespeare and the Emblem Writers* (1870), pp. 448 ff.
[2] Cf. W. B. D. Henderson, Parrott Presentation Volume (1935), pp. 142–4.

The Heauens themselues, the Planets, and this Center,
Obserue degree, priority, and place,
Insisture, course, proportion, season, forme,
Office, and custome, in all line of Order:
And therefore is the glorious Planet Sol
In noble eminence, enthron'd and sphear'd
Amid'st the other, whose med'cinable eye
Corrects the ill Aspects of Planets euill,
And postes like the Command'ment of a King,
Sans checke, to good and bad. But when the Planets
In euill mixture to disorder wander,
What Plagues, and what portents, what mutiny!
What raging of the Sea! shaking of Earth!
Commotion in the Windes! Frights, changes, horrors,
Diuert, and cracke, rend and deracinate
The vnity, and married calme of States
Quite from their fixure! O, when Degree is shak'd,
(Which is the Ladder to all high designes)
The enterprize is sicke. How could Communities,
Degrees in Schooles, and Brother-hoods in Cities,
Peacefull Commerce from diuidable shores,
The primogeniture, and due of Byrth,
Prerogatiue of Age, Crownes, Scepters, Lawrels,
(But by Degree) stand in Authentique place?
Take but Degree away, vn-tune that string,
And hearke what Discord followes: each thing meetes
In meere oppugnancie. The bounded Waters,
Should lift their bosomes higher than the Shores,
And make a soppe of all this solid Globe:
Strength should be Lord of imbecility,
And the rude Sonne should strike his Father dead:
Force should be right, or rather, right and wrong,
(Betweene whose endlesse iarre, Iustice recides)
Should loose their names, and so should Iustice too.
Then euery thing includes it selfe in Power,
Power into Will, Will into Appetite,
And Appetite (an vniuersall Wolfe,
So doubly seconded with Will, and Power)
Must make perforce an vniuersall prey,
And last, eate vp himselfe. Great *Agamemnon*:
This Chaos, when Degree is suffocate,

Followes the choaking:
And this neglection of Degree, it is
That by a pace goes backward in a purpose
It hath to climbe. The Generall's disdain'd
By him one step below; he, by the next,
That next, by him beneath: so euery step
Exampled by the first pace that is sicke
Of his Superiour, growes to an enuious Feauer
Of pale, and bloodlesse Emulation.
And 'tis this Feauer that keepes Troy on foote,
Not her owne sinewes. To end a tale of length,
Troy in our weaknesse liues, not in her strength.

Our examination of the sources, not only of this speech but of
the play as a whole, suggests that Shakespeare followed his usual
custom of reading all the accessible material on his theme and using one book to amplify another. Chaucer, Henryson, Homer,
Lydgate, and Caxton all contributed to themes and incidents in the
play; and a German critic, Miss Theleman,[1] even argues that
Shakespeare must have consulted De la Lande's translation of
Dictys, since his play has certain similarities of treatment with this
work which are not to be found in Lydgate or Caxton. It should be
mentioned, however, that there was at least one play on the same
theme before Shakespeare's, and some of the apparent similarities
with De la Lande may have been derived from this play. But
Shakespeare, as a general rule, took more pains than his contem-
poraries in the collection of source material, and he is more likely
than Chettle and Dekker to have gone to Caxton's source.

Shakespeare organized his heterogeneous material in the form
of a tragical satire. The play is complete in itself, and it is unnecessary to assume that the poet intended it as the first part of a
trilogy. Both the Greeks and the Trojans are depicted less heroic-
ally than they are by Caxton and Homer, though, as befits a play
with a Trojan hero, the Trojans are presented with rather more
sympathy. This was in accordance with medieval tradition, stem-
ming ultimately from Virgil.

[1] Cf. *Archiv*, cxxxiii (1915), pp. 91–6. The influence on the play of Shakespeare's
own *Sonnets* and *Lucrece* is discussed by K. Muir, *Shakespeare Survey 8*, pp. 28–39.

(9) All's Well that Ends Well

The source of *All's Well that Ends Well* was either Boccaccio's tale in the *Decameron* (III. 9) or William Painter's version of the same tale in *The Palace of Pleasure* (I. 38). The two versions differ very little. Painter tells how the Count of Rossiglione, because he is an invalid, keeps in his house a physician, named Master Gerardo of Narbona. The Count's son, Beltramo, is brought up with Gerardo's daughter, Giletta. She falls in love with the boy 'more than was meet for a maiden of her age'. When the Count dies, Beltramo, 'left under the royal custody of the King', is sent to Paris. Gerardo dies shortly afterwards, and Giletta would have liked to follow Beltramo to Paris, but she is 'diligently looked unto by her kinsfolk' because she is rich, and she refuses many suitors. She hears that the King suffers from a fistula, and she journeys to Paris with one of her father's remedies. She sees Beltramo first and then tells the King she can cure him within eight days 'by the aid and help of God'. The King at first refuses and she suggests that she shall be burnt if she fails, the King, for his part, promising to find her a husband. She stipulates that the husband shall be of her choosing 'without presumption of any of your children or other of your blood'. The cure is successful and she chooses Beltramo. At first he refuses her, but he finally accepts her under protest. He gets permission to return home to consummate the marriage, but goes instead to take service with the Florentines, who are at war with the Siennese.

Giletta goes to Rossiglione, where she wins the affection of her subjects by her wise rule. She sends word to Beltramo that if he has abandoned his country because of her she will depart from thence. He replies that he will not return till she has the ring from his finger, and a son in her arms begotten by him.

Giletta thereupon assembles the noblest and chiefest of her country and explains the position to them, and tells them she is going to spend the rest of her time in pilgrimages and devotion, so that Beltramo can return home. She goes to Florence and hears that Beltramo is in love with a poor girl. She tells the girl's mother that she will provide a dowry for her daughter if she agrees to her plan—to demand Beltramo's ring, to make an assignation with him, and to allow Giletta to take her place in bed. The mother consents and Giletta by this means consummates her marriage with Beltramo. (Painter adds that she slept with him many other times. Boccaccio mentions only one occasion.) When she knows she is pregnant Giletta gives the girl five hundred pounds and an equivalent value of jewels, and she is brought to bed of two sons. Meanwhile Beltramo has been called home, and in due course Giletta arrives with her babies while he is about to have a feast with many guests. She falls at his feet and urges him to fulfil his promise, explaining how she fulfilled the hard conditions. Beltramo, urged by his friends, acknowledges Giletta as his wife and they live happily ever after.

Helena, unlike Giletta, is poor; and we are told nothing by Shakespeare about other suitors. She does not see Bertram before her presentation to the King by Lafeu. After the cure the King lines up three or four lords for Helena to choose from, and Bertram had expressed a wish to go to the wars before he is married. Helena receives Bertram's harsh letter as soon as she arrives at Rousillon, and not in answer to a letter of hers; and she forthwith decides to leave for Florence, not after ruling for some months. Shakespeare, however, does not mention, as Painter does, that she hopes to fulfil the two conditions, and she tells no one about her plans. She meets with Diana and her mother on her first arrival, Shakespeare conflating Helena's hostess and Diana's mother. Shakespeare complicates the business of the rings by having Diana give Bertram the ring Helena received from the King. Bertram returns home because of the news of his wife's death, spread by Helena herself. Helena returns with Diana and her mother before the birth of her child and conveniently finds the King at Rousillon. Bertram is about to be married to Lafeu's daughter, to whom he gives Helena's ring, which is recognized both by Lafeu and the King. Bertram is arrested on suspicion of murdering Helena; Diana enters and claims his hand, and when he repudiates her as a harlot she demands her ring. Finally Helena enters and everything is explained. In addition to these complications in the last act Shakespeare introduces several important characters. Bertram's mother, his most sympathetic portrait of an old lady, and Lafeu both express a warm admiration for Helena; both feel that she is too good for Bertram. The rather feeble clown sings a song about Helen of Troy, which may be meant to suggest that the Helena of the play is extremely beautiful. Finally, there is

Parolles, the *Miles Gloriosus*, whose exposure is the first shock administered to Bertram's self-conceit and false values. He is as unable to choose a friend as he is to appreciate the woman he has married. His false values are revealed still further in his willingness to promise marriage to a girl in order to seduce her. Beltramo apparently makes no such promise.

The King's attitude, too, differs from that of his prototype. In the source the King is unwilling for Giletta to choose Beltramo—he thinks she has aimed too high; but the King in the play has an eloquent speech on the theme 'virtue is the true nobility'. It may be mentioned that Giovanni Battista Nenna's treatise on Nobility, translated by William Jones and published in 1595 under the title *Nennio*, is a debate on the subject of whether true nobility is founded on birth or on virtue. The conclusion is[1] that

> true and perfect nobilitie, doth consist in the vertues of the minde.

The disputant who argues this opinion points out that

> the body is lesse noble than the minde, of which two partes nature hath framed man, the one being subiect to corruption, the other eternallie dureable.

Nobility does not depend on birth since we are all descended from Adam:

> I reason then thus . . . that if Adam was noble, why then we are all noble . . . but if he were ignorant and base, we are so likewise.

It follows that

> true and perfit Nobilitie, is deriued from no other fountaine, then the vertues of the minde, and not from the worthinesse of bloud.

A king can ennoble any man he pleases, so that

> The dignity of a doctor is equall vnto the degree of a knight which hee obtaineth as a reward of his vertues.

We are reminded of Helena and her father. Indeed, Nenna points out that women also are noble by reason of their virtue:

> a Lady not borne of any noble bloud, but beautified with good

[1] The following quotations will be found on pp. 28, 32, 58, 92, 94, 97.

conditions, ought farre to be preferred before her whose birth is noble, and renowned, and by her vnordinate behauiour becommeth base, and infamous.

The King in *All's Well*, who points out that Helena is noble because she is virtuous and that he can himself give her the rank she lacks, agrees with Nenna and with other writers on the subject

that the nobilitie of the minde, is farre more true, and farre more perfect, than the nobility of blood conioyned with riches.

But the subject was much discussed and we cannot be certain that this particular book was used by Shakespeare.

Most critics feel dissatisfied with the play, as they are not with the source. Our sympathies are divided between Beltramo and Giletta, and when she succeeds in an apparently impossible task we feel she deserves the hand of the hero. Shakespeare transformed the conventional material of the story, and in so doing gave himself insoluble problems. Professor W. W. Lawrence, indeed, points out[1] the elements of the folk-tale in the play and he argues that the Elizabethans would have approved of Helena's trick. The trouble is, as Mr Middleton Murry has shown,[2] that Helena is by no means a medieval type, but created with 'delicate hesitation' as well as business-like resolution. Bertram, moreover, unlike Beltramo, is 'a cad, morbidly conscious of his birth, blind in his judgement of others, vicious in his morals, and, when cornered, a cowardly liar'—not, one would have thought, much of a prize.

But Professor Harold S. Wilson is, I believe, right in his interpretation[3] of the play. Shakespeare realized that Helena's actions in the second half of the play are liable to rob her of our sympathy. He arouses our admiration for her in the first acts both by her conduct and by the attitude of other characters to her, and in the second part of the play he removes her from the centre of the stage. Bertram's siege of Diana's chastity, the unmasking of Parolles, and the accusation of Bertram, 'successively provide the focus of interest while Helena works out her designs unobtrusively in the background'. It is necessary if the play is really to end well that Bertram should be converted, not just trapped, and the function of the Parolles scenes and of Bertram's final ordeal, in

[1] *Shakespeare's Problem Comedies* (1931), p. 51.
[2] *Shakespeare* (1936), p. 302.
[3] *H.L.Q.*, xiii, (1950), pp. 217. ff.

which he is revealed to all for what he is, is to bring him to a self-recognition, and so make him less unworthy of Helena.

Helena never loses our sympathy, especially when the play is performed. The way she releases the King from his promise, her quiet submissiveness when Bertram repudiates her, and her wish to save him from the dangers of war all prevent us from feeling that she is merely a Shavian heroine who hunts down her prey. In the scenes in which Bertram is tricked the emphasis is mainly on Helena's pathos, and Diana never seems to be merely a puppet in Helena's hands. As Mr Wilson says,[1]

> the controlling idea of the play that emerges is the conception of Helena's love as far stronger than Bertram's arrogance, a love which works unobtrusively but with humility toward an end that heaven favours.

We may feel in reading the play that Shakespeare did not quite succeed in his humanizing of his source-material. Some of the trouble may be due to imperfect revision and a poor text—Violante, for example, is given no words to say, and Bertram's final capitulation is given in an absurd couplet. But it is a play which acts much better than it reads, and the undertones (e.g. the feeling that the younger generation are inferior to their elders) and ambiguities, especially in the character of the heroine, may not be evidences of failure on the part of the dramatist but a deliberate deepening of his theme. If the Clown were given better jokes and Bertram a better speech at the end, the play would leave us with feelings of greater satisfaction.

(10) *Measure for Measure*

The first literary treatment of the plot[2] of *Measure for Measure* was Claude Rouillet's *Philanira* (1556), a Latin play which was translated into French seven years later. This was followed in 1565 by the version given in Giraldi's *Hecatommithi*, a collection of tales in which Shakespeare also found the plot of *Othello*.

---

[1] *H.L.Q.*, xiii (1950), p. 239.
[2] Cf. Mary Lascelles, *Shakespeare's 'Measure for Measure'* (1953), and the earlier studies, not altogether superseded, by F. E. Budd (*Revue de Littérature comparée*, 1931, pp. 711–36), by R. H. Ball (*University of Colorado Studies*, 1945, pp. 132–146), and by L. Albrecht (*Neue Untersuchungen zu Shakespeares Mass für Mass*, 1914).

There was a French translation by Gabriel Chappuys in 1584. Giraldi also wrote a dramatic version of the story, entitled *Epitia*, which was published posthumously in 1583; it was never acted. Meanwhile George Whetstone's play on the same theme, *Promos and Cassandra*, had been published in 1578, and this was Shakespeare's principal source. Three years later Thomas Lupton retold the story in the second part of *Siuquila*, and in 1582 Whetstone rehandled it as one of the tales in his *Heptameron of Civil Discourses*. There were other versions of the story, but they appear to have had no influence, direct or indirect, on Shakespeare's play.

It is probable that at the time he was working on *Othello* Shakespeare read the story of Epitia, and he may have read several of Giraldi's stories. From them, as Miss Mary Lascelles suggests,[1] he might have derived the idea of giving the story a happy ending, 'of the inclination to pardon which is to be looked for in the man of highest authority', and of the capacity of the victim of intolerable wrong to forgive the villain when he is at her mercy.

In Giraldi's tale the Emperor Maximian leaves Juriste as his deputy to govern Innsbruck. Vico is condemned to death for rape. His sister, Epitia, urges Juriste to pardon him, and when she returns to hear his decision he offers to spare Vico if she yields to his lust, hinting that he may afterwards marry her. On Vico's entreaty, and on his arguing that marriage will repair the wrong, Epitia consents to Juriste's proposal, and on the morning afterwards Vico is executed and the body is sent to his sister. Epitia sets out to find the Emperor; Juriste is confronted with his victim and brought to confess; Epitia and Juriste are married forthwith, and she pleads with the Emperor to spare the life of the man who has wronged her. Epitia and Juriste live happily ever after. Here Shakespeare would have found the main outlines of his plot, though Isabella only pretends to assent to Angelo's proposal, Claudio's offence is not rape but fornication, and his life is spared by a trick, and although Isabella pleads for Angelo, she does not marry him.

From Giraldi's story, we may suppose, Shakespeare turned to Whetstone's long and rambling play, written for the most part in rhymed doggerel. Cassandra, a young and virtuous maiden, goes to Promos to beg her brother Andrugio's life, who has been condemned for rape—though there is some suggestion that the offence should rather be described as fornication. Promos agrees

[1] op. cit., p. 35.

to pardon Andrugio and to marry Cassandra, on condition that she sleeps with him first.

Andrugio pleads; she consents; but after she has carried out her side of the bargain,

> Promos, as feareles in promisse, as carelesse in performance, with sollemne vowe sygned her conditions: but worse than any Infydel, his will satisfyed, he performed neither the one nor the other: for to keepe his aucthoritie vnspotted with fauour, and to preuent *Cassandraes* clamors, he commaunded the Gayler secretly, to present *Cassandra* with her brother's head. The Gayler, with the outcryes of *Andrugio*, abhorring *Promos* lewdenes, by the prouidence of God, prouided thus for his safety. He presented *Cassandra* with a Felons head newlie executed, who . . . was so agreeued at this trecherye, that at the pointe to kyl her selfe, she spared that stroke to be auenged of *Promos*.

The Argument goes on to describe how she told the King her story; and he ordered that Promos should marry her and afterwards be executed.

> This maryage solempnised, *Cassandra* tyed in the greatest bonds of affection to her husband, became an earnest suter for his life.

The King refuses to grant her suit until the disguised Andrugio discloses his identity. Shakespeare certainly read the play, for he derived his idea of the underplot from it; but he also read Whetstone's narrative version, which in the *Heptameron* is recounted by one Isabella. Miss Lascelles thinks[1] that Shakespeare may have read Lupton's version of the story, from which he could have got the idea of the disguised Prince, though in Middleton's *Phoenix*, acted not long before *Measure for Measure*, there is a disguised Prince who learns about the crimes and vices of society, and exposes them when he throws off his disguise. Lupton, however, hoped to legislate people into virtue, and he encouraged the use of informers. Shakespeare, if he read *Siuquila*, would have reacted violently against its spirit; and his reaction may have influenced his description of Angelo's rule in Vienna. Finally, there is more than a possibility that Shakespeare had read Giraldi's dramatic version, *Epitia*.[2]

---

[1] op. cit., pp. 22 ff., 36 ff.

[2] In addition to the critics mentioned on p. 101 *ante*, Madeleine Doran, *Endeavors of Art* (1954), pp. 385–9, and E. Schanzer, privately, have discussed the possible indebtedness of Shakespeare to *Epitia*. Miss Doran has a convenient table of eight

Reading Giraldi's story or Whetstone's two versions, Shakespeare would have been struck by the dramatic possibilities of the theme, but he must have realized that the psychology of Cassandra was theatrical and false. It is not easy to accept the spectacle of a virtuous girl forgiving a man who is both her seducer and the supposed murderer of her brother. Such a character could be interpreted only in terms of psychopathology. The marriage at the end of the play could be justified only if the character of Promos was whitewashed. Shakespeare was therefore faced with two alternatives. He could make a revenge-tragedy, ending the play with the death of the corrupt deputy. Or, he could by various means

---

points in which *Measure for Measure* agrees with *Epitia* while diverging from the other sources. In two of these points, however, Giraldi's novel also agrees with *Epitia*. There remain: the name of Juriste's sister, Angela; the fact that the Secretary protests to the Podestà about the harshness of the law and the severity of its prosecution, and that he comments in soliloquy on the rigour of those in power; discussion in both plays of justice and mercy, power and authority; the substitution for Vico of a criminal hopelessly evil; the fact that Angela pleads with Epitia for Juriste's life, as Mariana does with Isabella, and that Epitia distinguishes between the act and the intention; and the fact that the Captain of the Prison announces that Vico has not been killed, as the Provost does in *Measure for Measure*, though Claudio, unlike Vico, comes on the stage.

Epitia tells the Emperor, as Isabella tells the Duke, that the sentence on her brother was just. The closest verbal parallels are the following:

> Oh, I wil to him, and plucke out his eies . . .
> Vnhappie *Claudio*, wretched *Isabell*,
> Iniurious world, most damned *Angelo*.
> (IV. iii. 124, 126–7)
> Male ne hò detto à Iuriste, e poco meno
> Che non gli habbia cacciati ambiduo gli occhi,
> Accesa da giusta ira, e da vergogna . . .
> (III. ii.)
> O scelerato, ò traditore Iuriste,
> O doloroso Epitia, ò miserella.
> (III. i.)
> Whatsouer you may heare to the contrary, let Claudio
> be executed by foure of the clocke . . .
> (IV. ii.)
> Andai al Podestà ratto, ei mostromme
> Lettra di man d'Iuriste, & del sigillo
> Di lui segnata, che gli commetteva
> Che, senza udir cosa, che fusse detta,
> Levar gli fesse il capo.

In the same scene is another reference to the hand and the seal:

> Lettra, segnata del maggior Sigillo.

Vincentio, in a different context, shows the Provost the hand and seal of the Duke. As Ball says:

> The hand and seal, the letter with its order to disregard all other advice, the messenger, who is pictured arriving at the prison and bearing death when pardon is expected, are common only to *Epitia* and *Measure for Measure* and are not found in other sources.

The Emperor, on hearing Epitia's story, asks, 'E questo è vero?' and she replies

mitigate the guilt of Promos, and so be able to end the play with his marriage. But both these solutions would have been comparatively feeble. He had already in *Titus Andronicus* written a revenge-play in which the guiltless heroine is raped, and the result is shocking rather than tragic. In *Lucrece* the heroine commits suicide. But it would not have been a satisfactory theme for a play, as we can see from the attempts of Heywood and Obey. On the other hand, however much the guilt of Promos were minimized, his marriage with the heroine would lay her open to the suspicion that she did not dislike his proposal as much as she pretended. To remove the suspicion altogether Shakespeare made his heroine a novice with a passionate hatred of sexual vice. He decided to write a play on the subject of forgiveness—not the forgiveness prompted by sexual passion as in Whetstone, nor even the magnanimity suggested in some of Giraldi's stories, but Christian forgiveness—that is, the forgiveness of enemies.

By making his heroine a novice Shakespeare made the conflict in her mind, whether she should agree to Angelo's proposal, as violent as possible; and this obviously added to the dramatic intensity of the plot. On the other hand, it meant, of course, that Isabella could not possibly consent to Angelo's proposal. As a Christian, and still more as a novice, she ought not to commit

'Più ver, che il vero.' In the same way Vincentio tells Isabella 'Nay, it is ten times strange' and she replies:

> It is not truer he is Angelo
> Than this is all as true as it is strange.
> Nay, it is ten times true.

Later on Vincentio exclaims 'This is most likely!' and Isabella again replies:

> O that it were as like as it is true.

Schanzer points out that Angela's maid soliloquizes on the power of a beautiful young woman to obtain her petitions, and even take Jove's thunderbolt from his hands:

> che potrà levare
> I fulmini di mano al sommo Giove
> Quando più fier, che mai fulmina, & tuona.

This may have suggested both Lucio's speech on the power of maidens (I. iv. 80–4) and Isabella's speech beginning:

> Could great men thunder
> As *Ioue* himselfe do's . . .

In addition to some points already mentioned, Budd mentions three points of resemblance: *Epitia*, like *Measure for Measure*, is a dissertation on justice; Epitia's conduct may have suggested Vincentio's justification of his 'pandering' for Angelo and Mariana, that they were betrothed; and the Duke's speaking 'on the adverse side' at the opening of Angelo's trial finds a counterpart only in *Epitia*.

Some of these parallels are of doubtful validity; but the case that Shakespeare had read *Epitia* is a strong one.

fornication even to save her brother's life; for if he demanded, or even accepted, the sacrifice, she would believe him to be damned. (She might, of course, have done it without telling him, like the heroine of Clemence Dane's *The Way Things Happen*; but there the man who is saved from prison is furious with the woman who has bought his freedom.) Yet Claudio's life had to be saved, so a substitute for Isabella had to be found. Already in the source a substitute on the block is found for Claudio; Shakespeare finds a substitute, Ragozine, for this substitute, Barnardine, and a substitute for Isabella in the shape of Mariana. The device was doubtless suggested by the plot of *All's Well*, in which Helena tricks Bertram in the same way, and from which the name Mariana is taken. The bed-trick, as it has been called, offends modern susceptibilities; but Shakespeare in both cases uses the situation to show how sexual passion blinds the victim. Bertram imagined that it would be distasteful to share a bed with his wife, and the summit of human felicity to share one with Diana; yet, as Helena comments:[1]

> O strange men,
> That can such sweet vse make of what they hate,
> When sawcie trusting of the cosin'd thoughts
> Defiles the pitchy night! So lust doth play
> With what it loathes, for that which is away.

Similarly Angelo imperils his immortal soul by offering to spare Claudio's life in exchange for a night with Isabella, and yet in the dark is unable to tell the difference between Isabella and Mariana.

Shakespeare, then, had to find a suitable substitute for Isabella. It had to be someone who loved Angelo and had some right to his bed. What better choice than someone to whom Angelo had been betrothed, and whom he had rejected for some reason appropriate to his character and to the theme of the play? The reason was not far to seek. Claudio, contracted to Juliet, had postponed the marriage ceremony for the sake of a dowry. Angelo, with far less excuse, had repudiated Mariana because her dowry had miscarried. Claudio's fornication, for which he is condemned to death, is shown to be less sinful than the mercenary behaviour of Angelo, though the latter earns a reputation for uprightness and self-control. It is necessary to the scheme of the play that Angelo should commit the very sin for which he had condemned another to death.

[1] *A.W.* IV. iv. 21 ff.

The fact that Isabella is a novice would suggest Angelo's character. He has to be something of a puritan. He is a man of severe morals, sincerely respected both by the Duke and Escalus. He believes himself to be proof against the temptation to commit sins of the flesh:[1]

> whose blood
> Is very snow-broth: one, who neuer feeles
> The wanton stings, and motions of the sence;
> But doth rebate, and blunt his naturall edge
> With profits of the minde: Studie, and fast . . .

They say this *Angelo* was not made by Man and Woman, after this downe-right way of Creation. . . . Some report, a Sea-maid spawn'd him. Some, that he was begot betweene two Stock-fishes.

Shakespeare shows that chastity may proceed from meanness or cowardice. But it is wrong to regard Angelo as a villain. 'He is betrayed by the subtler temptation which would mean nothing to a grosser man. He is moved by the sight of the beauty of a distressed woman's mind'.[2] 'His boasted self-control' (as Professor L. C. Knights has shown[3]) 'is not only a matter of conscious will, but of a will taut and strained'. 'Once the precarious balance is upset', he is betrayed by the sexual instinct he despised. As Cadoux puts it:[4] 'His scheme of life has no decent place for sex, and therefore no foothold from which to fight its indecencies.' The puritanical streak in Angelo's character may have been suggested by the self-righteous and rigid attitude displayed by Lupton.

Until recently most critics have objected to Isabella's forgiveness of Angelo. Johnson and Coleridge for once were in agreement, and Bridges[5] thought the ending showed a lack of artistic conscience. Professor W. W. Lawrence excuses Shakespeare by saying[6] that it was customary in the drama of the period for the repentant villain to be married to the heroine. But Angelo, though he is morally guilty of lust and murder and actually guilty of hypocrisy, meanness, and treachery, is not really a villain; he is a 'sincere self-deceiver', as Mr J. I. M. Stewart says,[7] the kind of

---

[1] *M.M.* I. iv. 57 ff.; III. ii. 97 ff.
[2] J. Masefield, *William Shakespeare* (1911), p. 178.
[3] *Scrutiny*, X (1942), p. 222–33.
[4] A. T. Cadoux, *Shakespearean Selves* (1938), p. 81.
[5] R. Bridges, *The Influence of the Audience* (1927), p. 13.
[6] op. cit., p. 116.
[7] *Character and Motive in Shakespeare* (1949), pp. 14, 141.

person who is 'liable to the kind of aberration depicted'. Angelo, moreover, is not the central character of the play, and those recent critics who have justified the ending of the play have done so by showing that Isabella, who had pleaded with Angelo for her brother, is put in the position where she is called upon to forgive the man who has wronged her. She passes this test of the sincerity of her religion—a test which has been imposed by the Duke— after an agonizing struggle.

Shakespeare, by making his heroine a novice, involves Claudio also in a searching ordeal; and by making his Duke return in disguise to manipulate the action, he ensures that the characters shall be tempted without tragic results. Even Barnadine is spared, and only Lucio, who in spite of his corrupt charm is a cold-hearted lecher, informer, and slanderer, is treated with some severity. It is difficult to agree with Professor Ellis-Fermor that[1] 'the lowest depths of Jacobean cynicism' are touched in this play. Many of the minor characters are depicted sympathetically—the warm, forgiving Mariana, the humane Provost, the saintly Juliet. Shakespeare, indeed, was not without sympathy for Pompey the pimp, for Barnadine the drunken murderer, and for Mistress Overdone the bawd who looks after Lucio's bastard.

Dr Tillyard complains,[2] with greater justice, that the play falls into two disparate halves. After the scene between Claudio and Isabella most of the play is in prose, and what poetry there is, is greatly inferior to that of the first two acts. Theatrical intrigue takes the place of psychological profundity and great poetry. Dr Tillyard is right to point out the change in the second half of the play, but apart from the fact that the last two acts are highly successful on the stage, they may be defended on more respectable grounds. It is the intervention of the Divine in human affairs which transforms the style and pattern in the second half of the play. The characters become puppets, 'taking part in no common action',[3] and manipulated so that they all find judgement or salva-

---

[1] *The Jacobean Drama* (1936), p. 263.
[2] *Shakespeare's Problem Plays* (1950), p. 132.
[3] T. S. Eliot, *Murder in the Cathedral*. It may be added, as I have suggested elsewhere (*N.Q.*, 1956, p. 424), that a few minor details in *Measure for Measure* seem to have been derived from one of Erasmus's *Colloquia*. Shakespeare may have consulted the 'Funus' to obtain background information about friars and nuns. Erasmus tells us that a dying man's younger son is dedicated to St Francis, his elder daughter to St Clare (ed. 1571, p. 503: *Filius minor dicaretur S. Fransisco, filia maior S. Clarae*). This passage may have suggested making Isabella a votaress of St Clare, as the dative *Fransisco* suggested Francisca, Isabella's interlocutor. Nor is this all. In the same context Erasmus tells us that the dying man is visited by Bernardine, a Francis-

tion. In the first part of the play the characters blunder along in their human way, until they can be saved only by Providence Divine. Thereafter they are whirled about so swiftly that they do not have any time, even for poetry. The poetry is in the action itself.

---

can friar, and Vincentius, a Dominican friar. On the page next to the one which contains the reference to St Clare, Erasmus speaks of *Barnardino, tantundem Vincentio*. Here the misprint for *Bernardino* and the case in which Vincentius appears seem to have suggested the names Barnardine and Vincentio. William Burton's translation of seven of the *Colloquies*, including the 'Funus', did not appear until 1606, after the first performance of *Measure for Measure*.

(11) Hamlet

SHAKESPEARE's *Hamlet* was based on a lost play of the same title, perhaps by Shakespeare himself,[1] perhaps by an unknown dramatist; but *The Spanish Tragedy*, one of the most popular Elizabethan plays, which kept its place on the stage in spite of parody, resembles *Hamlet* so closely that it would appear that the source-play was written by Kyd[2] or a close imitator of his. Both plays begin with a ghost demanding vengeance; both are concerned with the madness, real or assumed, of the avenger; both contain the death of an innocent woman; both heroes blame themselves for their procrastination. We know very little about the *Ur-Hamlet*, except that the Ghost cried like an oyster-wife, 'Hamlet, revenge!' and that Hamlet is supposed to have said, 'There are things called whips in store'.[3] But although we have no certain knowledge of the *Ur-Hamlet*, we can deduce a good deal about it from a study of other versions of the Hamlet story. Its author was doubtless attracted to the plot because it enabled him to use some of the popular ingredients of *The Spanish Tragedy*. Instead of a father seeking to avenge his murdered son, he was provided with a son seeking to avenge his murdered father. The story given by Saxo Grammaticus and in Belleforest's *Histoires Tragiques* is substantially the same. The father of Amleth, a governor of Jutland, to whom the King of Denmark had given his daughter, Gerutha,

---

[1] A. S. Cairncross, *The Problem of Hamlet* (1936), even maintains that Shakespeare's play (c. 1588) was substantially the version of Q 2.

[2] Nashe's preface to Greene's *Menaphon* is thought by most, but not by all, critics to imply that Kyd was the author.

[3] This looks suspiciously like a misquotation of a passage from one of the late additions to *The Spanish Tragedy*:

> And there is Nemesis, and Furies,
> And things called whips,
> And they sometimes do meet with murderers.

Either the author of this passage was imitating the Ur-*Hamlet*, or Armin, who quotes the phrase, may have confused the two plays.

in marriage, won fame by slaying the King of Norway in single combat. His brother, Feng, murdered him, seized his office, and married his wife, thus 'adding incest to unnatural murder'. Young Amleth determined to avenge his father, but in order to gain time and allay his uncle's suspicions, he feigned 'a foolish and grotesque madness', so that all 'he did savoured of utter lethargy'. In his mad speech

> he mingled craft and candour in such a way that, though his words did not lack truth, yet there was nothing to betoken the truth and betray how far his keenness went.

Two attempts were made to pierce his disguise. A beautiful woman who had been friendly with him since his childhood was instructed to seduce him; but he was warned of the trap both by his foster-brother and also by the woman herself. The second attempt to pierce his disguise was made by one of Feng's friends, who undertook to spy upon him when he was talking with his mother in her chamber. From this trap Amleth was saved by crowing like a cock and flapping his arms like wings till he found the spy hidden under the straw mattress. He pierced him with his sword, cut up the body into little pieces, cooked them, and flung them through the mouth of an open sewer for the swine to eat. Then he upbraided his mother for her lustful conduct, comparing it to that of beasts who mate indiscriminately, and urged her to lament her own guilt rather than his madness. The mother repented of her sin, and Amleth won her over to his side. Feng next dispatched Amleth to Britain with two retainers, bearing a letter which instructed the King to put Amleth to death; but while they slept, Amleth searched their belongings, found the letter, and substituted fresh instructions, as in Shakespeare's play. When they reached Britain, Amleth's companions were hanged, and he married the Princess. A year later he returned to Jutland. Having made Feng and his followers drunk, he set fire to the palace, slew Feng, after changing swords with him—his own having been rendered useless by treachery—and the followers were burnt alive. The version of the story given in the *Histoires Tragiques* is much the same; but in that Gertrude and Fengon had committed adultery before the murder of Amleth's father and Belleforest speaks of Amleth's 'over-great melancholy'.

Whichever source the author of the *Ur-Hamlet* used he would have the germ of most of the characters—Claudius, Gertrude,

Polonius, Ophelia, Horatio, Rosencrantz, and Guildenstern—and
the basis for the feigned madness, the interview with Ophelia, the
closet-scene, the voyage to England, and the changing of weapons
in the final duel. If he used Belleforest he would have found there
Amleth's melancholy and Gertrude's adultery. But in neither
source was there a ghost, a *Mousetrap*, a Laertes, a Fortinbras;
there was no drowning of Ophelia, no pirates, no graveyard scene,
and no Osric. We may be sure that the author of the *Ur-Hamlet*,
imitating *The Spanish Tragedy*, invented the *Mousetrap*, the ghost
and the madness and death of Ophelia.

Some other characteristics of the source-play may be deduced
from a study of the piratical quarto of Shakespeare's play, which is
contaminated by an earlier version, and of the German version,
Fratricide Punished. When the bad quarto diverges from the good
quarto but agrees at that point with the source, it is reasonable to
assume that the bad quarto is following the *Ur-Hamlet*; and when
Fratricide Punished agrees with Belleforest and disagrees with
Shakespeare's play, it may possibly be reproducing something
which was in the *Ur-Hamlet*.

The character of the Queen seems to have been rather different
in the earlier play. After the death of Corambis (Polonius) she
blames herself for Hamlet's madness, and believes either that she
is thereby punished for her incestuous re-marriage, or else that her
marriage, by depriving Hamlet of the crown, has driven him mad
from thwarted ambition. Hamlet upbraids her for her crocodile
tears, and urges her to assist him in his revenge, so that in the
King's death her infamy should die. She replies:

> Hamlet, I vow by that maiesty
> That knowes our thoughts, and lookes into our hearts,
> I will conceale, consent, and doe my best
> What stratagem soe're thou shalt deuise.

Later on, when Hamlet returns from England, she sends him a
warning message by Horatio:

> Bid him a while
> Be wary of his presence, lest that he
> Faile in that he goes about.

Thus in the *Ur-Hamlet* the Queen apparently took positive steps
to aid the Prince in his revenge. In Shakespeare's play she conceals
Hamlet's secret and probably keeps herself from her husband's
bed, but she does nothing more positive to assist her son.

The version of the voyage to England given in *Fratricide Punished* differs both from Shakespeare's and Belleforest's. Hamlet embarks for England with his escort, and they are forced by contrary winds to anchor by an island, not far from Dover. They land on the island to enjoy the air and exercise, and the two ruffians tell Hamlet that they have orders to kill him. He pleads in vain; he attempts to seize a sword from one of the men, but is prevented; and he finally escapes by a trick. The villains plan to shoot him, one from each side. Hamlet gets permission to pray and promises when he is ready to die to raise his hands. But when he does so he throws himself forward so that his would-be assassins shoot each other, Hamlet finishing them off with their own swords. He then searches them and finds a letter from the King commanding that, should the first attempt on Hamlet's life miscarry, he should be put to death by the King of England. There is nothing about the forged commission, and nothing about the pirates. Hamlet makes his own way back to Denmark.

It has been argued that some such scene must have been in the *Ur-Hamlet*,[1] and this view receives some support from a few phrases in the bad quarto.

> Being crossed by the contention of the windes,
> He found the Packet sent to the king of England. . . .
> *Queene:* But what became of *Gilderstone* and *Rossencraft*?
> *Hor.:* He being set ashore, they went for *England*. . . .

Shakespeare seems to have invented the pirates, though not (as Mr Savage has argued) as an allegorical account of his own fight with the pirates of the printing trade and of the publication of the piratical quarto.[2] He avoided the dramatization of the island incident, if it was in the *Ur-Hamlet*, partly because of its absurdity, and partly because the visit to England could not be presented on the stage without making his longest play even longer. As his custom was, Shakespeare consulted more than one version of the stories he dramatized, and here he may have gone to Belleforest for the business of the forged commission and the killing of Rosencrantz and Guildenstern.

The *Ur-Hamlet*, therefore, so far as it can be reconstructed, seems to have been fairly close to Shakespeare's play in its main

---

[1] Cf. G. I. Duthie, *The 'Bad' Quarto of Hamlet* (1941).
[2] Cf, D. S. Savage, *Shakespeare and the Pirates* (1950).

outlines. The revelation of the ghost, the feigned madness, the play-scene, the closet-scene, the killing of Polonius, the voyage to England, the madness and suicide of Ophelia,[1] and the duel with Laertes were probably all to be found in the old play, and Shakespeare's additions (the pirates, Fortinbras, and possibly the grave-diggers), important as they are, are less significant than his intensification and subtilization of themes and motives present in his source—the effect of a mother's guilt on a son, the malcontent's satire under the guise of madness, the self-laceration of enforced delay, the contrast between the two avengers, Hamlet and Laertes, and the friendship between Hamlet and Horatio.

It used to be fashionable to assume that the real problem of *Hamlet* is not due to the character of the hero but to confusions caused by Shakespeare's inability to transform the intractable material of the old play, so that we have motives and incidents from the *Ur-Hamlet* (such as the murder of Rosencrantz and Guildenstern) side by side with the feelings and experience of Shakespeare's maturity. There are, too, certain discrepancies, such as Hamlet's varying age[2] and the varying knowledge of Horatio[3] which have been thought to indicate revision; and it has been suggested that in Shakespeare's earlier version of the play 'To be or not to be' was written for the first act, and that there was no graveyard scene.[4]

[1] Although the Ophelia of the source-play was probably drowned, it should be mentioned that when Shakespeare was fifteen there were three inquests of which he would have heard. On 6 July 1579 a William Shakespeare of Warwick was drowned while bathing in the Avon; a week later a John Shakespeare of Balsall hanged himself; and on 17 December Katharine Hamlet was drowned in the Avon at Tiddington, while getting water in a bucket. The surname of the third victim may have recalled her tragedy to Shakespeare while he was writing *Hamlet*, and this, rather than the source-play, might have been the origin of the manner of Ophelia's death.

[2] Hamlet's age is sometimes apparently 18, and sometimes 30. Østerberg, however, rightly points out that we cannot assume that the Gravedigger is accurate when he boasts that he has been a sexton for thirty years, and no audience would work out Hamlet's age from his statements. The general impression we have early in the play of Hamlet's youthfulness is partly due to the reference to Horatio as a fellow-student, and to the hero's wish to return to 'school' at Wittenburg. He may well have been a post-graduate student. It is nevertheless possible that Shakespeare altered Hamlet's age to suit Burbage, who was no longer young.

[3] At one point Horatio is a stranger to the Court, ignorant of Danish customs; at another moment he seems to know more about Denmark than Bernardo and Marcellus, and to have been acquainted with Hamlet's father. This apparent inconsistency would not be noticed in the theatre; and it may be said that an under-graduate friend of an English Prince of Wales might know of preparations for war, but might well be ignorant of the drinking habits of the Royal Family.

[4] Cf. W. J. Lawrence, *Speeding up Shakespeare* (1937), pp. 55 ff. As the soliloquy stands at present Hamlet refers to the bourne from which no traveller returns after he has talked with the Ghost. But, as Dover Wilson argues, Hamlet may be thinking that the Devil has assumed his noble father's person.

Santayana declares[1] that

> Some of Hamlet's actions and speeches seem anterior to his true character. They apparently remain over from the old melo-drama, and mark the points neglected by the poet and left untransmuted by his intuition. These survivals of cruder methods, if survivals they be, give a touch of positive incoherence to Hamlet's character, otherwise sufficiently complex.

But although we may concede that Shakespeare revised his own play, it is very doubtful whether he was at all hampered by his source-play. The view that he was is put in its bluntest form by Sir John Squire.[2] Hamlet, he complains,

> is crowded with faults. There are scenes which lead nowhere and the main theme is very confusingly handled.

He goes on to suggest that once the ghost was invented the feigned madness was unnecessary—though, as we have seen, the ghost is unlikely to have been Shakespeare's invention—and declares that we must perpetually remember that

> the play as we have it is new wine in an old bottle, that a new Hamlet has to fit an old plot, and that certain passages are retained either because they had already been successful in the theatre, or because Shakespeare was too slack, or thought he could not afford the time, to mend them.

Those who accept the argument of the present book will hardly share Sir John Squire's belief that Shakespeare was a lazy artist, and it is particularly difficult to square this belief with a *Hamlet* which is too long to have been performed in its entirety during the poet's lifetime. But even Professor Waldock thinks[3] that

> An old play is wrenched to new significances, significances, in places, that to the end it refuses to take. It was, perhaps, inevitable that the play should show signs, in fissures and strain, of all this forceful bending.

And Mr T. S. Eliot,[4] under the influence of J. M. Robertson, believed at one time the play was 'certainly an artistic failure'.

But whatever the defects of *Hamlet*, we cannot ascribe them to the intractability of the source-material. This material, difficult

[1] *Life and Letters*, i, (1928), p. 18.
[2] *Shakespeare as a Dramatist* (1935), pp. 77 ff.
[3] A. J. A. Waldock, *Hamlet: A Study in Critical Method* (1931) p. 97.
[4] *Selected Essays* (1932), p. 143.

but not intractable, had outstanding advantages. It was familiar, popular, and exciting, and required less adaptation than the sources of *Othello* or *King Lear*. Some characteristics of the play are doubtless survivals from the *Ur-Hamlet*, but there is no reason to believe that Shakespeare retained them casually and carelessly, or merely to please the groundlings. It seems likely that he wrote some passages and scenes so that he could express the whole of his theme, even though he knew that his work would be mangled by cuts. This concern with his art could not have existed side by side with the slapdash methods critics impute to him. We cannot explain the coarseness of Hamlet's words to Ophelia, both in the Nunnery scene and the Play scene, by the fact that her prototype was a lady of easy virtue. If, as is probable, Ophelia went mad in the *Ur-Hamlet*, she is unlikely to have been very different in her morals from Shakespeare's character; and even if she were, we can no more explain the coarseness of the words of Shakespeare's Hamlet by this fact, than we can the brutality of Othello by the fact that the Moor in the source watches the Ensign murder Disdemona with a stocking filled with sand. Nor can we explain the callousness of Hamlet's epitaph on Polonius by recalling that Amleth cut him up and fed him to the swine. The simple answer to those critics who say that Shakespeare's Hamlet would never have said such things, or done such things as the murder of his schoolfellows, is that Shakespeare's Hamlet did, and that we ought to explain these things in terms of the existing play. Shakespeare made himself responsible for any incidents or characteristics that he retained from the source-play.[1]

It is obvious that Shakespeare realized the dramatic advantages of contrasting the 'barbaric nature of his material' with 'the modern refinement and sophistication of his hero'[2] Nor was Shakespeare alone in this. The revenge play had by 1602 become a more complicated form than it had been ten or fifteen years earlier; and in the revenge plays of Marston, written about the same time as *Hamlet*, and in those of Webster, Tourneur, and Chapman, written soon afterwards, we can see something of the same complexity in the characters of the avengers.

Whether *Antonio's Revenge* was a debased version of Shakespeare's *Hamlet*, or *Hamlet* a refined version of Marston's play is immaterial to our present purpose, since both were ultimately

[1] Cf. Lascelles Abercrombie, *A Plea for the Liberty of Interpreting* (1930).
[2] E. M. W. Tillyard, *Shakespeare's Problem Plays* (1950), p. 29.

derived from *The Spanish Tragedy* and the *Ur-Hamlet*. The greater nobility and humanity of Shakespeare's hero are partly due to his doubt. Antonio pursues his revenge without misgiving, and after it has been achieved he complacently announces:

> Tis done, and now my sowle shal sleepe in rest,
> Sons that reuenge their fathers blood, are blest.

But in *The Malcontent*, published in the same year as the second quarto of *Hamlet* and acted by Shakespeare's company, the hero is a melancholy malcontent who in the end spares the villain out of pride:

> Slaue, take thy life
> Wert thou defenced, thorough blood and woundes,
> The sternest horror of a ciuell fight,
> Would I atcheeue thee: but prostrate at my feete
> I scorne to hurt thee: tis the heart of slaues,
> That daines to triumph ouer peasants graues.

In Beaumont and Fletcher's *The Pilgrim* a man is spared by his enemy for the same reason as Claudius is spared by Hamlet. In *The Maid's Tragedy* Amintor is prevented from avenging himself by his acceptance of the divine right of kings. In *The Revenger's Tragedy* Vindice is presented as morbid and unbalanced; and in *The Atheist's Tragedy* we have a ghost who urges his son to 'leaue reuenge vnto the King of Kinges'. When Charlemont is about to kill the murderer the ghost intervenes to stay his hand; and the hero is torn between the passion of his blood and the religion of his soul. The actual working out of the divine vengeance strains our credulity; when D'Amville lifts up the executioner's axe to slay Charlemont, he accidentally strikes out his own brains. In *The Revenge of Bussy D'Ambois* we have another variation on the revenge formula. Chapman's hero, Clermont, indulges in no self-accusations; he does not feign madness; nor is he the cause of the death of the innocent. Accepting the duty of avenging his brother's death he sends Montsurry a challenge, which is refused. Later on he doubts whether a private man should take the law into his own hands, and in the end he slays his enemy in fair fight and bids rest both to him and to the soul of his brother.

These different treatments of the revenge formula show that Shakespeare was not hampered by the expectations of the audience. The villain could be forgiven, as *Measure for Measure*, *The*

Tempest, and *The Malcontent* prove; revenge could be treated as a moral duty or as a sin; and the avenger could refrain from vengeance out of Senecan pride or on Christian grounds. The fascination of the revenge theme to the Elizabethans was due to the conflict between the revenge code and the more civilized code formulated by classical moralists and Christian theologians.[1] Private vengeance was forbidden by Church and State, and their prohibition was reinforced by classical writers. Seneca, for example, in his essay on Anger,[2] declared that for a man to harbour desire of revenge is not consonant to his nature:

> A man ought to correct him that offendeth by admonitions, forcible reprehensions, friendly but effectual speech.

We ought to redeem offences with mercies. Personal revenge is always wrong, and we ought to be too proud to stoop to it:

> It is the part of a great mind to despise iniuries: it is a contumelious kinde of reuenge, that he thought him vnworthy to reuenge himselfe on. . . . That man is great and noble, that after the manner of a mightie wilde beast, listneth securely the barking of lesser Dogges. . . . So then we ought to auoid wrath whether it bee with our equall, with our superiours or inferiours. To striue against our equals is a matter doubtful, against our superiours is furie, against our inferiours is basenes. . . . Anger . . . is the canker of humane nature. . . . A man that is truly valiant, and knoweth his owne worth, reuengeth not an iniurie, because he feeleth it not. . . . How farre more worthy a thing is it to despise all iniuries and contumelies, as if the minde were impregnable. Reuenge is a confession of paine. The minde is not great which is animated by iniurie.

The view of preachers and moralists on the subject of revenge was not necessarily identical with that of an audience. It has even been suggested that the popularity of the revenge play is a sign of the survival of more primitive modes of thought; and the prevalence of duelling, particularly after the accession of James I, both on and off the stage, is a sign that popular feelings about revenge differed from the more official views. Many dramatists seem to have assumed that revenge was a kind of wild justice; and though the avenger usually has to expiate his actions—particularly

---

[1] Cf. F. Bowers, *Elizabethan Revenge Tragedy* (1940), *passim*.
[2] tr. T. Lodge, pp. 514, 519-21, 547-9, 556.

if they have involved the death of innocent people—the dramatist seldom flatly condemns revenge.[1]

Shakespeare was, of course, fully conscious of the difference between religious and philosophical attitudes to revenge and those used by some dramatists; but the revenge play became so varied that we could not, even if Shakespeare were not exceptional, predict the precise way in which he would treat the Hamlet story. We do not know the precise attitude of the author of the *Ur-Hamlet*; we do not know what Shakespeare's first-night audience expected; and we do not know the extent to which he fulfilled or cheated their expectations. Just as the Greek audiences were interested in the variant treatments by Aeschylus, Sophocles, and Euripides of the theme of the *Oresteia*, and just as part of Racine's audiences would be intrigued by his variations on a theme of Euripides, so Shakespeare's audience must have expected him to present variations on the theme of Leir or Amleth. They would not mind alterations, provided they justified themselves by being more effective than the original. The extent to which Hamlet's madness was real or assumed, the exact amount of the Queen's complicity in the murder of his father, the nature of Hamlet's love for Ophelia, and many other details, could be settled in accordance with Shakespeare's dramatic design. The character of his hero could vary from that of a primitive avenger who unquestioningly carried out his father's commands to that of a stoic or Christian who morally disapproved of revenge. There is nothing impossible in Professor Lawlor's argument[2] that the Elizabethan audience would assume that Hamlet's failure to act was due to a scruple about the justice of revenge.

The wonder is not that Shakespeare retained so little of the spirit of the earlier play, but that he was able to make use of so many of its episodes. The primitive materials formed a strange basis for a sophisticated play; and nothing better illustrates Shakespeare's genius than the way he made use of primitive episodes for his own purposes. In the *Ur-Hamlet*, for example, the hero spared the King at prayers, we may assume, to avoid sending him straight to heaven. Shakespeare's hero offers precisely the same avowed reason; but hardly any critic believes him.

The main outlines of his plot being settled by the source-play, Shakespeare concerned himself with a re-creation of the charac-

[1] Cf. F. Bowers, op. cit., *passim*.
[2] Cf. J. J. Lawlor, *R.E.S.* (1950), pp. 97–113.

ters. As part of this process he turned to Dr Timothy Bright's *Treatise of Melancholy*. Some scholars think that he might have picked up the information about melancholy from several other books, but it is difficult to brush on one side the evidence set out by Professor J. Dover Wilson.[1] Bright tells us, for example, that

> The ayre meet for melancholicke folke, ought to be thinne, pure and subtile, open and patent to all winds: in respect of their temper, especially to the South, and South-east.

This lends point to Hamlet's remark—

> I am but mad north-north-west; when the wind is southerly I know a hawk from a handsaw.

More significant, perhaps, is the resemblance between Bright's phrase, 'the braine as tender as a posset curd', and the ghost's account of the effect of his brother's poison—

> And with a sudden vigour it doth *posset*
> And *curd*, like eager droppings into milk.

Bright mentions the importance of exercise and uses Hamlet's phrase 'custom of exercise'. He shows how the melancholy man ponders and debates long, but when he acts, he acts vigorously. Unnatural melancholy, he tells us,

> raiseth the greatest tempest of perturbations and most of all destroyeth the braine with all his faculties, and disposition of action.

With melancholy men desperate fury is sometimes joined with fear:

> Which so terrifieth, that to auoid the terrour, they attempt sometimes to depriue them selues of life: so irksome it is vnto them through these tragicall conceits, although waighing and considering death by it self without comparison, and force of the passion, none more feare of then they.

This 'sharpe kind of melancholie' makes 'rage, reuenge, and furie' to possess both heart and head, and the whole body is 'carried with that storme, contrarie to persuasion of reason'. The melancholy man is dull of deed, with a reasonably good memory, 'if fancies deface not';

[1] *What Happens in Hamlet* (1935), pp. 309 ff.

firme in opinion, and hardly remoued, wher it is resolued: doubtfull before, and long in deliberation: suspicious ... giuen to fearefull and terrible dreames: in affection sad, and full of feare.

Yet he is sometimes 'merry in appearance, through a kind of Sardonian, and false laughter'. He is apt to see 'phantasticall apparitions' and he is apt to be

doubtfull, suspitious, and thereby long in deliberation, because those domesticall feares, or that internal obscuritie, causeth an opinion of daunger in outwarde affaires, where there is no cause of doubt.

Finally, 'the whole force of the spirite' being 'close vp in the dungion of melancholy darkenes, imagineth all darke, blacke and full of feare'.

One is reminded of numerous passages in *Hamlet*—of the Prince's fear that the Devil is making use of his melancholy to abuse him with a 'phantastical apparition', of his bad dreams and thoughts of suicide, of his feeling that Denmark is a prison, of his belief that the world is a foul and pestilent congregation of vapours, of his wit and sardonic humour. In a very real sense Shakespeare was depicting a melancholy man as he appears in Bright's treatise.[1]

For his treatment of the supernatural Shakespeare relied partly on Reginald Scot and partly on Lavater's *Of Ghosts and Spirites*.[2] In his account of the drinking habits of the Danes he was echoing Nashe's *Pierce Penilesse*.[3] For the account of the portents, as we shall see, he combined hints from Plutarch, Virgil, and Ovid, and possibly from Lucan.[4] In Laertes's advice to Ophelia he inadvertently echoed Henry Swinburne's *Treatise on Wills*;[5] and in Polonius's advice to Laertes he imitated either Lyly's *Euphues* or Greene's *Gwydonius* or similar passages in other works.[6] For Æneas's tale to Dido he used Marlowe's *Dido* and probably Virgil as well. For Hamlet's third soliloquy and for some other ideas in the play he may have made use of *Cardanus Comforte* translated by

[1] T. Bright, op. cit., pp. 257, 13, 130, 124.
[2] J. D. Wilson, op. cit., pp. 60–84.
[3] Cf. A. Davenport as cited Chapter 1, p. 10.   [4] Cf. p. 197 *ante*.
[5] Cf. Chapter 1, p. 7.
[6] Cf. J. Lyly ed. Bond, ii. 31; Greene ed. Grosart, iv. 21; Florio, *Second Frutes*, pp. 92–105.

Thomas Bedingfeld.[1] Other ideas may be derived from Montaigne, though Florio's translation was not published until 1603.[2] The scene with Osric appears to be based on Florio's *Second Frutes*[3] and the attack on cosmetics resembles a passage in Guazzo's *Civill Conversation*.[4] These examples out of many will be enough to suggest the range of reading which contributed to the richness of the play.

(12) Othello

The source of *Othello* is Giraldi's *Hecatommithi* (III. 7). As there is a version of the story which formed the plot of *Measure for Measure* in the same collection, and as that play was probably written soon after *Othello*, it is likely that Shakespeare read Giraldi's book in the first years of the seventeenth century. It is possible, of course, that there was an English version of the story, though there is no evidence of this. It is also possible that there was an Italian dramatic version known to the Elizabethans.[5] But in the absence of evidence it is safer to assume that Giraldi's tale was the immediate source of *Othello*. There was a French translation by Gabriel Chappuys, but from one passage in the play which is closer to the Italian than it is to the French, it seems probable that Shakespeare read the original Italian.[6] Othello's words—

---

[1] Cf. H. Craig, *H.L.B.* (1934), pp. 17 ff.
[2] Cf. G. C. Taylor, *Shakespeare's Debt to Montaigne* (1925).
[3] Cf. K. Muir, *N.Q.* (1952), pp. 493 ff.
[4] tr. G. Pettie (Tudor Translations ed.) II, pp. 10–13:

Ad hereto that bewty breedeth temptation, temptation dishonour: for it is a matter almost impossible, and sieldome seene, that those two great enimies, bewty and honesty agree togither . . . And though it fall out often that bewty and honesty are joyned togither, yet it falleth out sieldome, but that exquisite bewty is had in suspition . . . Those which vse artificiall means, displeasure God much, in altring his image, and please men neuer a whit, in going about to deceiue them. I know of no man of iudgement, but setteth more, by ods, by a naturall bewty that sheweth but meanly, then by a painted artificiall bewty that shineth most gallantly . . . We will maintayne then, that a woman taking away and changing the coolour and complexion which God hath giuen her, taketh vnto her that which belongeth to a harlot.

[5] As M. Praz points out (*Machiavelli and the Elizabethans*, 1928), Giraldi's play *Altile* has a villain named Astano who ruins Norrino by his treachery in the same way as Iago ruins Othello, and he had vainly loved Altile in much the same way as the Ensign had loved Disdemona.
[6] Cf. W. Wokatsch, *Ar.* clxii (1932), pp. 118–19.

> Villaine, be sure thou proue my Loue a Whore—
> Be sure of it: Giue me the Ocular proofe
> Or, by the worth of mans eternall Soule,
> Thou had'st bin better haue bin borne a Dog
> Than answer my wak'd wrath . . .
> Make me to see't . . .

are based on the words Giraldi gives to the Moor:

> Se non mi fai, disse, vedere cogl' occhi quello, che detto mi hai,
> viviti sicuro, che ti farò conoscere, che meglio per te sarebbe,
> che tu fossi nato mutulo.

Chappuys's version is not so close:

> Si tu ne me fais voir ce que tu m'as dit, assure-toi que je te
> ferai connoistre, que mieux t'eût valu être né muet.

The probability that Shakespeare read the Italian text is reinforced
by his use of the word *acerbe*,[1] for Giraldi tells us that the love
which his villain had borne Disdemona 'turned to the bitterest
hatred'—*in acerbissimo odio*. Smart argued[2] that Shakespeare derived his account of the handkerchief from Ariosto's description
of Cassandra in the last canto of *Orlando Furioso*:

> Una donzella de la terra d' Ilia
> Ch' avea il furor profetico congiunto
> Con studio di gran tempo, e con vigilia
> Lo fece di sua man di tutto punto.

Harrington, in his version, does not translate the phrase *il furor
profetico*, though 'prophetic fury' is used by Sylvester.

In Giraldi's story Othello is called the Moor, Iago the Ensign,
and Cassio the Captain. Only Disdemona is given a name; but to
avoid confusion between the military terms—Ensign, Ancient,
Captain, Lieutenant—it will be convenient in the following summary to give Giraldi's characters their Shakespearian names.

Disdemona is a virtuous lady of great beauty who falls in love
with the Moor, not out of lust or feminine appetite, but because of
his virtues. Her relations try to persuade her to take another husband, but she insists on marrying the Moor and they live in Venice
'in such harmony and peace that no word ever passed between
them that was not affectionate and kind'. The Moor is appointed

---

[1] I. iii. 345. F. substitutes the commoner word 'bitter'.
[2] J. S. Smart, *Shakespeare: Truth and Tradition* (1928), p. 183.

to the command of the Cyprus garrison, and he is sad at the prospect of leaving his wife behind or of exposing her to the dangers of the sea, but Disdemona, on learning the reason for his sadness, insists on accompanying him. The Moor embraces her, exclaiming 'God keep us in this love for a long time!'[1]

Iago and his wife and Cassio accompany Othello and Disdemona to Cyprus, sailing in the same boat. The Moor loves both Iago and Cassio, and Disdemona is very fond of the young and beautiful Emilia. Iago is handsome, but depraved:

> Despite the malice lurking in his heart, he cloaked with proud and valorous speech and with a specious presence the villainy of his soul with such art that he was to all outward show another Hector and Achilles.

Cassio dines often at the Moor's house, and Othello entirely approves of his wife's friendship with their guest. Meanwhile Iago falls in love with Disdemona, and meeting with no response he imagines that she must be in love with Cassio. To avenge himself on Disdemona, whom he now hates, to destroy Cassio, and to prevent Othello from enjoying Disdemona since he himself cannot, Iago hits on the plan of accusing her of adultery with Cassio. Before he has the opportunity of putting his plan into action, Othello deprives Cassio of his rank for having wounded another soldier while on duty.

Disdemona tries many times to restore Cassio to favour, and when Othello tells Iago that he will ultimately consent, Iago begins to hint that Cassio and Disdemona are lovers. When Disdemona next solicits her husband for Cassio, the Moor is very angry, and declares that he will take vengeance for the injuries she has done him. He then goes to Iago and demands that he shall speak openly; and he replies that Disdemona has committed adultery, partly because she is tired of the Moor's colour,[2] and that when Cassio boasted of his conquest he would have slain him if he had not been afraid of the Moor's anger. Othello demands ocular proof of the accusation, and Iago promises to try and provide it. One day when Disdemona is visiting Emilia he steals an embroidered handkerchief from Disdemona's girdle while she is fondling his infant daughter. He hides the handkerchief in Cassio's house; and he, knowing it to be Disdemona's, goes to return it to

---

[1] II. i. 187-92.   [2] I. iii. 210-50 and III. iii. 232-42.

her. But hearing the Moor's voice he hurriedly departs without seeing Disdemona, though the Moor thinks he recognizes Cassio.[1] Othello asks Iago to sound Cassio;[2] and one day, when the Moor is watching, Iago jests with Cassio and afterwards tells the Moor that Cassio was boasting of his success with Disdemona,[3] and telling him that on the last occasion they slept together she had given him the handkerchief. Othello asks his wife for the handkerchief and she searches for it in vain.

Disdemona talks with Emilia of Othello's strange conduct,[4] and says that she is afraid she will prove a warning to young ladies not to marry against the wishes of their relations, and that Italian women will learn of her not to wed a man 'whom nature, heaven and mode of life estrange from us'. Emilia knows of Iago's plot, but although she is too frightened of him to reveal it to Disdemona, she warns her to avoid giving any occasion of suspicion to Othello.

Cassio has a woman[5] in his house who is skilful with her needle, and knowing that the handkerchief is Disdemona's, she decides to copy the embroidery before it is returned. Iago takes Othello past the house where the woman sits at the window at her task. Othello bribes Iago to kill Cassio, and one night when he is coming from a harlot's house Iago attacks him and wounds him in the leg.[6] Cassio draws his sword and calls for help, and Iago flies, returning with the crowd to sympathize with the wounded man. Incensed with Disdemona because she grieves for Cassio, Othello decides to murder her in such a way that he will not be called to account for the crime. He agrees to Iago's plan; and one night while he is in bed with his wife he tells her to investigate a noise in the adjoining room. Iago, who is waiting for her, batters her with a stocking filled with sand; and the two men conceal the crime by making part of the ceiling fall.

Othello, however, is stricken with remorse and begins to hate Iago, who goes to Cassio, now fitted with a wooden leg, and informs him that it was the Moor, suspecting him of adultery, who had wounded him and murdered Disdemona. Cassio accuses Othello before the Signiory; he is arrested, brought to Venice, and tortured, but he denies everything. Sentenced to perpetual banishment, he is eventually killed by Disdemona's kinsmen. Some time

---

[1] III. ii. 28–41.   [2] III. iii. 243–4.   [3] Cf. IV. i.
[4] Cf. III. iv. 100–7; IV. iii. 9 ff.   [5] Cf. p. 131 post.
[6] Cf. V. i. 27; but see p. 135 post.

afterwards Iago is involved in another crime of bearing false witness, and he dies wretchedly after being tortured.

Thus did God avenge the innocence of Disdemona. All these events were related by the Ensign's wife, who was privy to the whole.

At first sight, perhaps, the story does not seem to afford a suitable plot for a tragedy. The colourless heroine, the melodramatic villain, the sordid *crime passionel*, the clumsy nemesis which overtakes villain and hero, and the leisurely tempo of the story are all obstacles to dramatic treatment. Above all, the Moor himself lacks most of the dimensions of the tragic hero: a man who arranges to have his wife battered to death with a sandbag is not likely to retain the sympathy of an audience. But Shakespeare as a poet was attracted and stimulated to his greatest efforts by the sheer difficulties of a situation. When the difficulties were not in the source (as in *Macbeth*) he imported them from outside. The problem he set himself in that play was to reveal how a noble character came to commit a murder. The more lofty the character and the more atrocious the crime, the more difficult, and therefore the more stimulating, was the problem to the imagination. So in reading Giraldi's story he would have been challenged by the magnitude of the difficulties involved in making a tragedy from it, but he would have found several hints for methods of treatment—the suggestion that Disdemona had fallen in love with the Moor's virtues and not from sexual appetite, her decision to brave the dangers of the sea, her later remark about mixed marriages, and the statement after the murder that the Moor loved her more than life.

Shakespeare stressed the apparent unnaturalness of the marriage, so unnatural that Brabantio can accuse Othello of having made use of drugs or charms, and Iago can pretend that Desdemona is a supersubtle Venetian, a society lady who seeks a new thrill by running off with a coloured man, and who would realize the error of her choice when she was sated with his body. Shakespeare blackens the marriage before the appearance of Othello and Desdemona and reinstates it by Othello's account of his wooing, by his disclaiming that he wishes to take his wife to Cyprus to please the palate of his appetite, and by Desdemona's declaration that she 'saw Othello's image in his mind'. Yet the very fact that the marriage has been smeared prepares the way for the operation of Iago's poison. In the fairy-tale Beauty marries the Beast, and the Beast is transformed into a handsome young man; but the disparity between Othello and Desdemona remains. The very feeling of 'otherness', which can be a recurrent miracle in marriage, can also be the seed from which distrust will spring. In a marriage of two races the 'otherness' can be distorted and warped into alienation. The act of faith and commitment can be interpreted as a perversion, the strangeness can come to seem as a mask hiding the real self. This was the psychological basis of Iago's plot.

Shakespeare would have seen other opportunities in Giraldi's story. The contrast between the apparent honesty and the actual villainy of the Ensign provided an opportunity of exploring once again the nature of 'seeming', fresh as Shakespeare was from Hamlet's discovery that one may smile and be a villain, and just before he created the character of Angelo. Above all he must have been struck by the dramatic possibilities of making a noble hero kill the woman he loved.

Several of Shakespeare's alterations were designed to raise the stature of the hero. He is introduced on the night of his elopement, sought by Brabantio's men and quelling a brawl with eleven words, and sought at the same time by the Senate's messengers. The urgency of the summons on account of the Turkish danger—invented by Shakespeare—displays Othello's value to the State. His nobility is manifested by his defence against the charge of witchcraft. For this Shakespeare went to Holland's translation of Pliny's *Natural History* where he found the story of C. Furius Cresinus,[1] a former bondslave,[2] who was accused of acquiring great possessions

> by indirect means, as if he had vsed sorcerie,[3] and by charmes and witchcraft drawne into his owne ground that encrease of fruits.

Cresinus's defence begins with the words 'My Maisters',[4] and pointing to his plough and other implements he says:

> Behold, these are the sorceries, charmes, and all the inchauntments that I vse[5] . . . I might besides alledge mine owne trauell

---

[1] Cf. E. H. W. Meyerstein, *T.L.S.* (1942), p. 72.
[2] Cf. 'Bond-slaues, and Pagans shall our Statesmen be' (I. ii. 99).
[3] Cf. 'indirect, and forced courses' (I. iii. 111).
[4] Cf. 'My very Noble, and approu'd good Masters' (I. iii. 77).
[5] Cf. 'what Charmes, What Coniuration, and what mighty Magicke . . . This onely is the witch-craft I haue vs'd' (I. iii. 91–4, 169).

and toile that I take, the earely rising and late sitting vp so ordinarie with mee, the carefull watching that I vsually abide, and the painefull sweats which I daily endure.[1]

Other details of Othello's defence—the men whose heads grew beneath their shoulders and the anthropophagi—may be derived from another chapter of Holland's translation.[2]

There was a third source[3] of Othello's defence—Sir Lewes Lewkenor's translation of Cardinal Contareno's *The Commonwealth and Gouernment of Venice* (1599). In his Address to the Reader, Lewkenor speaks of his pleasure in conversing with travellers:

of which sorte it hath been my happinesse to be beholding to sundry nations for their friendly conversation, who neuer were so willing at any time to speake, as I euer was ready to receiue their discourses with an attentiue eare.

Lewkenor also contrasts the 'soft beds' of those who stay at home with the hardships of travellers, the

many carefull thoughtes, industrious peniuries and painefull inconueniences.

He refers to

the description of forreine regions, the manners & customes of farre distant countries, the diuersitie of their complections, humor, diet and attire, and such like other singularities, espe-

---

[1] Cf. 'A Naturall and prompt Alacritie I finde in hardnesse' (I. iii. 231).

[2] VII. ii. But see *P.M.L.A.* (1934), p. 807 and *P.Q.* (1938), p. 351, where other possible sources are suggested. It is generally agreed that the image of the Pontic Sea is derived from Holland's Pliny. I have argued (*N.Q.* 1953, pp. 513–14) that Shakespeare's text can be amended by reference to Holland. Shakespeare would have found in the same source an account of the coloquintida, of the Arabian trees, of the mines of sulphur, of a statue made of chrysolite, of mandragora, and of earthquakes (XIX. 5; II. 14–5; XXXV. 15; XXXVIII. 13; XV. 13; II. 80). T. W. Baldwin, however, in 'Shakespeare's Use of Pliny' (*Parrott Presentation Volume*, ed. H. Craig, 1935, pp. 157 ff.) argues that Shakespeare read Pliny in the original Latin, probably using Dalecampinus's index to the work; and he states that he has found 'nothing anywhere to indicate that Shakespeare did use Holland'. He argues that the Arabian trees come from Ovid (*Metam.* X); that the 'antres vast' probably come from the *Æneid* (e.g. I. 52; III. 617); that the word *antres* may come from an unidentified translation of Pliny; and that 'deserts idle' comes from the Latin, not from Holland. In spite of these arguments it is surely significant that there are so many Pliny echoes just after the publication of Holland's translation, and there are some indications that Shakespeare was influenced by Holland's phrasing. (Cf. Meyerstein's article and my note cited above). I have not been able to discover any parallels with the earlier digest of Pliny. It is possible, no doubt, that Shakespeare used the sixteenth century French translation—*antres*, after all, is nearer to the French than to the Latin.

[3] Cf. K. Muir, *R.E.S.* (1956), p. 182.

cially if they come from the mouth of a wise and well speaking traueller, to whose tongue I would willingly endure to haue mine eares enclined.

Lewkenor confesses, 'My education hath been in the wars'. In the Epistle Dedicatory he apologizes for 'the vntuned harshnesse of my disioynted stile' and speaks of 'the violence of my own fortune'.

In the same way Othello apologizes for his 'rude' speech, and excuses it by his education in the wars. Desdemona would 'seriously incline' to hear his tales and 'with a greedy ear' she devoured up his discourse. Othello speaks of his hardships and contrasts the 'flinty and steele couch of Warre' with the 'thrice-driuen bed of Downe' of civilians. Desdemona in the same scene refers to her 'downe-right violence, and storme of Fortunes'.

Malone was the first to suggest that Shakespeare had read Lewkenor's book in his notes on 'officers of the night' (I. i. 183) and 'double as the Duke's' (I. ii. 14). H. C. Hart pointed out that Lewkenor used the word 'weaponed' (cf. V. ii. 266). He also uses the word *intentiue*, and Shakespeare's sole use of *intentiuely* is in *Othello*.

Presumably Shakespeare consulted the book for background information about Venice, but he may also have derived from it another interesting suggestion. In Kiffen's dedicatory sonnet, Venice is praised as a city

> Where all corrupt means to aspire are curbd,
> And officers for vertues worth elected.
> The contrarie wherof hath much disturbd
> All states, where the like cause is vnrespected.

Iago's complaint that he has been passed over in favour of Cassio is a motive not given by Giraldi, and it is noteworthy that he contrasts the good old days, when promotion was by merit, with the degenerate times in which he lives.

Shakespeare emphasizes Othello's stature by several other means. The discussion of his appointment by the people at Cyprus and their enthusiastic welcome show that Iago's views are not shared by other soldiers, and Othello's intervention in the fight between Cassio and Montano exhibits his calm authority. The worst blot in the character of Giraldi's Moor is eliminated by Shakespeare's alteration of the murder of Desdemona. Giraldi's

Moor is careful to arrange that it should appear to be an accident, and the actual butchery is carried out by the Ensign. Othello's sacrificial killing is done with his own hand, he allows Desdemona to pray, and he makes no attempt to escape the responsibility for his deed. Giraldi's Moor apparently remains unaware of Disdemona's innocence, and he refuses to confess to his murder. Othello hears the truth about the handkerchief from Emilia, he tries to kill Iago, and he commits suicide and dies upon a kiss.

Shakespeare makes fewer changes in the character of Desdemona, but these, too, are significant. He makes her a motherless girl, and he makes her elope with Othello instead of having her marry with the reluctant consent of her relations. This deception of Brabantio, which breaks his heart, has a triple function. It enables Othello to be accused of witchcraft, and so evokes his defence before the Senate, it provides an opportunity for Desdemona to defend the purity of her love, and it provides Iago later with some plausible evidence that Desdemona is a deceiver. By making the elopement take place on the same night as Othello's appointment to the command at Cyprus, Shakespeare not merely economizes in time—a single meeting of the Senate dealing with the elopement and the Turkish question—but also by making the meeting take place at night he increases the dramatic tension. Desdemona's appearance and behaviour exhibit her as Othello's 'faire Warriour'. But the greatest dramatic advantage afforded by this change is that it eliminates the period of happy married life in Venice. By not allowing Othello to obtain this day-to-day knowledge of his wife, he provides the only possible basis for Iago's plot.

The arrival of Desdemona at Cyprus, her anxiety for Othello, their reunion, her solicitude for his 'headache' in the scene where she loses the handkerchief, her warm advocacy of Cassio's reinstatement (though Giraldi mentions this), her lack of resentment of Othello's brutal treatment, her refusal to wish she had never married him—this wish is transferred to Emilia—and her forgiveness of her murderer as shown by her immortal lie all display the depth and purity of her love for Othello. Her conversation with Emilia after the brothel-scene and Cassio's emphasis on her modesty underline her essential innocence.

The third main character also undergoes significant alterations. The Ensign's sole motives in the novel are his thwarted lust for Desdemona, and his belief that his lack of success is due to the

Captain. Shakespeare retains at least a trace of the first of these motives, but he adds several others—his envy at Cassio's promotion, his suspicion that both Othello and Cassio have cuckolded him, his wish to infect Othello with the jealousy he has himself experienced, his hatred of goodness.[1] He is introduced in the first scene of the play in company with Roderigo, a character possibly suggested by the necessity of providing a motive for Cassio's brawl. Shakespeare took a hint from *Twelfth Night*, written not long before. Sir Toby Belch uses Sir Andrew as his purse by promising to assist him in his wooing of Olivia, as Iago had promised to help Roderigo. The marriage of Desdemona means, of course, that Roderigo now aims at adultery; and this provides Iago with an additional motive for his actions. Mr Flatter, indeed, argues that Iago does not really hate Othello at all, and that he is led to destroy Desdemona merely to avoid his own exposure, Roderigo having threatened to ask her for the return of the presents Iago had intercepted. Although this motive is present, it is obvious that Iago does hate Othello. The creation of Roderigo makes the incident of the brawl a deliberate device to get Cassio dismissed, and not merely a lucky accident which the Ensign makes use of for his own purposes.

Although Iago is an opportunist he controls events more completely than his prototype. It is he who suggests to Cassio to solicit Desdemona—in the source the Captain does not ask Desdemona to plead for him—and he uses Cassio's visit as a starting point for his temptation. In the novel the Ensign secures the handkerchief because the Moor has been clamouring for proof. He hides it in the Captain's chamber, and after the conversation watched by the Moor he tells him that the Ensign has told him that Disdemona had given him the handkerchief. It is only after this that the Moor asks his wife for the handkerchief. Shakespeare alters the order of events. Iago asks Emilia to filch the handkerchief and actually obtains it before Othello demands proof; he tells the story of Cassio's dream—not in the source—before mentioning the handkerchief; and he hides it in Cassio's lodging after he has told that he has seen Cassio wipe his beard with it. Cassio asks Bianca to copy the embroidery—in the novel it is the woman's[2] own idea—and Bianca brings the handkerchief back to

[1] Cf. K. Muir, 'The Jealousy of Iago', *English Miscellany* (1951), pp. 65-83.
[2] Some critics assume that the *donna* of the novel is Cassio's wife. Perhaps Shakespeare made the same assumption and so referred in the first scene to Cassio as 'A Fellow almost damn'd in a faire Wife'. If so, he afterwards decided to discard the

him during the overlooked conversation with Iago. The dramatic advantages of these changes are obvious. The events are more closely linked together. Iago's plot becomes at once more plausible and more ingenious, in spite of the element of luck; an unnecessary character is eliminated; the harlot, instead of being a shadow, is given a significant role; Iago's conversation with Cassio, being about Bianca, plausibly hoodwinks Othello into thinking that they are talking about Desdemona; and the production of the handkerchief by Bianca is infinitely more dramatic than the glimpse of it through the window. That Cassio has given the treasured love-token to his whore adds a final touch to Othello's hatred and disgust. In the novel the villain works only on the Moor: in the play he also manipulates Roderigo, Cassio, and Emilia.

In one respect the Ensign appears to rely less on accident than Iago does. He steals the handkerchief himself, whereas Iago urges his wife to steal it, and she only does so because Desdemona lets it fall. This is Giraldi's account:

> The Moor's wife went often, as I have said, to the Ensign's wife's house, and abode with her a good part of the day. Whence this man seeing that she sometimes bore about her a handkerchief which he knew that the Moor had given her, the which handkerchief was wrought in moorish wise most subtly, and was most dear to the lady, and likewise to the Moor, he bethought him to take it from her secretly, and thence to prepare against her final ruin. And he having a girl of three years old, which child was much beloved by Disdemona, one day that the hapless lady had gone to stay at the house of this villain, he took the little girl in his arms and gave her to the lady, who took her and gathered her to her breast. This deceiver, who was excellent at sleight of hand, reft the handkerchief from her girdle so cunningly that she was unaware of it, and departed from her right joyful. Disdemona, knowing not this, went home, and being busy with other thoughts took no heed of the handkerchief. But some days thence, seeking for it and not finding it, she was right fearful lest the Moor should ask it of her, as he was often wont to do.

Swinburne discussed why Shakespeare forbore to make use of this

wife as superfluous. It may be added that Florio, *Second Frutes*, p. 191, has a proverb which may have suggested Iago's line:

> He that a white horse and a fayre wife keepeth,
> For feare, for care, for ielousie scarce sleepeth.

'terribly beautiful passage', since he regarded the substituted incident as less probable and less tragic. He came to the conclusion
that the sole reason for the change is that it is impossible to imagine Iago fathering a child.[1]

> In Shakespeare's world as in nature's it is impossible that mon
> sters should propagate: that Iago should beget, or that Goneril
> or Regan should bring forth.

However this may be—and Lady Macbeth had given suck and
Goneril seems to have conceived—a good case can be made out
for the superiority of Shakespeare's version of the loss of the
handkerchief. There is, first, a purely theatrical reason. Shakespeare's stage children are never as young as three, and a much
older child would hardly have done in this scene. Moreover, the
introduction of a child would have involved a passage of dialogue
which would have lessened the intensity of the temptation scenes;
and to make Desdemona visit Emilia's house would have altered
the relationship between the two women. Desdemona would suffer
if we thought she was an intimate of the worldly and cynical
Emilia. Shakespeare allows Desdemona to forget the handkerchief
in the only circumstances where her neglect of the love-token is a
proof of her love. She offers to bind Othello's forehead with it,
and he brushes it aside because it is too small. As Mr Middleton
Murry says:[2]

> Shakespeare transformed accident into inevitability and inven
> tion into imagination. By that one change it is the perfection of
> Desdemona's love for Othello that destroys her. . . . In such a
> cause . . . to remember her handkerchief would be a blemish.
> For what is it now? . . . a thing that has failed in the only use
> of a thing—to serve her beloved.

Giraldi does not state, though he may imply, that the handkerchief was a love-token. Shakespeare mentioned that it was Othello's first gift to Desdemona, and his account of its magical
properties contributes significantly to the atmosphere of the play
and links up with other references to magic and witchcraft:

> That Handkerchiefe
> Did an Ægyptian to my Mother giue:
> She was a Charmer, and could almost read

---

[1] A. C. Swinburne, *Three Plays of Shakespeare*, p. 34.
[2] *Shakespeare* (1936), pp. 315-16.

The thoughts of people. She told her, while she kept it,
'Twould make her Amiable, and subdue my Father
Intirely to her loue: But if she lost it,
Or made a Guift of it, my Fathers eye
Should hold her loathed, and his Spirits should hunt
After new Fancies. She dying, gaue it me,
And bid me (when my Fate would have me Wiue)
To giue it her. I did so; and take heede on't,
Make it a Darling, like your precious eye:
To loose't, or giue't away, were such perdition
As nothing else could match . . .
'Tis true: There's Magicke in the web of it:
A *Sybill* that had numbred in the world
The Sun to course two hundred compasses,
In her Prophetticke furie sew'd the Worke:
The Wormes were hallowed that did breede the Silke,
And it was dyde in Mummey which the Skilfull
Conseru'd of Maidens hearts.

The handkerchief, of course, symbolizes love. But the magic in the web of it, in which Othello and possibly Desdemona believe, symbolizes both the fate that brought them together and the fate that finally destroyed their marriage. Because of what he believes about the handkerchief, Othello accepts fatalistically when Desdemona loses it that his marriage is destroyed; and this accounts for his blind neglect to discuss with Desdemona the reasons for his suspicions. The fact that Desdemona believes, or half believes, in the magic accounts for her foolish lie, which Othello takes as a further proof of her guilt.

There are some modifications in the character of the villain's wife. In the source she knows of the plot against Desdemona, but she dare not reveal it. Emilia, on the other hand, is ignorant of Iago's real character, and as soon as she realizes the truth she sacrifices her life for love of her mistress. Yet she appears to be coarse-grained beside the 'divine Desdemona'; she purloins the handkerchief to please the fantasy of her 'wayward husband', as she thinks him; and she does not confess to finding the handkerchief in spite of Desdemona's distress and Othello's anger.

Cassio's drunkenness was Shakespeare's invention. It is used to explain his lapse from duty without too much alienation of our sympathies. The main lines of the character were determined by his innocence with regard to Desdemona, by his appointment as Othello's lieutenant, by his love of Othello, and by the fact that he is wounded when returning from a harlot's house. Shakespeare combines the copier of the handkerchief with the harlot, and apart from its dramatic economy this has the advantage, as we have seen, of adding to Othello's sense of outrage.

Giraldi has nothing about the arrival of Lodovico with the news that Othello is to be recalled, the emergency being over, and Cassio to be appointed in his place. By choosing Cassio for the post Shakespeare indicated that Iago's resentment of his previous promotion was unjustified. The brothel-scene is Shakespeare's invention: he realized that if Othello had made a direct accusation earlier in the play we should have wondered why Desdemona did not make the inquiries which would have exposed Iago's plot. In *reading* the play we are struck with the improbability of Iago's luck; but in *seeing* the play we are impressed more by the diabolical ingenuity of his scheming.

In the source the Ensign attacks the Captain single-handed. In the play the complication of the plot by the invention of Roderigo enables Iago to use his dupe in the attempt to 'remove' Cassio. Roderigo bungles the job, and Iago wounds Cassio from behind,[1] slays Roderigo, and on Bianca's arrival suggests that she is an accomplice.

The manner of Desdemona's murder, as we have seen, was Shakespeare's invention. The dénouement of the story is completely transformed by the insertion of the willow-song scene, of Desdemona's forgiveness, of the immediate discovery of the murder, of Emilia's exposure of Iago and her consequent death, of the news of Brabantio's death, and of Othello's suicide. Shakespeare, moreover, brings Iago to justice for his crimes—not as in the source for another crime altogether.

These changes of character and incident are less important, however, than certain other dramatic and poetic qualities infused by Shakespeare into the plot. Attention has been called to these by many different critics. There is, for example, the pervasive use of irony of which Giraldi is completely innocent. For Othello to entrust his wife to Iago for the voyage to Cyprus and for Desdemona and Cassio to ask his advice are dramatic strokes of singular felicity. The continuous iteration of *honest* and its derivatives

---

[1] So the editors assume; but there is no direct indication of this in the original texts.

enables Professor Empson to conclude somewhat fancifully that Iago is 'a critique on an unconscious pun'.[1]

Professor Charlton stresses the way in which Shakespeare speeds up the plot.[2] He eliminates (as we have seen) the matrimonial happiness in Venice and dispatches Othello to Cyprus on the same day as his elopement. Whereas Giraldi allows time in Cyprus for Iago to fall in and out of love with Disdemona, and for Disdemona to get into the habit of visiting his wife, more time before Disdemona notices the loss of her handkerchief, more time before the Moor asks to see it, more again before he sees the woman at the window, more before the attack on Cassio, and more before the murder of Disdemona, Shakespeare condenses the Cyprus scenes into a couple of days. Iago's temptation begins a few hours after the dismissal of Cassio, the handkerchief is seen in Bianca's hands a few hours after that, and the final tragedy comes before nightfall. The sheer technical mastery displayed throughout the play is admitted by all critics,[3] even by those, such as Bridges and Stoll, who resent the way Shakespeare hypnotizes us into believing impossibilities. Shakespeare laid up trouble for himself by his determination to achieve speed at all costs, and presumably he felt that apart from the resultant intensity it was desirable to leave no time for Othello—or the audience—to ask inconvenient questions.

Many critics have pointed out that there was in fact no occasion when Cassio and Desdemona could have committed adultery. They travel to Cyprus on different ships, and Iago begins his accusation on the morning after Othello's marriage has been consummated. How are we to answer this point? Are we to assume that Shakespeare blundered, and that he ought to have made Cassio travel to Cyprus on the same ship as Desdemona? Or, as Bridges suggested, that Othello's ship should have been delayed a week by the storm? Or are we meant to think that Othello was extraordinarily stupid? Or shall we accept the theory of double-time, that Shakespeare was using two clocks so as to increase the speed of the action, and that he relied on getting away with this trick in the theatre?

This last was Stoll's opinion. He argued that the noble and rational hero of the first two acts of the play would not have suc-

---

[1] *The Structure of Complex Words* (1951), pp. 218 ff.
[2] *Shakespearian Tragedy*, pp. 130–2.
[3] Rymer, it will be remembered, regarded the play as 'a bloody farce'.

cumbed to Iago's temptation with such incredible facility; that Othello, far from being 'not easily jealous', displays all the characteristics of jealousy mentioned by Coleridge; that to trust Iago and believe the worst of wife and friend is a sign of pathological credulity; that Iago's temptation is absurdly unconvincing and that in real life his lies would have rapidly been exposed; that the psychology of all the characters is false and unreal; and that Shakespeare was relying on an absurd theatrical convention—that the calumniator is always believed.

It seems to me that Stoll underestimates the dramatic force and coherence of the temptation scene. He assumes that an honest man who undertakes to tell you of your wife's adultery will make a clean breast of it, and not behave as Iago does. But surely an irresolute friend, torn between two loyalties, might behave on the surface not very differently from Iago. Secondly, we might expect some difference of behaviour between the academic world of Minneapolis—or of Liverpool—in the twentieth century and what the Elizabethans expected of a Florentine acting as a professional soldier in the Venetian army. Thirdly, Elizabethan conceptions of psychological probability, and particularly their ideas about jealousy, differed from our own, and differed still more from those of the nineteenth century. Fourthly, a dramatic poet is not concerned with giving a realistic picture of human behaviour. He can be as unrealistic as he pleases, provided the general effect on the audience is that of truth to life. One can only appeal to common experience on the question of these scenes. With very few exceptions almost every member of almost every audience accepts Iago's conduct not as how an honest man would behave, but as how a villain pretending to be an honest man would behave in these circumstances; and they accept Othello's behaviour as what a noble and credulous Moor would do in the face of such a temptation. Once, moved to exasperation by Othello's blindness, a member of an audience cried out: 'O you great black fool, can't you *see*?' And in Russia a coal-miner in the audience shouted: 'Shooting's too good for such a bastard'. His neighbour, not realizing he was referring to Iago, reproved him sternly, the *Moscow News* informs us. But these unsophisticated reactions show us not that the temptation is incredible, but rather that Shakespeare is able to persuade his audience of the vivid reality of the scene. As Professor Peter Alexander says:[1]

[1] *Shakespeare's Life and Art* (1938), p. 166.

Shakespeare had set before himself a much more 'philosophical' end than the realization of historical probability. He has to reveal the heart of a human situation, a situation in which, he makes clear to us, the seeds of suspicion and jealousy might easily take root. To create an elaborate replica in material terms to satisfy the intelligence, when the imagination can gather all it needs of the situation from what Shakespeare can spare for mere exposition, would be a breach of artistic economy, and would distract attention from the inner train of events.

Alexander goes on to suggest that not only do the liberties Shakespeare takes with time pass unnoticed during a performance, but also they are the means he employs, as legitimate as perspective, to concentrate attention on the essentials of his story.

This is not, perhaps, the whole truth about double-time. Othello accuses Desdemona of committing 'the act of shame' with Cassio a thousand times, which implies a liaison of at least a year's standing. But other passages, such as Iago's account of Cassio's dream, imply that the alleged intrigue dates from after Desdemona's marriage. Shakespeare may be deliberately ambiguous on this point, but I think the usual explanation is too ingenious. The fact is Shakespeare deliberately deprived the Moor of the slightest rational ground for jealousy. Iago makes no attempt to provide any circumstantial evidence of Desdemona's guilt until Othello is no longer in a fit state to think logically about it. His various suggestions, improvised, are graded very carefully. He first picks up Desdemona's mention of the fact that Cassio had come a-wooing with Othello, warns Othello against jealousy, and then hints that Desdemona is too friendly with Cassio. Up to this point Iago can withdraw his imputations and protest that he has been misunderstood. Othello can assume that Desdemona has been mildly flirting with Cassio during his own wooing.

But the seed of suspicion has been planted, and before Iago resumes the temptation he comes into possession of the handkerchief. He does not use it at once. He waits to see how far Othello's mind is poisoned, and gives his account of Cassio's dream, which suggests that Desdemona had committed adultery. He recounts this dream only when Othello by his talk of stolen hours of lust and by his demand for ocular proof has shown that he has gone much further in his imagination than Iago has done in his accusations. For, as Mr Stewart has said, 'Iago's villainy draws its potency from Othello's own mind . . . Iago is a device of Othello's by which Othello hears an inner voice that he would fain hear and fain deny'.[1]

Iago might still retreat even after the story of Cassio's dream. It might be a true account of the dream, as Iago himself points out, and yet not prove the Lieutenant's guilt. It would merely prove that he had committed adultery in his heart, as many of us do. But from Othello's reactions, Iago knows he can safely mention the handkerchief. If he had mentioned it first, Othello might have assumed that Desdemona had mislaid it. By this time Othello is so blinded with passion that he can believe impossibilities. This seems to me to be a more satisfying and plausible explanation than double-time, although it would be impossible to deny that Shakespeare does use two clocks. According to some indications the Cyprus scenes appear to be spread over several weeks; according to others they last only a couple of days. We have Bianca complaining of Cassio's long absence when he has apparently been on the island for only a couple of hours. But such difficulties do not obtrude themselves during a performance.

The general effect of Shakespeare's alterations is more important than the various things we have discussed—the speeding up of the action, the tightening of the plot, the alteration of the characters, and the increasing of the dramatic tension. He completely transforms the story and converts a sordid melodrama with a commonplace moral into a tragedy of love. He does this by convincing us poetically of the nobility of Desdemona and the Moor and by making the jealousy of Othello as much a shattering of his faith as a crude sexual possessiveness. He convinces us by means of poetry. Several critics have analysed the use of imagery in the play. Bethell, by examining the diabolic images, has shown that the theme of hell originates with Iago 'and is passed to Othello later as Iago succeeds in dominating his mind'.[2] Other critics have pointed out that the prevalent animal imagery is likewise transferred from Iago to Othello.[3] Heilman has analysed the opposition between light and dark throughout the play and the imagery relating to economics and theft.[4] To these discussions we may add that there are fifteen references to witchcraft, a continuous iteration of free and liberal,[5] a group of images relating food and

---

[1] op. cit., p. 102.   [2] *Shakespeare Survey 5*, pp. 62–80.
[3] e.g., Spurgeon and Clemen.
[4] *E.C.* (1951), pp. 315 ff; *P.M.L.A.* (1953), pp. 555–71. These essays now form part of *Magic in the Web* (1956).   [5] Cf. K. Muir, *N.Q.* (1954), pp. 20–1.

poison to sexual appetite and jealousy, and a frequent reference to fate. Elsewhere I have tried to show that the imagery of the last scene is used to retain the sympathy of the audience for the hero.[1] But the imagery is, of course, only one aspect of the poetry. What Wilson Knight calls the 'Othello music' is equally important.

[1] Cf. K. Muir, *Penguin New Writing* (1946), No. 28, pp. 101–21. But J. Money, *Shakespeare Survey 6*, pp. 94–105, argues that the imagery underlines Othello's self-deception.

❖ VI ❖

GREAT TRAGEDIES II

(13) King Lear

WE do not know what first gave to Shakespeare the idea of writing a play about King Lear. It is possible that the original inspiration came not from the Lear story at all but from Sidney's story of the Paphlagonian King in *Arcadia*.[1] He may even have been prompted by the true story of Sir Brian Annesley, who in October 1603, a year before Shakespeare began his play, was reported to be unfit to govern himself or his estate. Two of his daughters tried to get him certified as insane, so that they could obtain his estate; but the youngest daughter, Cordell, appealed to Cecil, and when Annesley died the Court of Chancery upheld his will. Although Cordell afterwards married Sir William Harvey, the step-father of the Earl of Southampton, and although the Fool's remark 'Winters not gon yet, if the wild Geese fly that way' may be an allusion to Annesley's eldest daughter, Lady Wildgoose, it is unsafe to assume that this topical story was the genesis of the play.[2]

Years before, when he was writing his history plays, Shakespeare would have come across the Lear story both in Holinshed's *Chronicles* and in *The Mirror for Magistrates*. In 1590 he could have read Spenser's version in *The Faerie Queene*. He may have known the version in Gerard Legh's *Accedens of Armoury*; and, about the time he was writing the play, Camden was retelling part of the story in his *Remaines*. There was, finally, the old chronicle play, *King Leir*, with which the poet was certainly familiar. As this seems not to have been published before 1605, he must either have seen it in manuscript or on the stage. I have elsewhere suggested that he may have acted in it.[3] It is true that there is no evidence that the

[1] F. Pyle, *M.L.R.* (1948), pp. 449–55.
[2] Cf. G. M. Young, *Shakespeare and the Termers* (1947).
[3] ed. *King Lear* (1952), p. xxxii.

play belonged to Shakespeare's company. But if it did not, we have to assume either that there was an edition in 1594 when the play was entered in the Stationers' Register, or else that somehow Shakespeare obtained access to the manuscript. Too little is known about Shakespeare's early career for us to be certain that he never belonged to the company which owned the play.

I have examined elsewhere[1] the evidence that Shakespeare was acquainted with all these sources, but it may be as well to summarize it here. We do not have to rely on probabilities. Sir Walter Greg has detailed[2] some forty parallels between *King Lear* and the old chronicle play. One of these will be sufficient to show that Shakespeare knew the old play. Perillus upbraids Gonorill with the words:

> Nay, peace thou monster, shame vnto thy sexe,
> Thou fiend in likenesse of a human creature.

Shortly afterwards, Leir asks Ragan, 'Knowest thou these letters?' She snatches them and tears them up. In one scene of *King Lear* (IV. 2) Albany urges his wife in similar terms:

> See thy selfe, diuell:
> Proper deformitie shows not in the Fiend
> So horrid as in woman.
> Thou changed and selfe-couer'd thing, for shame,
> Be-monster not thy feature
>   . . . howere thou art a fiend,
> A womans shape doth shield thee.

In the last scene of the play he says to her:

> Shut your mouth Dame,
> Or with this paper shall I stople it . . .
> Thou worse than any name, reade thine owne euill!
> No tearing, Lady, I perceiue you know it.
> . . . Most monstrous! O,
> Know'st thou this paper?

In both plays we have *shame* and *fiend*; *monster* is echoed in *be-monster* and *monstrous*, *sex* in *woman*, and *Knowest thou these letters?* in *Know'st thou this paper?* The action of tearing is echoed in Albany's *No tearing*.

From Holinshed's *Chronicles* Shakespeare took the ducal titles

---

[1] ed. *King Lear* (1952), pp. xxvi ff.   [2] *The Library*, xx, pp. 386–97.

of Cornwall and Albany (Albania) and perhaps a hint for Goneril's first speech:

> she loued him more than toong could expresse.

From *The Faerie Queene* Shakespeare derived the form of Cordelia's name, and the manner of her death, by hanging.[1] In Holinshed and *The Mirror for Magistrates* she stabs herself. From *The Mirror for Magistrates* Shakespeare took about ten minor details, including the forms Albany and King of France, and there is one significant verbal parallel. The lines describing Cordila's life in prison—

> From sight of princely wights, to place where theues do dwel:
> From deinty beddes of downe, to be of strawe ful fayne—

may be compared with Cordelia's lines—

> And wast thou *faine* (poore Father)
> To houell thee with Swine and Rogues forlorne,
> In short, and musty *straw*?

Oddly enough, there is some evidence[2] that Shakespeare consulted both the 1574 and the 1587 editions of *The Mirror for Magistrates*, since some of the parallels are only with one edition, and some only with the other. The evidence that Shakespeare consulted Camden's *Remaines*, Legh's *Accedens of Armoury*, and Geoffrey of Monmouth[3] is inconclusive.

On the whole it seems likely that the idea of re-dramatizing the Lear story came from Shakespeare's acquaintance with the old play, though he must have recognized from the first that the plot would have to be considerably modified. The author of *King Leir* had dramatized only half of the story given by the chroniclers. He ends the play with the restoration of Leir to the throne, and omits the tragic sequel: years later, after the death of the King, Cordelia is deposed by her nephews and cast into prison, where she takes her own life. Shakespeare was faced with a real difficulty. Cordelia's death takes place so long after the main events of the story that to dramatize it meant a sacrifice of dramatic unity and the introduction of new characters. Even though the death of Cordelia could be represented as the working of nemesis, the despair and suicide of the virtuous heroine could hardly satisfy our sense of poetic justice. On the other hand, to end the play with the

---

[1] Perhaps suggested to Spenser by the rhyme.
[2] K. Muir, *ed. cit*. p. xxxvi.   [3] ibid., p. xxxvi.

restoration of Lear would seem to those who knew the sequel only an interim conclusion.

The dramatic problem confronting Shakespeare was therefore clear. He had to avoid the seven years that elapsed in the chronicle between the restoration of Lear and the death of Cordelia.[1] He had to make the death of Cordelia a logical result of Lear's original error and of her refusal to flatter. He had to make Lear pay for his sin by death, a death which is hastened by the killing of the daughter he had wronged. Cordelia could not be allowed to commit suicide, and therefore she must be murdered.

Shakespeare solved the problem by bringing forward the death of Cordelia, so that she dies before her father; and the man who orders her murder does so because he hopes for the throne. This situation can arise only if Cordelia is defeated in battle—in the sources she is successful in this battle and defeated seven years later—not by her nephews but by the armies of Goneril and Regan. If Lear and Cordelia are to die, then the wicked sisters must die too; and, since they are victorious in the battle, they must be killed by the working out of their own evil passions. Shakespeare makes them quarrel about their shares of the kingdom and also about Edmund. He has one sister poison the other, and then commit suicide—to kill herself, in fact, as the Cordelia of the Chronicles had done. But she would do this only if she were foiled and reduced to despair. So Shakespeare makes Goneril's husband a man of integrity, and for this alone she would wish to get rid of him. Already one can see the character of Albany emerging, and one can also see the need for an attractive upstart with whom both sisters will fall in love. Shakespeare even makes use of the sources' version of Cordelia's death by making it the 'official' story, spread by Edmund as a cover to the murder.

For the scene of the division of the kingdom Shakespeare relied mainly on the old play, but he condensed its first eight scenes into the second part of his own first scene. Leir plans a sudden stratagem to trick Cordella into marriage; the plot is betrayed to Gonorill and Ragan, who promise to marry anyone their father chooses; Leir decides to divide the kingdom between the wicked daughters, but not to banish Cordella; the Gallian King visits Brittayne in disguise and woos Cordella, and in the meanwhile Cornwall and Cambria draw lots for their shares of the kingdom and Perillus makes an unsuccessful attempt to prevent Cordella

[1] Cf. R. W. Chambers, *King Lear* (1940).

from losing her share, but he is not banished, and he decides not to desert Leir. Shakespeare by his ruthless telescoping leaves Lear's motives in some obscurity and he does not explicitly state that Goneril and Regan had been informed beforehand of Lear's stratagem. He makes the love-test an afterthought and it is apparently not a device to persuade Cordelia to marry. He may have felt that Lear's irrationality would be more credible on the stage than Leir's stupid cunning, and as he was adding an underplot and continuing the play to the death of Cordelia he could not afford more time for exposition. The banishment of Kent and his subsequent serving of Lear in disguise are more dramatic than the continuation of Perillus in Leir's service.

Shakespeare borrowed comparatively little from the remainder of *King Leir*. Leir is ill-treated by the wicked daughters. Ragan bribes a man to kill him, but the would-be murderer is stricken with remorse. Cordella and her husband, about to visit Britain in disguise, encounter Leir and Perillus faint with hunger. Leir and Cordella forgive each other; and this scene of reconciliation in which they kneel to each other was remembered by Shakespeare in the fourth act of his play. The Gallian King invades Britain on behalf of Leir, defeats the armies of Cornwall and Cambria, and reinstates Leir, who apparently lives happily ever after. There is no underplot, no storm, no Fool, no madness, and no deaths.

Shakespeare's play opens with the introduction of Edmund to Kent. For the story of Gloucester and his sons Shakespeare borrowed an episode from Sidney's *Arcadia*, which provided a perfect parallel to the Lear story; and, by making use of the artistic law that two similar improbabilities are more credible than one, he forced the audience retrospectively to accept Lear's strange conduct in the first scene of the play by duplicating it in the subsequent conduct of Gloucester in the second scene. The two plots are closely linked throughout the play. Plexirtus, re-christened Edmund, provided Shakespeare with a murderer of Cordelia, and a lover of the two evil sisters. His brother becomes the unwitting immediate cause of Lear's madness, and the man who exposes Goneril and Regan to Albany, so bringing about their downfall. Gloucester's fortunes are linked with those of the King, and he is blinded because he takes the King's side. But the plots are linked in other ways. Tate's ending, deplorable as it was, had a certain dramatic logic about it. The man who had received evil from his father and had nevertheless succoured him was wedded to the child who had received evil from her father. In both plots we have a credulous father who believes the evil child and disinherits the good. In both plots the father receives ill from the favoured child and good from the disinherited. Lear's madness is suitably balanced with Gloucester's blindness; for, whereas Lear was mad when everyone thought him sane and acquired wisdom only when he was apparently mad, Gloucester was spiritually blind when he possessed his eyesight and only learnt to see clearly when he had lost both his eyes. In a sense, then, the scene which has been blamed as dramatically unnecessary and inorganic—the meeting of the blind Gloucester with the mad Lear—is the symbolic climax of the play.

Whatever comparison we make of Shakespeare's play with the sources, we cannot help being struck by Shakespeare's genius for picking out the most suitable incidents and characters and inventing others where no suitable ones were to hand. To make Edmund boast of his bastardy, for example, and to give Gloucester some light-hearted comments on Edmund's mother, goes a long way to humanize the character of the bastard; and Shakespeare had the tact not to have him present at the blinding of his father. He repents at the end, whereas Sidney's Plexirtus only feigns repentance.

Not only did Shakespeare take the outlines of his underplot from the story of the Paphlagonian King, but he took some hints from it for other parts of the play. The death of Lear, too, owes something to *Arcadia*. Both Gloucester and Lear die of joy, Gloucester after his reconciliation with Edgar, and Lear in the belief that Cordelia is not dead. The hint for both scenes is to be found[1] in Sidney's account of the death of the Paphlagonian King, 'his hart broken with vnkindnes and affliction, stretched so farre beyond his limits with this excesse of comfort'.

It has been argued, moreover, that the duel between Edgar and Edmund may have been suggested by other episodes in *Arcadia*, and that the stratagem by which Edmund deludes his father may have been derived from the story of Plangus, King of Iberia. Between this story and that of the Paphlagonian King there is a dialogue in *terza rima* between Plangus and Basilius on the subjects of suicide, the justice of the Gods, and the slaughter of the innocent, which is reflected in Shakespeare's account of the attempted suicide of Gloucester and his treatment of Cordelia's

[1] Cf. R. W. Chambers, *King Lear* (1940), p. 44.

death.[1] For Gloucester's attempted suicide he may have remembered, too, Seneca's *Thebais*, which opens with a long scene in which the blinded Oedipus asks Antigone to let him fall over a precipice, and a scene in Marston's *Malcontent* in which Pietro, in disguise, describes his own feigned suicide by leaping from a cliff into the sea.[2] But the leap from Dover Cliff certainly owes something to a passage in Holinshed's *Chronicles*, a few pages before the Leir story, in which there is an account of how Corineus wrestled with Gogmagog. He

> did so double his force that he got the vpper hand of the giant, and cast him downe headlong from one of the rocks there, not farre from Douer, and so dispatched him: by reason whereof the place was named long after, *the fall or leape of Gogmagog*, but afterward it was called *The fall of Douer*.

It is possible, too, that Edgar's description of the imaginary fiend with eyes like two full moons was influenced by Holinshed's account of Gogmagog.[3]

The dialogue between Plangus and Basilius mentioned above coalesced in Shakespeare's mind with the opening scene of *Julius Caesar*.[4] Sidney mentions a stage 'where chaunge of thoughts one foole to other shews', the cries of the new-born infant, 'the presage of his life', and the 'blockish braine' of the man who does not grieve. In *Julius Caesar* we have the sequence of *cobbler*, *surgeon*, *shoes*, *blocks*, *shout*, and *weep*. In the King Lear context we have a reference to *boots*, to the new-born infants wawling and crying, to 'this great stage of Fooles', to 'a good blocke', to the stratagem of shoeing 'a Troope of Horse with Felt', and to surgeons. Perhaps the scaffold suggested the executioner's block, and thence the boot-block, the mounting-block and the hat-block, and these different blocks combined to suggest the words '*shoe* a troop of *horse* with *felt*'.

The storm, for which there is in the source-play only a rudimentary thunder-clap—dissuading Ragan's emissary from the murder of Leir—may have been suggested by the 'extreame and foule storm' and the 'fury of the tempest' in the *Arcadia* episode, though the storm-scenes owe most to Harsnett's *Declaration of Egregious Popishe Impostures*.[5]

[1] Cf. Muir and Danby, *N.Q.* (1950), pp. 49–51.   [2] IV. iii.
[3] Cf. K. Muir, *N.Q.* (1955), p. 15.   [4] Cf. K. Muir, *T.L.S.* (1953), p. 73.
[5] Cf. K. Muir, *R.E.S.* (1951), pp. 11–21.

Dr Samuel Harsnett, Chaplain to the Bishop of London, had already exposed the Puritan exorcist, John Darrell, when in 1603 he turned to attack the Jesuit exorcists in his famous, but little-read, book. It has been generally recognized by editors, since Theobald pointed it out, that

> The greatest part of Edgar's dissembled lunacy, the names of his devils, and the descriptive circumstances he alludes to in his own case, are all drawn from this pamphlet, and the confessions of the poor deluded wretches.

Several editors and critics have pointed out parallels overlooked by Theobald, but there seems to have been no thorough investigation of Shakespeare's indebtedness until recently, though it may be argued that Harsnett's book contributed more to the texture of *King Lear* than the source-play, Holinshed, Spenser, or Sidney.

One of the first things that is likely to strike a reader of Harsnett's *Declaration* is his detailed and unclerical knowledge of the theatre. There are not only several references to Plautus and Seneca,[1] but also to the miracle plays and to various stage technicalities. His description of the Vice is one of the most vivid we have:[2]

> It was a pretty part in the old Church-playes, when the nimble Vice would skip vp nimbly like a *Iacke an Apes* into the deuils necke, and ride the deuil a course, and belabour him with his woodden dagger, til he made him roare, whereat the people would laugh to see the deuil so vice-haunted. This action, & passion had som semblance, by reason the deuil looked like a patible old *Coridon*, with a payre of hornes on his head, & a Cowes tayle at his breech; but for a deuil to be so vice-haunted, as that he should roare, at the picture of a vice burnt in a pece of paper, especially beeing without his hornes, & tayle, is a passion exceeding al apprehension, but that our old deere mother the Romish church doth warrant it by Canon. Her deuils be surely some of those old vice-haunted cassierd woodden-beaten deuils, that were wont to frequent the stages, and haue had theyr hornes beaten of with *Mengus* his clubbe, and theyr tayles cut off with a smart lash of his stinging whip, who are so skared with the *Idea* of a vice, & a dagger as they durst neuer since looke a paper-vice in the face.

[1] e.g. pp. 70, 73.

[2] pp. 114-15.

It may also be mentioned that Harsnett, after describing how the devil had been driven into a woman's toe-nail, remarks of the credulous spectators [1]—

> that neuer an vnhappy fellow in the company shewed so much vnhappie wit, as to offer to take a knife, and pare away the deuil, lying in the dead of the nayle, and throw him into the fire, for acting his part so badly.

This passage was, of course, written after the allusions in *Henry V* and *Twelfth Night* to paring the nails of the devil.

But Harsnett's acquaintance with the stage can best be gauged from the way he continually returns to his comparison, made on the first page, of the tricks of the exorcists to a stage performance. There are scores of references to actors, comedians, players, tragedians, cue-fellows, playing, acting, performing, feigning, counterfeiting, acts (of a play), dialogue, prompter, cue, *plaudites*, puppets, scenes, hangings, &c. Altogether there are some 230 words derived from the theatre in the first 170 pages of the book, apart from references to characters in Plautus and Seneca. Harsnett may have derived this knowledge, superfluous for a Bishop's Chaplain, from his undergraduate days at Cambridge; he may have frequented the playhouse in London; but as Chaplain to the Bishop of London he had the job of licensing books for the press —sometimes a dangerous occupation, as he discovered to his cost [2] —and he read plays as part of his job; and it happens that his publisher, James Roberts, had a number of plays in his list, including the Second Quarto of *Hamlet*. Perhaps Harsnett's use of the word Deuillmastix [3] is a sign that he had some knowledge of the War of the Theatres.

The events described in Harsnett's *Declaration* had taken place in 1585–6, though the examination of Sarah and Friswood Williams and Anne Smith—three chambermaids in the family of Edmund Peckham—by the Ecclesiastical Commissioners had been made in 1598 and 1602. The three girls had been exorcised by the Jesuit Edmunds, alias Weston; and it is obvious from their evidence, and from that of Tyrrell and Richard Mainy, that 'they were drawn by' the priests' 'cunning carriage of matters, to seeme as though they had been possessed, when as in truth they were

---

[1] p. 61.
[2] *C.S.P. (Domestic)*, 1598–1603, pp. 405, 452–3.
[3] p. 51. One of the plays read by Harsnett as part of his duties was *Every Man Ou of his Humour*.

not'.[1] The alleged motive of the priests was to persuade the supposed demoniacs and others to become reconciled to the old Church, and they met with considerable success.

The girls were said to be possessed by several devils at once; and Edgar tells Gloucester that 'five fiends have been in Poor Tom at once', including Fliberdigibbet, 'who since possesses chambermaids and waiting-women'.[2] It is generally agreed that Shakespeare was alluding to the cases described by Harsnett. It is probable, too, that the name of Edgar's wicked brother, who is called Plexirtus in Sidney's *Arcadia*, was derived from the Edmunds and the Edmund Peckham who figure so prominently in Harsnett's *Declaration*.

When Edmund announces his brother's first appearance he says that his 'cue is villanous melancholy, with a sigh like Tom o' Bedlam'.[3] According to Harman, some of the Abraham men[4]

be merry and very pleasant, they will dance and sing; some others be as cold and reasonable to talk withal.

But Marwood, one of the alleged demoniacs, is described as 'pinched with penurie, & hunger' and as 'a melancholicke person'; Captain Pippin, Marwood's devil, is said to be like 'a melancholick *Priuado*'; all the demoniacs are melancholy rather than cheerful; and Harsnett begins a chapter with 'a question moued by Scaliger':[5]

Why men of a melancholick constitution be more subiect to feares, fancies, and imagination of deuils, and witches, then other tempers be?

One of the Fool's songs in the first act uses the phrase 'play at bo-peep' and the word 'apish'.[6] Both these are to be found in Harsnett's *Declaration*, and the first is not elsewhere used by Shakespeare.[7]

When Edgar decides to disguise himself as Poor Tom he uses several phrases which recall Harsnett:[8]

> the basest, and most poorest shape
> That euer penury in contempt of man,
> Brought neere to beast. . . .
> The Windes and persecutions of the skie. . . .
> Bedlam beggers, who with roaring voices,

---

[1] p. 250. [2] IV. i. 63. [3] I. ii. 121.
[4] J. D. Wilson, *Life in Shakespeare's England* (1949), p. 303.
[5] pp. 24, 47, 131. [6] I. iv. 181–93.
[7] pp. 148, 166. Cf. p. 61. [8] II. iii. 7 ff.

Stick in their num'd and mortified bare Armes
Pins, Wodden-prickes, Nayles . . .
And with this horrible obiect, from low Farmes . . .
Inforce their charitie.

Harsnett mentions 'penurie', as we have seen; he declares that[1]

There is neither Horse, nor Asse, nor Dogge, nor Ape if he had
been vsed, as these poore seely creatures were, but would haue
been much more deuillishly affected then they.

he speaks of 'what wind or weather so euer',[2] and of thunder,
lightning, and hail; he uses the word '*Bedlam*';[3] he describes frequently the roaring of the devils possessing the demoniacs;[4] he
tells how 'there were two needles thrust into' the leg of one of the
girls and quotes Friswood Williams' complaint that a priest 'did
thrust a pinne into her shoulder';[5] he tells us of a demoniac who
thought he was 'rent with a thousand nayles',[6] and of another who
would[7]

winch, skip, and curuet, hauing so many fiery needles in his skin
at once;

and he uses the phrase 'mortified patience'.[8]

In the next scene the Fool, seeing Kent in the stocks, exclaims:[9]

Horses are tide by the heads, Dogges and Beares by th' necke,
Monkies by th' loynes, and Men by th' legs: when a man's ouer-
lustie at legs, then he weares wodden nether-stocks.

With this we may compare Harsnett's words,[10]

as men leade Beares by the nose, or Iacke an Apes in a string;

the name of one of the devils, Lustie Dickie, and the mention of
'neather-stocks'—used by Shakespeare on only one other occasion.[11] Another word, used only in *King Lear*, is to be found a few
lines later—

They summon'd vp their *meiney*.

This word is used more than once by Harsnett[12]—

now the many, rascality, or black-guard of hell . . .
this deuice of an huge many of deuils. . . .

[1] p. 41.   [2] p. 52.   [3] p. 116.   [4] pp. 38, 45, 72, 127.
[5] pp. 42, 214.   [6] p. 73.   [7] p. 93.   [8] p. 41.
[9] II. iv. 7 ff.   [10] pp. 106–7.   [11] pp. 50, 100, 199.   [12] pp. 50, 52.

and, it may be added, the name of one of the supposed demoniacs was 'Maynie'.[1]

A few lines later Lear cries:[2]

> O, how this Mother swels vp toward my heart!
> *Hysterica passio*, downe, thou climing sorrow,
> Thy Elements below!

Shakespeare does not elsewhere use the term 'hysterica passio', but Harsnett refers to it several times. Richard Maynie[3]

> had a spice of the *Hysterica passio*, as seems from his youth, hee himselfe termes it the Moother . . . a poore passion of the Mother, which a thousand poore girles in England had worse.

In his confession Maynie says[4]—

> When I was sick of this disease in Fraunce, a Scottish Doctor of Physick then in *Paris*, called it, as I remember, *Vertiginem capitis*. It riseth (as he said, and I haue often felt) of a wind in the bottome of the belly, and proceeding with a great swelling, causeth a very painfull collicke in the stomack, and an extraordinary giddiness in the head.

Later in the same scene, in the lines—

> She hath tied
> Sharpe-tooth's vnkindnesse, like a vulture heere!

there is a reference to the torture of Prometheus, to which Shakespeare does not elsewhere directly refer. He knew the story, of course, but the later reference to 'a wheele of fire'[5] suggests that the tortures of Prometheus and of Ixion may have been recalled to the poet's mind by Harsnett's words:[6]

> Was euer *Prometheus* with his Vulture, *Sisyphus* with his stone, *Ixion* with his wheele in such a case?

When we turn to the storm scenes Shakespeare's indebtedness to Harsnett is much more obvious. It may even be suggested that the thunderstorm itself was partly derived from Harsnett. In the old play of *King Leir*, as we have seen, the murderer is frightened into repentance by a sudden clap of thunder, and in Sidney's account of the Paphlagonian king there is a storm, but without thunder or lightning. But Harsnett mentions 'a shelter against

---

[1] pp. 38, 48, 54, 257 ff.   [2] II. iv. 56-8.   [3] p. 25.
[4] p. 263.   [5] IV. vii. 47.   [6] p. 73.

what wind or weather so euer' and 'lightning from heauen';[1] he speaks of [2]

> in steede of thunder, and lightning to bring *Iupiter* vpon the stage . . . thundring, clapping, and flashing out . . . hearing the huge thunder cracke of adiuration:

and he says that a devil

> is so violent, boystrous, and bigge, as that he will ruffle, rage, and hurle in the ayre, worse then angry God *Æolus* euer did, and blow downe steeples, trees, may-poles.

Shakespeare twice uses the word 'ruffle' and three times the word 'rage'—twice about the storm and once about the foul fiend—and in one of these contexts there is a mention of 'steeples'.[3] Shakespeare uses 'vaunt-courier' only once,[4] and the word is to be found in Harsnett's *Declaration*[5]—

> Six parts in this comedie: the harbinger, the host, the steward, the vauntcourrier, the sacrist, and the Pandar.

Hiaclito, a devil who describes himself as 'Monarch of the World', is accompanied by 'two men and an vrchin boy'. Harsnett comments:[6]

> It was little beseeming his state (I wis) beeing so mighty a Monarch, to come into our coasts so skuruily attended, except hee came to see fashions in England . . . or els that he was of the new Court cut, affecting no other traine then two crasie fellowes, and an vrchin butter-flie boy.

Lear is similarly attended, and when Gloucester asks 'What, hath your Grace no better company?' Edgar replies that 'The Prince of Darknesse is a Gentleman'. Harsnett twice refers to 'the Prince of darknes'.[7] Moreover, this passage may have suggested the juxtaposition of *court news* and *butterflies* in the last scene of the play.

It is probable that the words 'all these sensible accidents should be made pendulous in the ayre' influenced the lines[8]—

> Now all the plagues that in the pendulous ayre
> Hang fated o're mens faults light on thy Daughters!

[1] pp. 52, 73. [2] p. 108.
[3] p. 18. Cf. II. iv. 304; II. vii. 43; III. i. 8; III. ii. 1–3; III. iv. 131.
[4] III. ii. 5.
[5] p. 12. Kent is a harbinger, Gloucester a host, Oswald a steward and pandar.
[6] p. 47.   [7] pp. 147, 168. Cf. III. iv. 154.   [8] p. 159.

Lear comments on Edgar's lack of clothes and tells him[1]

I do not like the fashion of your garments.

as though, like Hiaclito, he was come 'to see fashions in England'. The Fool's 'Court holy-water'[2] means 'flattery';[3] but Harsnett mentions holy-water in its religious sense several times.[4] In his prayer to the 'poore naked wretches'[5] Lear urges Pomp to take physic—

> Expose thy selfe to feele what wretches feele,
> That thou maist shake the superflux to them,
> And shew the Heauens more iust.

Harsnett in his preface speaks of [6]

> These lighter superfluities, whom they disgorge amongst you . . . in the fashion of great Potentates, vntill Gods reuengefull arme doth vncase them to the view of the world, and then they suffer the mild stroke of iustice with a glorious ostentation.

Edgar, hiding in the hovel, grumbles in the straw; Harsnett mentions that 'there was a pad in the straw, the poore man would faine haue out',[7] Marwood[8]

> did lie but a night, or two, abroad in the fieldes, and beeing a melancholicke person, was scared with lightning, and thunder, that happened in the night, & loe, an euident signe, that the man was possessed . . . this pittifull creature.

Harsnett says that a girl with 'a little helpe of the Mother, *Epilepsie*, or *Cramp*' can learn to[9]

> role her eyes, wrie her mouth, gnash her teeth, startle with her body, hold her armes and hands stiffe, make anticke faces, girne, mow, and mop like an Ape, tumble like a Hedgehogge, and can mutter out two or three words. . . .

Sara Williams, in her efforts to escape from the priests,[10]

> attempted to runne from the house, and to wade through a brooke, half a yard deepe of water.

Friswood Williams, when she was examined, said[11]

---

[1] III. vi. 28.   [2] III. ii. 10.
[3] J. Eliot, *Ortho-Epia Gallica*, has: 'I shall be sprinckled with the Court holy-water, that is to say, I shall haue a deluge of ceremonies, but as many apes tailes as dinners and breakefasts'.
[4] pp. 100 &c.   [5] III. iv. 28 ff.   [6] Sig. A3.   [7] p. 62.
[8] p. 24.   [9] p. 136.   [10] p. 43.   [11] p. 219.

that one *Alexander* an Apothecarie, hauing brought with him from London to *Denham* on a time a new halter, and two blades of kniues, did leaue the same, vpon the gallerie floare in her Maisters house. . . . *Mainy* in his next fit said, as it was reported, that the deuil layd them in the Gallery, that some of those that were possessed, might either hang themselues with the halter, or kil themselues with the blades.

One of the demoniacs cried out:[1]

> How doost thou vexe, how dost thou wring me? thou art neuer but plaguing me with torment and fire.

Harsnett uses the words 'devil-blasting',[2] 'sparrow-blasting',[3] 'sprite-blasting',[4] and 'owle-blasted';[5] and he refers to whirlwinds several times. He also speaks of the 'foule-mouthed fiend'.[6] From these and similar passages Shakespeare derived the material for Edgar's speech:[7]

> Whom the foule fiend hath led through Fire and through Flame, through Ford and Whirle-Poole, o're Bog and Quagmire; that hath laid Kniues vnder his Pillow and Halters in his pue . . . Blesse thee from Whirle-Windes, Starre-blasting, and taking, do poore *Tom* some charitie, whome the foule Fiend vexes.

The word 'pue' in this speech means 'gallery', not a church-pew. Harsnett uses the word 'pue-fellow',[8] and Shakespeare later uses a similar compound, 'yoke-fellow',[9] also found in Harsnett.

Maynie, Harsnett tells us, had 'his haire curled vp', and Weston cried, 'Loe heere comes vp the spirit of pride'.[10] Later we are given another account of the same episode. Maynie, it is said,[11]

> curled his haire, and vsed such gestures, as Ma. Edmunds presently affirmed that that spirit was *Pride*.

According to Friswood Williams,[12]

> the priests at theyr departure from *Denham*, took euery one thence his woman with him.

Maynie, according to Sara Williams, tried to seduce her.[13] In his own deposition Maynie recalled how Edmunds had told him he was possessed by[14]

[1] p. 73. [2] p. 107. [3] p. 136. [4] p. 137.
[5] p. 141. [6] p. 114. [7] III. iv. 50 ff. [8] p. 77.
[9] III. vi. 38. Cf. p. 195. [10] p. 54. [11] p. 278.
[12] p. 236. [13] p. 190. [14] p. 141.

the Maister-deuils of the seauen deadly sinnes, and therefore his deuils went out in the forme of those creatures, that haue neerest resemblance vnto those sinnes: as for example; the spirit of *Pride* went out in the forme of a *Peacocke* (forsooth): the spirit of *Sloth* in the likenesse of an *Asse*: the spirit of Enuy in the similitude of a *Dog*: the spirit of Gluttony in the forme of a *Woolfe.*

Vp commeth another spirit, singing most filthy and baudy songs: euery word almost that hee spake, was nothing but ribaldry. They that were present with one voyce affirmed that deuill to be the author of *Luxury.*

Although only the wolf represents the same sin in Harsnett and Shakespeare, we may compare with the above passages Edgar's description of himself as[1]

A Seruing-man, Proud in heart, and minde; that curl'd my haire; . . . One that slept in the contriuing of Lust, and wak'd to doe it: . . . Hog in sloth, Foxe in stealth, Wolfe in greedi-nesse, Dog in madnes, Lyon in prey.

Fliberdigibbet is mentioned several times by Harsnett, though he is described as a dancing devil, without the attributes ascribed to him by Edgar.[2] Smulkin appears as Smolkin, who came out 'at *Trayfords* right eare in the forme of a *Mouse*'.[3] Mado and Mahu are derived from Modu and Maho, the devils of Maynie and Sara Williams. Maho was the 'generall *Dictator* of hell'.[4]

Mr Edmund Blunden has demonstrated[5] that the word *Modo* recalled a passage in one of Horace's *Epistles* in which it occurs twice.

> Ille per extentum funem mihi posse videtur
> Ire poeta, meum qui pectus inaniter angit,
> Irritat, mulcet, falsis terroribus implet,
> Ut magus; et modo me Thebis, modo ponit Athenis.
>
> (*Epist.* II. i.)

Mr Blunden argues that 'Riding over four-inched bridges' and 'Modo' recalled this passage, and that this in turn led to the men-tion of 'learned Theban' and 'good Athenian' and the allusion to 'Persicos odi, puer, apparatus'.[6] Professor T. W. Baldwin has

[1] III. iv. 94. ff. [2] pp. 49, 119, 181. [3] pp. 47, 141.
[4] pp. 46, 48, 50, 54, 59, 90, 119.
[5] *Shakespeare's Significances* in *Shakespeare Criticism* (1919–35) ed. A. Bradby, pp. 327 ff. [6] III. vi. 82.

pointed out that *magus* is defined in Cooper's *Thesaurus* as 'a great
learned philosopher' in Persia, and this would serve as a link with
Horace's ode. Mr Blunden's theory can be supported by the fact
that Harsnett quotes from Horace's next epistle—

> Somnia, terrores, magicos, miracula, sagas,
> Nocturnos lemures portentaque Thessala rides?—

a passage which he versifies in the lines:

> Dreames and Magicall affrights,
> Wonders, witches, walking sprights,
> What Thessalian Hags can doe,
> All this seemes a iest to you.

The two passages are linked, apart from their proximity, by the
reference in the first to 'falsis terroribus' and the 'magus' who in-
spires them, and the reference in the second to 'somnia, terrores,
magicos, miracula'.

Edgar's first speech in the next storm scene contains the sentence:

> *Frateretto* cals me, and tells me *Nero* is an Angler in the Lake of
> Darknesse.

Harsnett mentions Frateretto several times.[1] Mr F. E. Budd has
demonstrated that the reference to Nero was not derived from
Rabelais[2] or Pausanias,[3] but from Chaucer, who mentions that
Nero was an angler,[4] and Harsnett who speaks of a Fiddler, a few
pages after a reference to the '*stygian* lake'.[5]

> our *stygian* Imposters goe farre beyond that *stygian* lake. . . .

> *Frateretto*, *Fliberdigibbet*, *Hoberdidance*, *Tocobatto* were foure
> deuils of the round, or Morrice, whom *Sara* in her fits, tuned
> together, in measure and sweet cadence. And least you should
> conceiue, that the deuils had no musicke in hell, especially that
> they would goe a maying without theyr musicke, the Fidler
> comes in with his Taber, & Pipe, and a whole Morice after him,
> with mostly visards for theyr better grace.

---

[1] pp. 49, 119, 181, 185.   [2] Cf. *R.E.S.* (1935), pp. 428–9.
[3] E. Sitwell, *A Notebook on William Shakespeare* (1948), p. 48.
[4] 'The Monk's Tale', 485–6.
[5] pp. 45, 49. Budd does not mention that in the story of Cordelia in *The Mirror
r Magistrates* there is a 'darksome Stygian Lake', nor that Nero was guilty of
atricide, whilst Edgar was accused of parricide.

It may be added that between these pages Harsnett mentions that Pippin, Marwood's devil, is 'of a *Caesars* humor,[1] and there are later references to the bottomless pit.[2]

A few lines after the reference to Nero Lear cries—

> To haue a thousand with red burning spits
> Come hizzing in vpon 'em.

Harsnett mentions [3]—

> So many fiery needles . . . swords, darts, and speares of fire, pointed with grisly death . . . the Furies . . . fire in theyr hands . . . and a huge bunch of a thousand snakes.

Lear's 'thousand' and 'hizzing' seem to have been suggested by the 'thousand snakes', and the 'red burning spits' were derived from the 'fiery needles', the 'speares of fire' and the fire in the hands of the Furies.

Harsnett on the page after a description of a feigned haunting mentions a nightingale;[4] and elsewhere he speaks of Hoberdidance or Haberdidance.[5] He recounts Sara Williams's testimony that when[6]

> shee was troubled with a wind in her stomacke, the priests would say at such times, that then the spirit began to rise in her . . . If they heard any croaking in her belly, (a thing whereunto many women are subiect, especially when they are fasting) then they would make a wonderful matter of that. One time shee remembreth, that shee hauing the said croaking in her belly, or making of herselfe some such noyse in her bed, they said it was the deuill that was about the bedde, that spake with the voyce of a Toade.

Shakespeare seems to have combined 'voyce of a Toade', nightingale, Hoberdidance, 'belly' and 'croak' for Edgar's speech:[7]

> The foule fiend haunts poore *Tom* in the voyce of a nightingale. Hoppedance cried in *Toms* belly for two white herring. Croke not, blacke Angell, I haue no foode for thee.

Just before his first mention of Hoberdidance, Harsnett says that[8]

> the deuill is like some other good fellowes in the world, that will not sweare, except he allow theyr Commission that tenders him his oath.

[1] p. 47. [2] p. 116. [3] pp. 93–4. [4] p. 225.
[5] pp. 49, 140, 180. [6] pp. 194–5. [7] III. vi. 30. [8] p. 49.

So Lear before the commission takes his oath that Goneril kicked the poor King her father.[1] Immediately before this speech Edgar uses the name of another of Harsnett's devils, Purre.[2] A few lines later, overcome with pity for the King, he says:[3]

> My teares begin to take his part so much
> They'll marre my counterfeiting.

Harsnett uses the phrases 'marred the play',[4] 'spoyle the play',[5] 'spoiled a good play',[6] 'marred a good play',[7] 'spoiled the play',[8] and 'the play be mard'.[9] In one passage he speaks of those who are able[10]

> so cunningly to act, & feigne the passions, and agonies of the deuil; that the whole companie of spectators shal by his false illusions be brought into such commiseration and compassion, as they shall all weepe, crie, and exclaime, as loude as the counterfet deuil.

Lear's dog, Tray, may have been suggested by the Trayford who is frequently mentioned by Harsnett. Edgar's 'Auaunt, you Curres!' was perhaps suggested by the devils in Harsnett who take the form of dogs, and by such phrases as 'your dogs being curres'.[11] Harsnett also mentions 'mad dogges', 'spaniel', 'hound', and various other dogs,[12] and he uses the phrase, 'tag, and ragge, cut and long-tayle:[13] all these may have contributed to Edgar's charm to rid himself of the imaginary dogs:[14]

> Tooth that poisons if it bite . . .
> Hound or Spaniell, Brache or Lym,
> Bobtaile tyke, or Trundle-tail . . .

Captaine Philpot, Trayford's devil, was a Centurion and 'had a hundred vnder his charge'.[15] Lear proposes to enrol Edgar as one of his hundred, and in a later scene there is a reference to a Century.[16] Shakespeare does not elsewhere use the terms 'hundred' or 'century', though Lear himself may have been thinking of the hundred knights he had reserved for himself when he divided the kingdom. Harsnett uses the epithet 'corkie',[17] and Cornwall in the next scene applies it to Gloucester's arms.

[1] III. vi. 39, 48. [2] pp. 50 &c. [3] III. vi. 60. [4] p. 19.
[5] p. 22. [6] p. 61. [7] p. 89. [8] p. 91.
[9] p. 130. [10] p. 74. [11] p. 76. [12] pp. 139, 89.
[13] p. 50. [14] III. vi. 67. [15] p. 47. [16] IV. iv. 6.
[17] p. 23. Cf. III. vii. 29.

The five fiends mentioned by Edgar in IV. i. are all taken from Harsnett's *Declaration*, Obidicut, the only one not mentioned earlier, being a corruption of Hoberdicut.[1] The phrase 'mopping and mowing' in the same speech was doubtless an echo of one of the following passages:[2]

> . . . to frame themselues iumpe and fit vnto the Priests humors, to mop, mow, iest, raile, raue, roare.

> . . . make anticke faces, girne, mow, and mop like an Ape, tumble like a Hedgehogge, and can mutter out two or three words.

> . . . a Sisternity of mimpes, mops, and idle holy women . . . and be as ready to cry out, at the mowing of an apish wench.

The passage in IV. vi. describing the lechery of women and the contrast between their rational minds and their irrational lusts has been thought by some critics to reflect Shakespeare's own revulsion against sexuality; but it may equally well have been suggested by Harsnett's account of the way the exorcists pretended that Sara Williams, at a time of menstruation, was possessed with a devil 'in a peculiar part of the body' and of the[3]

> Canon for lodging the deuil, that you be sure to lodge him not in the head, nor stomack, but in the inferiour parts.

The poor girl complained of the smell of the filthy relics[4]—

> the Priests did pretend, that the deuill did rest in the most secret part of my body: whereuppon they deuised to apply the reliques vnto that place—

and of the burning of sulphur underneath her nose. Harsnett mentions 'filthy fumes',[5] 'the bottomlesse pit of hell',[6] 'scalded',[7] 'thicke smoake & vapour of hell',[8] 'brimstone . . . burning',[9] and 'Brimstone . . . vgly blackness, smoake, scorching, boyling and heate'.[10] So Lear cries that[11]

> Beneath is all the fiend's.
> There's hell, there's darknesse, there's the sulphurous pit; burning, scalding, stench, consumption.

It may be worth while to add that Shakespeare uses 'benedic-

---

[1] p. 119. [2] pp. 38, 136, 166. [3] pp. 62–3. [4] p. 122.
[5] p. 45. [6] p. 61. [7] p. 68. [8] p. 94.
[9] p. 95. [10] p. 109. [11] IV. vi. 129 ff.

tion' three times in *King Lear*, though never before, and that this word is frequently used by Harsnett;[1] that 'fire vs hence like Foxes'[2] may have been suggested by[3]—

> fire him out of his hold, as men smoke out a Foxe out of his burrow.

and that Kent's words[4]—

> Vex not his ghost, O let him passe, he hates him
> That would vpon the racke of this tough world
> Stretch him out longer—

may echo Harsnett's juxtaposition of 'tormented' with 'tough weather-beaten spirit'.[5] Finally it may be mentioned that *propinquity*, *auricular*, *carp* (vb), *gaster*, and *asquint*, words used by Shakespeare for the first time in *King Lear*, are to be found in Harsnett's book,[6] that *sainted* used in *Measure for Measure* and *Macbeth*, is also there,[7] and that 'like the sentinel in a watch' and 'forelorn hope'[8] may have suggested Cordelia's 'poor perdu'. The Harsnett influence lasted right down to the end of Shakespeare's career and left its traces on *Pericles* and *The Tempest*.[9]

Lear's madness, as we have seen, may have been suggested by the Annesley story, but Shakespeare took some details—the gilded fly, the archery, the imaginary petition, and the words 'I am not mad; I know thee well enough'—from a scene in *Titus Andronicus*.[10] From the same play Shakespeare may have taken some hints for his portrait of Edmund from the character of Aaron, and the idea of the intrigue with Goneril from the Aaron–Tamora–Saturninus triangle.

Shakespeare perhaps took Edgar's dialect in IV. 6 from a play performed by his company entitled *The London Prodigal*, though such a dialect is used in other plays.[11]

From the fact that Shakespeare uses for the first time more than a hundred words[12] to be found in Florio's translation of Montaigne (including *amplify*, *avouched*, *bastardising*, *catastrophe*, *compeer*, *contentions*, *depositaries*, *derogate*, *disnatured*, *Epicurism*, *evasion*, *handy-dandy*, *hereditary*, *justicer*, *planetary*, *reciprocal*, *sophisticated*, and *windowed*) it

---

[1] p. 41.   [2] V. iii. 23.   [3] p. 97.   [4] V. iii. 313–15.
[5] p. 66.   [6] pp. 143, 9, A3ᵛ, 135, 96.   [7] p. 119.   [8] pp. 61, 119.
[9] p. 10. Cf. *Per.* IV. vi. 118–19; p. 136. Cf. *Temp.* II. ii. 5–12.
[10] Cf. K. Muir, ed. *King Lear*, p. xlii.
[11] Cf. H. Kökeritz, *Proc. Yorks Dialect Soc.* (1951), p. 17.
[12] Cf. K. Muir, ed. *King Lear*, pp. 249 ff.

seems probable that he had been reading the translation not long before he wrote *King Lear*. Several critics have argued that certain ideas in the play owe something to Montaigne. He exposes the weakness of unaccommodated man, he considers the influence of the stars on human destiny, he discusses the effect of dizzy heights, and he may have provided some of the material for Lear's attacks on authority—the fact that a dog is obeyed in office, the way big sinners pass judgement on lesser sinners, and the lust of women.

Shakespeare created *King Lear* from the most heterogeneous materials. As was his custom, he amplified and complicated his original fable by using incidents, ideas, phrases, and words from a variety of books. He found material for his purposes in the most unlikely places. Some critics, it is true, have complained that the play suffers from a weakness of structure. Bradley compared it in this respect to *Timon of Athens*; Allardyce Nicoll compared it unfavourably with the source-play;[1] and Richard H. Perkinson complained[2] that Shakespeare was content to use the loose episodic structure of the chronicle-play. But I think it may be truthfully claimed that there is no more impressive example of Shakespeare's skill as a dramatic craftsman. The way in which he combined a chronicle play, a prose chronicle, two poems, and a pastoral romance without any sense of incongruity is quite masterly, even for him; and the resulting play is interfused with ideas and phrases from his own earlier work, from Montaigne, and from Samuel Harsnett. Although the scene is laid in prehistoric times, it deals continually with topical ideas. The dangers of a disunited kingdom were particularly relevant at a time when King James was trying to get Parliament to approve of the union of England and Scotland;[3] the counterfeit demoniacs exposed by Harsnett in his books directed against puritan and catholic exorcists were a subject of violent controversy; the plight of the beggar was one of the main social problems at the beginning of the seventeenth century; and the conflict between two theories of nature—the view that nature is benignant, rational, and divinely ordered, and the view of the rationalists that man is governed by appetite and self-interest—was a much-discussed topic of the day; and all these matters were dramatized by Shakespeare in *King Lear*. The invention of the storm, the invention of Edgar's disguise as Poor Tom, and the

---

[1] *Studies in Shakespeare* (1927), pp. 154-5.
[2] *P.Q.* xxii (1943), pp. 315-29.
[3] J. W. Draper, *S.P.* (1937), pp. 176-85.

creation of a part for Robert Armin, the subtle Fool, enabled
Shakespeare to have the madness of the elements as a kind of pro-
jection of the mad king, the mad fool, and the beggar counterfeiting madness. The use of the main plot to lend verisimilitude to
the sub-plot is notable in the third act, where Gloucester's blinding
is the punishment for his alleged treachery; and the sub-plot assists
in the working-out of the main plot by disposing of one of the
villains, and thus intensifying the jealousy between Regan and
Goneril. It has recently been argued[1] that the death of Cornwall
brings about the destruction of the anti-Lear faction because he is
the only man strong enough to hold the others together. Edmund
forthwith works to gain absolute power, and Regan's intention of
marrying him compels Goneril to act hastily. Moreover, the death
of Cornwall puts the British forces into the hands of Albany,
while the news of the blinding of Gloucester fills him with loath-
ing for Edmund, Regan, and Goneril. Cornwall is killed by the
First Servant, who is driven to rebel only by the fiendish cruelty of
Cornwall and Regan. So that the working out of the plot turns
on the character of the First Servant—to what extent he will
acquiesce in his master's cruelty.

If one compares the reconciliation of Lear and Cordelia, the
best scene in the old play, with Shakespeare's version of it—and
for this scene he had no other source—one can see his immeasure-
able superiority. The earlier dramatist was hampered by the presence of the King of France, who like Cordelia was disguised. He
is hampered still more by the presence of a comic character called
Mumford, who kneels in parody of the other characters. Above
all, the earlier dramatist did not know when to stop. Different
characters kneel five times in the space of fifty lines:

> *Leir:* O, no mens children are vnkind but mine.
> *Cor.:* Condemne not all, because of others crime:
>   But looke, deare father, looke, behold and see
>   Thy louing daughter speaketh vnto thee.
> *Leir:* O, stand thou vp, it is my part to kneele,
>   And aske forgiuenesse for my former faults.
> *Cor.:* O, if you wish I should inioy my breath,
>   Deare father rise, or I receiue my death.
> *Leir:* Then I will rise, to satisfy your mind,
>   But kneele againe, til pardon be resigned.

[1] Cf. A. J. Price, *N.Q.* (1952), p. 313.

Cor.: I pardon you: the word beseemes not me:
But I do say so, for to ease your knee.
You gaue me life, you were the cause that I
Am what I am, who else had neuer bin.

Leir: But you gaue life to me and to my friend,
Whose dayes had else, had an vntimely end.

Cor.: You brought me vp, when as I was but young,
And far vnable for to helpe my selfe.

Leir: I cast thee forth, when as thou wast but young,
And far vnable for to helpe thy selfe.

Cor.: God, world and nature say I do you wrong,
That can indure to see you kneele so long.

King: Let me breake off this louing controuersy,
Which doth reioyce my very soule to see.
Good father, rise, she is your louing daughter,
And honours you with as respectiue duty.
As if you were the Monarch of the world.

Cor.: But I will neuer rise from off my knee,
Vntill I haue your blessing, and your pardon
Of all my faults committed any way,
From my first birth vnto this present day.

Leir: The blessing, which the God of *Abraham* gaue
Vnto the trybe of *Iuda*, light on thee,
And multiply thy dayes, that thou mayst see
Thy childrens children prosper after thee.
Thy faults, which are iust none that I do know,
God pardon on high, and I forgiue below.

Cor.: Now is my heart at quiet, and doth leape
Within my brest, for ioy of this good hap:
And now (deare father) welcome to our Court,
And welcome (kind *Perillus*) vnto me,
Myrrour of vertue and true honesty.

Leir: O, he hath bin the kindest friend to me,
That euer man had in aduersity.

Per.: My toung doth faile, to say what heart doth think,
I am so rauisht with exceeding ioy.

King: All you haue spoke: now let me speak my mind,
And in few words much matter here conclude:
If ere my heart do harbour any ioy,
Or true content repose within my brest,
Till I haue rooted out this viperous sect,

And repossest my father of his Crowne,
Let me be counted for the periurdst man,
That euer spake word since the world began.

Mum : Let me pray too, that neuer pray'd before;
If ere I resalute the Brittish earth,
(As (ere't be long) I do presume I shall)
And do returne from thence without my wench,
Let me be gelded for my recompence.

King : Come, let's to armes for to redresse this wrong:
Till I am there, me thinks, the time seemes long.

The scene is not without pathos, and Shakespeare deliberately retained the most memorable feature of it, where Lear and Cordelia kneel to each other. As Granville-Barker says,[1] it is 'a daring and unmatchable picture, for it is upon the extreme edge of beauty; one touch further and it might topple over into the absurd'. As, of course, it does in the original play.

Although, as we have seen, several critics have complained of looseness of structure in *King Lear*, there are few plays which are more closely knit. One test is a simple one to apply. If in producing the play you begin cutting out scenes or lines you soon come to realize how impossible it is to find a superfluous line. Shakespeare's fellows, one hopes after his retirement, made a number of cuts. Each one is disastrous from the dramatic point of view. They cut out, for example, the mock trial of Goneril and Regan in the third act of the play, a trial which is manifestly necessary for our understanding of Lear's development, as it is essential to the symbolic pattern of the play. Then they cut out the dialogue between the two servants after the blinding of Gloucester:

Second Serv. : Ile neuer care what wickednes I do
If this man come to good.

Third Serv. : If she liue long,
And in the end meet the old course of death,
Women will all turne monsters.

Second Serv. : Lets follow the old Earle, and get the Bedlam
To lead him where he would: his rogish madnes
Allows it selfe to any thing.

Third Serv. : Goe thou; Ile fetch some flaxe and whites of egges
To apply to his bleeding face. Now heauen helpe
him!

[1] H. Granville-Barker, *Companion to Shakespeare Studies* (1934), p. 77.

How much the scene would lose by the omission of this choric comment by ordinary humanity on the cruelty of Regan and Cornwall, how necessary it is to end the scene and the act quietly rather than violently, and how desirable it is to prepare the way for Poor Tom's meeting with Gloucester! Then the actors apparently omitted the whole of IV. iii., the scene in which an anonymous gentleman describes to Kent Cordelia's grief at the way her father has been treated. At first sight it seems to be a passage which could be omitted without loss. But Cordelia's part is so very short that her next appearance requires a preparation and build-up. The ineffectiveness of the Cordelia in many modern productions is largely due to the omission of this preparatory scene. Apart from that, the audience needs to be informed of the reason why Lear refuses to see Cordelia, and Kent's comment on the influence of the stars is necessary to the atmosphere of the play, though it is not intended as the whole truth:

> It is the stars,
> The stars aboue vs, gouerne our conditions;
> Else one self mate and make could not beget
> Such different issues.

It is therefore an illusion to suppose that Shakespeare employs the loose episodic structure of the chronicle play. The main plot and the sub-plot are not merely parallel; they are closely linked. In the first two acts Lear is deceived by Goneril and Regan into disinheriting Cordelia; he realizes his mistake and is driven out into the storm. Meanwhile Gloucester is deceived by Edmund into disinheriting Edgar, and Edgar, like Kent, returns in disguise to succour the man who has wronged him. In the third act the outcasts of the main plot encounter the outcast of the sub-plot; Lear goes mad, and Gloucester is blinded for taking his part. In the fourth act the mad Lear encounters the blinded Gloucester; Cordelia and Edgar succour their fathers; and the evil daughters quarrel over the evil son. In the last act both fathers die of joy, after being reconciled to the children they have wronged; and Edgar brings about the ruin of the three evil children. The only accident in the play—the only event which does not spring from man's greed, or lust, or pride—is the encounter of Edgar and Oswald, which betrays the plot to kill Albany; and even this accident is used by Shakespeare to illustrate Oswald's character.

(14) Macbeth

It is reasonable to assume that Shakespeare chose the subject of *Macbeth* because James I was reputed to be descended from Banquo, and it is quite possible that Shakespeare had been informed of the King's interest in Matthew Gwinn's entertainment performed at Oxford on 27 August 1605, in which three sibyls prophesied to Banquo's descendants *imperium sine fine*, an empire without end. If Shakespeare was at Oxford in the summer of 1605 —and there is some reason to believe that he was[1]—he would

[1] Cf. H. N. Paul, *The Royal Play of Macbeth* (1950), pp. 15–16. Davenant, who claimed that Shakespeare was his father, was baptized on March 3, 1606. An additional piece of evidence for Shakespeare's presence in Oxford may be worth mentioning. Among the plays performed during the King's visit was *Arcadia Reformed*—afterwards known as *The Queenes Arcadia*—by Samuel Daniel. It was performed before the Queen at Christ Church on August 30. The King wisely chose to visit the University library instead of watching the play. There is one parallel between this play and *Macbeth* which may suggest that Shakespeare had read it, or seen it. In the third act Daphne visits the quack, Alcon, and afterwards soliloquizes:

> O what
> Can Physicke doe to cure that hideous wound
> My lusts haue giuen my Conscience? which I see
> Is that which onely is diseas'd within
> And not my body now, that's it doth so
> Disquiet all the lodging of my spirits,
> As keepes me waking, that is it presents
> Those onely formes of terror that affright
> My broken sleepes, that layes vpon my heart
> This heauy loade that weighes it downe with griefe;
> And no disease beside, for which there is
> No cure I see at all, nor no redresse.

Macbeth complains of the terrible dreams that shake him nightly and of the torture of the mind on which he lies. In the last act the Doctor explains that Lady Macbeth

> is troubled with thicke-comming Fancies
> That keepe her from her rest.

Macbeth replies:

> Cure her of that.
> Can'st thou not Minister to a minde diseas'd,
> Plucke from the Memory a rooted Sorrow,
> Raze out the written troubles of the Braine,
> And with some sweet Obliuious Antidote
> Cleanse the stuft bosome, of that perillous stuffe
> Which weighes vpon the heart?

The Doctor tells him:

> Therein the Patient
> Must minister to himselfe.

The parallel may be discounted to some extent by the fact that both poets were expressing medical commonplaces. But the words

> that layes vpon my heart
> This heauy loade that weighes it downe with griefe . .

seem to be echoed in the last line of Macbeth's speech.

have heard that the King had exhibited a dislike of long plays and he would have heard of the subjects suggested for debate before the monarch—whether the morals of nurses were imbibed by babies with their milk, whether the imagination can produce real effects, whether nicotine has medicinal uses, and so on.[1]

Shakespeare then turned to the story in Holinshed's *Chronicles* on which Gwinn had based his *Tres Sibyllae*. There he would have found that Banquo was himself involved in the conspiracy to murder Duncan, and this would never do, for three good reasons: it would remind everyone that the King's ancestor had been guilty of treason; it would have been impossible to depict him sympathetically because King James believed that rebellion was never justified, even against a wicked king;[2] and the assassination of Duncan by Macbeth and his friends was dramatically unsatisfactory. The open assassination by the conspirators who felt that the naming of Malcolm as Prince of Cumberland was defrauding Macbeth 'of all maner of title and claime, which he might in time to come pretend vnto the crowne' was lacking in inward conflict. Banquo, therefore, had to be cleared of complicity in the crime, and Macbeth had to be deprived of the excuse that he had 'a just quarrell so to doo (as he tooke the matter)'.

More promising was the single reference by Holinshed to Lady Macbeth: 'but speciallie his wife lay sore vpon him to attempt the thing, as she that was verie ambitious, burning in vnquenchable desire to beare the name of a queene'. With this passage in mind, Shakespeare remembered the story of Donwald and his wife; or perhaps in reading the Scottish chronicles for local colour his eye was caught by the marginal notes less than twenty pages before the Macbeth story: 'Donwald's wife counselled him to murther the king. . . . The womans euill counsell is followed'. He must have seen immediately that the murder of King Duff by Donwald, the 'capteine of the castell' in which he was staying, had more dramatic possibilities than the open killing of Duncan. It also offered him the means of whitewashing Banquo.

Donwald's wife is the instigator of the crime, though her motive is revenge for the death of her kinsmen. She it is who 'shewed him the meanes whereby he might soonest accomplish' the murder. Donwald, 'being the more kindled in wrath by the words of his wife', determined 'to follow her aduise'. Holinshed tells us that

---

[1] Cf. H. N. Paul, *The Royal Play of Macbeth* (1950), p. 18.
[2] Cf. K. Muir, ed. *Macbeth*, p. lxii.

the day before his purposed departure the King was at prayers till late into the night (from which Shakespeare may have got the idea of stressing Duncan's holiness) and bestowed gifts upon Donwald and others. The two chamberlains, having escorted him to bed, 'fell to banketting with Donwald and his wife'. Their possets are not drugged, but they go drunk to bed. Donwald, 'though he abhorred the act greatlie in heart', bribed four servants to murder the King, and they conveyed the body out of the castle. In the morning, when the alarm is given, Donwald found 'cakes of bloud in the bed', and he slew the chamberlains,

> and then like a mad man running to and fro, he ransacked euerie corner within the castell.

A few pages later Shakespeare would have read how after King Kenneth had slain his nephew he was afraid the crime would be discovered:

> For so commeth it to passe, that such as are pricked in conscience for anie secret offense committed, haue euer an vnquiet mind.

A voice was heard telling him that his crime was known to God and that both himself and his issue would suffer punishment.

> The King, with this voice being striken into great dread and terror, passed that night without anie sleepe comming in his eies.

This passage may have suggested the voice that cried 'Sleep no more' and the terrible dreams of which Macbeth speaks.

Liddell,[1] followed by Paul,[2] argued that Shakespeare had also read the corresponding passage in Buchanan's Latin *History*:

[1] Mark H. Liddell's edition of *Macbeth* (1903) is not easily accessible. His note on the Buchanan passage reads as follows:

> Shakespeare, in describing Macbeth's mental torture, employs verbiage that sounds very like a rough translation of Buchanan's Latin; one can almost fancy him reading it: 'animus conscientia sceleris inquietus'—his mind in 'restless ecstasy' with the consciousness of his guilt—'nullum solidum et sincerum ei gaudium esse permittebat'—kept him 'dwelling in doubtful joy',— 'sed foedissime interdiu vexabatur'—and he was continually 'tortured'—'cogitationibus sceleris'—by thoughts of his wicked deed in 'sending' Malcolm 'to his peace'—'intercursantibus per otium'—and could 'gain no peace' for himself,—'et visa horroris plena'—but 'terrible dreams' and 'visions'—'observantia'—'afflicting' him—'per somnum quietam interpellabant'—'shook him nightly';—'sive vere vox coelo edita est'—either he heard a voice from heaven crying 'sleep no more', Kenneth doth murder sleep—'sive'—or—'turbatus

His soul disturbed by a consciousness of his crime, permitted him to enjoy no solid or sincere pleasure; in retirement the thoughts of his unholy deed tormented him; and, in sleep, visions full of horror drove repose from his pillow. At last, whether in truth an audible voice from heaven addressed him, as is reported, or whether it were the suggestion of his guilty mind, as often happens with the wicked, in the silent watches of the night, he seemed thus to be admonished.

Although this may seem to be closer than Holinshed's account to Shakespeare's picture of the tortures of Macbeth's mind, it should be said that the nightmares of the wicked are a commonplace and Shakespeare had already depicted them in *Richard III*, a play which, as we shall see, was very much in Shakespeare's mind when he wrote *Macbeth*.

It has been argued by Mrs Stopes[3] and Professor Dover Wilson[4] that Shakespeare was acquainted with William Stewart's *Buik of the Cronicles of Scotland*, a huge poem which remained in manuscript until the middle of the nineteenth century. Mrs Stopes declared that 'in every case in which Stewart differs from Holinshed, Shakespeare follows Stewart'. But since any poet expanding the bare facts of the story would be driven to develop Lady Macbeth's character in the same way, the resemblances are likely to be accidental. Already in Holinshed Shakespeare was provided with two women urging their husbands to regicide, and one of the husbands had moral scruples. Almost any dramatist would make the wife call the husband a coward, bid him play the hypocrite, and pretend indignation after the murder. The one verbal parallel of any significance 'til the warldis end' and 'the crack of doom' (IV. i. 117) is not very substantial. Holinshed speaks of 'long order of continuall descent'; James I himself expressed the hope that his posterity might 'rule over you to the world's end'; Lance-

---

animus'—his 'diseased mind'—'ipse eam speciem sibi finxerat'—itself 'informed' thus to his guilty ears, &c.

It will be apparent that not all Liddell's parallels are valid.

[2] Paul, op. cit., p. 216. The passage reads as follows:

Tamen animus, conscientia sceleris inquietus, nullum solidum et syncerum e gaudium esse, permittebat: sed, intercursantibus per otium cogitationibus sceleris foedissimi, interdiu vexabatur: et per somnum obuersantia, visa horroris plena quietam interpellabant. Tandem, siue vere (quod quidam tradunt) vox coelo edita est, siue turbatus animus eam sibi ipse speciem finxerat.

[3] *Shakespeare's Industry* (1916), pp. 102-3.
[4] ed. *Macbeth*, pp. xvii ff.

lot Andrewes, in his sermon on the coronation, prayed that the King's descendants would 'stretch their line to the world's end'— the closest parallel of all; and Gwinn, as we have seen, used the phrase *'imperium sine fine'*.

It is not absolutely impossible that Shakespeare got hold of a copy of Stewart's manuscript poem; but if we must have a source for Lady Macbeth's tactics with her husband, John Bellenden's translation of Boece's *Chronicles* would be more likely:[1]

> Attoure, his wyfe, impacient of lang tary, as wemen ar to all thing quhair thai sett thame, gaif him grete artacioun to persew the samyn, that scho mycht be ane qwene; calland him oft tymes febill cowart and nocht desyrus of honouris, sen he durst nocht assailye the thing with manhede and curage quhilk is offerit to him be beneuolence of fortoun, howbeit sindry vtheris offeris thame to maist terribill ieopardeis, knawing na sikkirnes to succede thereftir.

Dover Wilson, however, has been converted more recently to Paul's view that Shakespeare's other source was not Stewart but Buchanan. Paul points out[2] that Buchanan is more explicit than Holinshed about Macbeth's good qualities. Holinshed speaks of him as

> a valiant gentleman, and one that if he had not beene somewhat cruell of nature, might haue beene thought most woorthie the gouernement of a realme.

Buchanan says he

> was a man of penetrating genius, a high spirit, unbounded ambition, and, if he had possessed moderation, was worthy of any command however great; but in punishing crimes he exercised a severity, which, exceeding the bounds of the laws, appeared oft to degenerate into cruelty.

Later on he adds that before Macbeth's dream of the three women 'of more than mortal stature' he had 'cherished secretly the hope of seizing the throne'. It is perhaps true that Buchanan's account of Macbeth's character is nearer to Shakespeare's than Holinshed's; but Shakespeare in creating a tragic hero would naturally

---

[1] ed. 1941, p. 151.
[2] op. cit., p. 213.

> Erat enim Macbethus acri ingenio, animo prorsus excelso, et magnarum rerum cupido: cum si moderatio accessisset, quamuis magno imperio dignus erat.

depict him as valiant and noble as possible to make his downfall more dramatic; and Holinshed's phrase when Malcolm is given the title of Prince of Cumberland might be taken to imply, or at least might have suggested to Shakespeare, that Macbeth had secretly hoped for the throne:

> Mackbeth sore troubled herewith, for that he saw by this his hope sore hindered (where, by the old lawes of the realme, the ordinance was, that if he that should succeed were not of able age to take charge vpon himselfe, he that was next of bloud vnto him should be admitted).

It should be mentioned,[1] however, though Paul overlooks the point, that Buchanan says that

> This appointment highly incensed Macbeth, who thought it an obstacle thrown in the way of his ambition, which—now that he had obtained the two first dignities promised by his nocturnal visitors—might retard, if not altogether prevent, his arriving at the third, as the command of Cumberland was always considered the next step to the crown.   (tr. 1827)

Macbeth in the play seems to echo this passage:

> The Prince of Cumberland: that is a step,
> On which I must fall downe, or else o're-leape,
> For in my way it lyes.

Buchanan tells us that Macbeth's mind 'was daily excited by the importunities of his wife, who was confidante of all his designs'. Shakespeare's account might easily have been developed from Holinshed's. Buchanan suggests that the reason why Macbeth's good rule was changed to a tyranny was his feelings of guilt about the killing of Duncan:[2]

> The murder of the king—as is very credible—haunting his imagination, and distracting his mind, occasioned his converting the government, which he had obtained by perfidy into a cruel tyranny.

---

[1] Cf. K. Muir, N.Q. (1955), pp. 511–12.

> Id factum eius Macbethus molestijs, quam credi poterat, tulit, eam videlicet moram sibi ratus iniectam, vt priores iam magistratus, iuxta visum nocturnum, adeptus, aut omnino a regno excluderetur, aut eo tardius potiretur: cum praefectura Cumbriæ velut aditus, ad supremum magistratum, semper esset habitus.

[2] Regiæ (vt credibile est) cædis stimulis animum elatum in præceps impellentibus imperium, perfidia partum, in crudelissimam tyrannidem vertit.

But Holinshed's account is closer to Shakespeare's:

Shortlie after, he began to shew what he was, in stead of equitie practising crueltie. For the pricke of conscience (as it chanceth euer in tyrants, and such as atteine to anie estate by vnrighteous means) caused him euer to feare, least he should be serued of the same cup, as he had ministred to his predecessor.

Editors have compared the lines:

> This euen-handed Iustice
> Commends th' Ingredience of our poyson'd challice
> To our owne lips.

It should be added that in the margin Holinshed called attention to Macbeth's 'guiltie conscience', to his 'dread', and to the fact that his cruelty was 'caused through feare'.

Paul then refers to the reasons given by Buchanan for the murder of Banquo:

Igitur veritus, ne homo potens et industrius, et Regio iam sanguine imbutus, exemplum ab ipso propositum imitaretur.

This is translated by Paul as follows:

Whereupon (Macbeth) fearing lest (Banquo, who was) a powerful man and a very resourceful one and with royal blood in his veins, might imitate the example set by himself.

But Buchanan does not say that Banquo had royal blood in his veins, but that his hands were stained with royal blood—and that he was therefore not likely to shrink from killing Macbeth. It cannot therefore be said that this passage suggested Shakespeare's phrase—

> in his Royaltie of Nature
> Reignes that which would be fear'd—

unless we assume that he also mistranslated the passage. Buchanan does, however, say that Macbeth invited Banquo and Fleance to supper *familiariter*, and this touch, absent from Holinshed, may have suggested the tone of Macbeth's invitation in the play.

There is nothing in the account of Donwald given by Buchanan that Shakespeare seems to have noted. But, on the whole, and in view of Shakespeare's usual habits of composition, it is quite likely that he consulted Buchanan.

There is little to suggest that he knew Skene's *Scots Acts*. Paul, however, argues[1] that Skene's description of Duncan as 'a gud and modest Prince', who was slain traitorously by Macbeth who 'in the beginning of his reigne . . . behaved himselfe as a gud and just Prince, bot thereafter . . . degenerated into a cruell tyrant', is the basis of Shakespeare's portrayal of the two men. Holinshed's Duncan is weak, and he is slain in a fight, and Macbeth's good deeds at the beginning of his reign were a 'counterfeit zeal of equity'. But Duncan's goodness was necessary as a dramatic contrast; once his murder was conflated with that of Duff the deed became more treacherous, and although Macbeth may be noble before the murder, Shakespeare deliberately omits the ten years of good rule.

Paul is on much stronger ground when he argues[2] that Shakespeare knew Leslie's *De Origine, Moribus, et Rebus Gestis Scotorum*, published at Rome in 1578. Leslie describes how Macbeth heard the prophecy about Banquo's descendants from certain devils disguised as women—which may have given Shakespeare a hint for his treatment of the weird sisters; he stresses the unbroken series of kings descended from Banquo (*series perpetuo filo contexta*), and he provides an interesting genealogical tree of Banquo's descendants, with roots, leaves, and fruit. Paul is probably right in thinking that this tree left its mark on the imagery of Acts III and IV:[3]

Banquo (III. i. 5) rephrases the prophecy concerning his children as he sees himself 'the *root* and father of many kings'. Macbeth's fears stick deep (are deeply rooted) in Banquo (III. i. 49) because he is to be 'father to a *line of kings*'. . . . The tree of Banquo in the cut bears not only leaves and flowers, but globular fruit, eight of which united in a direct line are crowned; and Macbeth sees that he has murdered Banquo only to make these '*seeds*' of Banquo kings. Macbeth's thwarted ambition imagines the serpentine trunk of the tree as drawn in the cut to be a 'snake' he cannot kill (III. ii. 13), or a 'serpent' (III. iv. 29). The picture of this trunk showing '*quam justa serie Reges nostri ex Regibus parentibus continenter fuerint nexi*' is seen as 'that great bond' which keeps Macbeth pale and which he wishes 'torn to pieces' (III. ii. 49). And finally, in the fourth act it is a show of eight (not nine) kings, for the title of the cut speaks of a series '*octo posteriorum regum*'.

Not all these points are equally convincing and some readers will be sceptical of Paul's interpretation of 'that great bond'. But the

---

[1] op. cit., p. 221.   [2] op. cit., pp. 171 ff.   [3] op. cit., p. 175.

case for Shakespeare's having seen Leslie's book is a good one, and it can be strengthened by a few additional points.

Leslie makes no mention of Macbeth having accomplices in the murder of Duncan (presumably because he, like Shakespeare, wished to hush up Banquo's part), but he stresses Lady Macbeth's influence. She, as in Shakespeare's play, overcomes her husband's fears by showing how he can ensure a successful outcome. Leslie refers to the 'most holy king Duncan' and says that Macbeth 'impiously' slew him:

> Verum non multos post dies spiritus ita Machabeo inflauit inanis quaedam gloria, animumque vesana quaedam dominandi libido distrinxit, vt (vxore illum meticulosum spe felicis euentus excitante) Duncanum sanctissimum Regem (qui illum tanto honore ornarat) impiissime trucidarit, anno eius regni sexto.

Leslie's account of Macbeth's reign of terror is also worth quoting:

> Verum . . . tandem admissi sceleris conscientia agitatus, a propinquis tantopere sibi timuit, vt mutata naturae suauitate, Nobiles suos vel aperta vi truculentus extingueret, vel occulto consilio ad mutuam caedem vafer excitaret. At cum sibi a Banquhone, ac Makduffo in primis periculum imminere putaret, illum quamprimum tollit: huic insidias subdolus struit. Quid plura? Tyrannorum more, omnes timet, ac ab omnibus timetur.

The major alterations made by Shakespeare in the Macbeth story as told by Holinshed are for the most part easily explicable on dramatic grounds. Once he decided to graft the Donwald story on to the Macbeth story he would make Duncan more virtuous and deprive Macbeth of his grievance, which in any case would have been difficult to explain to an English audience.[1] Banquo's innocence was determined both by dramatic and politic necessity. Several changes are explained by considerations of dramatic economy: the battles at the beginning and end of the play are condensed; the ten years of good rule by Macbeth are omitted, partly, no doubt, because Shakespeare could not afford to give his hero a respite of this kind; Macduff offends Macbeth by not attending the coronation and refusing to come to court—his offence is not with regard to the building of Dunsinane Castle; and the prophecies in Act IV are ascribed to the weird sisters, not to a wizard.

---

[1] As Dover Wilson points out, the principles of succession were different.

Law lists thirty-five incidents not to be found in Holinshed,[1] but most of these are inevitable results of a dramatization of the story—for example, the introduction of the weird sisters, Macbeth's letter to his wife, Lady Macbeth's welcome of Duncan, and Banquo's suspicions that Macbeth has murdered Duncan. Others are more significant. According to Holinshed, Macduff comes to England, knowing that his family have been killed. Shakespeare by making Rosse bring the news after the testing of Macduff by Malcolm makes the scene more plausible, as Malcolm could hardly suspect Macduff of being a spy if he knew that Macbeth had murdered his family.

There is nothing in Holinshed to suggest Lady Macbeth's invocation of the murdering ministers, her sleep-walking, or her death. There is nothing about the knocking on the gate or the drunken porter and nothing about the appearance of Banquo's ghost at the banquet. It is possible that the translation of De Loier's *Treatise of Specters*, published in 1605, may have given Shakespeare the idea of the ghost at the banquet.[2] There tyrants are mentioned among those who 'are perplexed and terrified with a million of feares' after they have put to death persons 'they suspected to bee men of noted vertue and honestie'. Such murderers

> haue bin troubled and tormented with most horrible phantasmes and imaginations, which do com into their heads both sleeping and waking: . . . How often haue they supposed and imagined, that they haue seene sundry visions and apparitions of those whom they haue murthered, or of some others whome they haue feared?

De Loier goes on to describe how King Thierry, having slain Simmachus, saw

> on an euening as he sat at supper . . . the face of Simmachus in a most horrible shape and fashion, with great mustachoes, knitting his browes, frowning with his eyes, biting his lippes for very anger, and looking awry vpon him.

From this tiny hint and the invitation of Banquo to supper mentioned by Holinshed Shakespeare may have constructed his scene, but he added the arrival of the murderer, the pledging of the missing guest, the double appearance of the ghost, Lady Macbeth's

---

[1] R. A. Law, *University of Texas Studies in English*, 1952, pp. 35–41.
[2] Cf. Paul, op. cit., pp. 58–9.

attempt to call her husband to his senses, and their exhaustion
after the guests have departed.

The Porter scene, though Shakespeare's invention, takes the
form it does because it was written at the time of the trial of the
Gunpowder conspirators when Father Garnet's equivocation was
being everywhere discussed. Another question of topical interest,
touching for the King's evil, was to be found in the account of
Edward the Confessor given by Holinshed. Presumably Shakespeare turned to this section of the *Chronicles* in search of background material for the scene at the English court. He saw that it
would provide a good supernatural element to contrast with the
evil supernatural of the weird sisters, the more interesting to an
audience as James I had with reluctance begun to touch for the
Evil. James was also interested in hounds, but the passage in III. i.
was probably based not on the royal proclamation but on one of
Erasmus's *Colloquies* which compares the different kinds of men
with the different species of dogs, as Macbeth does, and uses the
phrase *naturae benignitas*, rendered by Shakespeare as 'bounteous
Nature'.[1]

There is some evidence that Shakespeare had been reading
several of King James's own works.[2] In the *Counterblast to Tobacco*
James had compared the King to a Physician:

> It is the King's part (as the proper Phisician of his Politicke-
> bodie) to purge it of all those diseases, by Medicines meete for
> the same.

This idea is used four times in *Macbeth*, as in the lines:

> If thou could'st Doctor, cast
> The Water of my Land, finde her Disease,
> And purge it to a sound and pristine Health,
> I would applaud thee to the very Eccho.

The idea was not, of course, peculiar to Shakespeare and his
sovereign, and the resemblance may be accidental. Other parallels
have been listed with *The True Law of Free Monarchies* and *Basilikon
Doron*, and it has even been suggested that the theme of the play
was based on a passage in the latter book in which James contrasts
the good king with the tyrant whose own subjects become his
executioners.[3] But although it is highly probable that Shakespeare

[1] Cf. J. D. Rea, *M.L.N.*, xxxv (1920), p. 378.
[2] Paul, op. cit., p. 391.
[3] ed. Muir, p. lxii.

did not neglect to read his royal patron's works, this theme could have been derived from the facts given by Holinshed.

We are on much surer ground when we turn to another work by the King. *Daemonologie* has clearly left its mark on all those scenes in which the weird sisters appear, though some of his knowledge Shakespeare may have derived from Reginald Scot and others. He would have read in *Daemonologie*[1] that

> as to the diuells foretelling of things to come, it is true that he knows not all things future, but yet that he knowes part;

that witches might

> foretell what commonweales shall florish or decay; what persones shall be fortunate or vnfortunate; what side shall winne anie battell;

that the Devil makes himself

> so to be trusted in these little thinges, that he may haue the better commoditie thereafter to deceiue them in the end with a tricke once for all; I meane the euerlasting perdition of their soul and body;

that he

> will make his schollers to creepe in credite with Princes, by foretelling great thinges; parte true, parte false. For if all were false he would tyne credite at all handes; but alwaies doubtsome, as his Oracles were;

that

> at their thirde meeting, he makes a shew to be carefull to performe his promises;

and that he is able to

> deceaue vs to our wracke.

So Banquo explains in the play that

> oftentimes, to winne vs to our harme,
> The Instruments of Darknesse tell vs Truths,
> Winne vs with honest Trifles to betray's
> In deepest consequence.

[1] Cf. K. Muir, 'The Dramatic Function of Anachronism' (*Proc. Leeds Phil. and Lit. Soc.*) 1951, pp. 529–33.

There is no reason to doubt that Shakespeare had perused *Dae-monologie*.

It has recently been argued[1] that Shakespeare was influenced by another of King James's works, *A Fruitfull Meditation* (1603), a commentary on the book of *Revelation* xx. 7-10; and certainly James touches on a number of themes which are to be found in *Macbeth*. He points out, for example, that

> all that doe euill, are inspired by Sathan, and doe vtter the same in dyuers degrees, according as that vncleane spirite taketh possession in them, and by diuers obiects and means, allureth them to doe his will, some by ambition, some by enuie, some by malice and some by feare.

These words might be applied to all Macbeth's crimes.

James, moreover, quotes a number of biblical passages which Shakespeare appears to echo. 'Wide is the waye that leadeth to destruction' recurs in the Porter scene; some of the imagery concerning blood and babes in *Macbeth* may be coloured by memories of *Revelation*; there is one unmistakable, and several possible, allusions to the story of Saul,[2] who like Macbeth made use of witchcraft; and Jeremiah's denunciation of a man who listens to false prophets, 'Write this man destitute of children', may underlie Macbeth's complaint of his barren sceptre, though his childlessness is implicit in the story. Yet Shakespeare did not need to read the works of King James to be reminded of the stories of Herod and Saul, or of the Sermon on the Mount, and his use of *A Fruitfull Meditation* remains, I believe, unproven.

There are biblical echoes in all Shakespeare's plays, but those in *Macbeth* are particularly interesting. One group is linked with the line:[3]

> What Hands are here? Hah: they pluck out mine Eyes.

It was suggested by the verses in *Matthew* xviii:

> Wherefore, if thy hand or thy foote cause thee to offend, cut them off, and cast them from thee: it is better for thee to enter into life, halt, and maymed, then hauing two hands, or two

---

[1] Jane H. Jack, *E.L.H.* (1955), pp. 173 ff.

[2] Cf. *I Sam.* xxiv. 12. 'The Lord be iudge betwene thee & me' and *Macb.* IV. iii. 120-1: 'But God aboue Deale betweene thee and me'.

[3] Cf. Muir, ed. *Macbeth*, pp. 51, 57, 80, and R. Walker, *The Time is Free* (1949), pp. 71-2.

feete, to be cast into euerlasting fire. And if thine eye cause thee to offend, plucke it out, and cast it from thee: it is better for thee to enter into life with one eie, then hauing two eyes to be cast into hell fire.

This passage was linked with others. In *Matthew* v and *Mark* ix there is the same injunction to pluck out the eye to avoid the fires of hell. In *Matthew* vi and *Luke* xi there is another passage about the eye:

The light of the body is the eye: if then thine eye bee single, the whole body shalbe light. But if thine eye be wicked, then all thy bodie shall be darke.

A few verses later in St Matthew's Gospel, and a few verses earlier in St Luke's, there is the injunction 'Knocke, and it shall be opened'. In St Matthew's Gospel this is followed by a reference to the primrose path:

Enter in at the strait gate: for it is the wide gate, and broad way that leadeth to destruction: and many there be which goe in thereat.

In the same chapter in St Luke's Gospel, between the references to knocking and the eye, Beelzebub is mentioned three times. So in *Macbeth* the line quoted above follows and precedes the knocking at the gate, and the Porter speaks of Hell Gate, Beelzebub, and those who 'goe the Primrose way to th'euerlasting Bonfire'.

There are a number of echoes from adjacent verses from the Sermon on the Mount in Act III; and a famous speech in V. v. contains several echoes from *Job* and the *Psalms*.[1]

The other main influence on the texture of the play is Seneca. Both the *Hercules Furens* and the *Agamemnon* appear to have left their marks on *Macbeth*. The echoes from the former play tend to come in pairs,[2] and as one such echo appears to be closer to the Latin than to Heywood's translation, it looks as though Shakespeare had read the original;[3] but, on the other hand, the echoes from the *Agamemnon* are clearly of the translation.[4] It is possible that Shakespeare re-read Seneca's plays with the intention of writing a more classical play than his previous tragedies. The Hercules

[1] Cf. Muir, op. cit., p. 160.
[2] ed. J. D. Wilson, p. xliii (quoting Grierson and Smith).
[3] ibid., II. ii. 59–63 N.
[4] Cf. K. Muir, N.Q. (1949), pp. 214–15.

who slays his own family in a fit of madness gave Shakespeare
some emotional parallels with his own hero. The healing powers
of sleep, the murderer's horrified re-awakening after the deed, the
sense of guilt, the feeling that all the oceans of the world would
not cleanse the blood from his hands, the contrast between the
tyrant and the good king all find expression in Seneca's play.[1]

In the *Agamemnon* Shakespeare found a prototype for Lady
Macbeth. The translation of the first chorus had been echoed in
Richard II, and there are many reminiscences of it in *Macbeth*.[2]

> No day to Scepters sure doth shine, that they might say,
> To morrow shall wee rule, as wee have done to day.
> One clod of croked care another bryngeth in,
> One hurly burly done, another doth begin: ...
> O how doth Fortune tosse and tomble in her wheele
> The staggring states of Kynges, that readdy bee to reele?
> Fayne woulde they dreaded bee, and yet not setled so
> When as they feared are, they feare, and lyve in woe.
> The silent Lady nyght so sweete to man and beast,
> Can not bestow on them her safe and quiet rest:
> Sleepe that doth overcome and breake the bonds of griefe,
> It cannot ease theyr heartes, nor mynister reliefe:
> What castell strongly buylt, what bulwarke, tower, or towne,
> Is not by mischyefes meanes, brought topsy turvye downe?
> What ramperd walles are not made weake by wicked warre?
> From stately courtes of Kings doth justice fly afarre: ...
> The bloudy Bellon those doth haunt with gory hand,
> Whose light and vaine conceipt in paynted pomp doth stand.
> And those Erinnys wood turmoyles with frensyes fits,
> That ever more in proud and hauty houses sits,
> Which ficle Fortunes hand in twinkling of an eye,
> From high and proude degre drives downe in dust to lye.
> Although that skyrmishe cease, no banners be displayed
> And though no wyles be wroughte and pollecy be stayed,
> Downe paysed with theyr waight the massy things do sinke.

This passage appears to have influenced several speeches in *Macbeth*—'When the Hurley-burley's done', 'To morrow and to morrow. . . . The way to dusty death', 'Can'st thou not Minister to a

---

[1] op. cit., 735–6, 1065–81, 1260, 1323.
[2] Cf. K. Muir, *N.Q.* (1949), pp. 214–15.

mind diseas'd', 'thy bloodie and inuisible Hand', 'Though Castles topple on their Warders heads',

> Hang out our Banners on the outward walls,
> ... our Castles strength,

Macbeth's tyranny springing from fear, and the numerous references to insomnia.

In the same play Clytemnestra's adage[1]—

> The safest path to mischiefe is by mischiefe open still—

is echoed by Macbeth:

> Things bad begun, make strong themselues by ill.

The Nurse's adage[2]—

> The thing he feares he doth augment who heapeth sinne to sinne—

might almost be taken as the epigraph of *Macbeth*. Finally it may be suggested that Cassandra's foreseeing of the future[3] in Act V has affinities with two memorable passages in *Macbeth*—the aside in which he describes the onset of temptation and the soliloquy of the visionary dagger:

> my prophesying spright
Did never yet disclose to mee so notable a sight:
I see the same, and am thereat, and busied in the broyle,
No vision fond fantasticall my senses doth beguile:
... The King in gorgyous royall robes on chayre of State doth sit,
And pranckt with pryde of Priams pomp of whom he conquerd it.
Put of this hostile weede, to him, (the Queene, his wyfe gan say,)
And of thy loving Lady wrought weare rather thys aray.
This garment knit. It makes mee loth, that shivering heere I
  stande.
O shall a King be murthered, by a banisht wretches hand? ...
The gubs of bloude downe dropping on the wynde shall powred
  be.

So Macbeth conceives the murder of Duncan:

> My Thought, whose *Murther* yet is but *fantasticall*,
> *Shakes* so my single *state* of Man,
> That Function is smother'd in surmise.

[1] I. 115.   [2] II. 71.   [3] Cf. Muir, N.Q. (1956), pp. 243–4.

In the later soliloquy he addresses the dagger:

> Art thou not, fatall *Vision*, sensible
> To feeling as to *sight*? or art thou but
> A Dagger of the Minde, a false Creation,
> Proceeding from the heat-oppressed Braine?
> *I see thee yet* . . .
> *Mine Eyes are made the fooles o' th' other Sences,*
> *Or else worth all the rest: I see thee still;*
> And on thy Blade, and Dudgeon, *Gouts of Blood,*
> Which was not so before.

It is possible that the vision of the imaginary dagger with its gouts of blood was suggested by Cassandra's vision of the murder of Agamemnon with 'gubs of bloude'. Perhaps even

> Shall blow the horrid deed in euery eye
> That teares shall drowne the winde

may be coloured by the last line of the above quotation and the words 'detestable deede' used by Cassandra a few lines later.

Shakespeare also drew on his own previous work for some of the detail of *Macbeth*.[1] It was natural that he should echo ideas and images from *Richard III*, for *Macbeth* is a more subtle form of the tragedy of a man who kills to win a throne. Both Macbeth and Richard are murderers and usurpers, both are cruel and treacherous tyrants, and both are called 'hell-hound'. Both suffer from insomnia as a result of their bad consciences; both use the image of wading through a sea of blood; both talk of sending their victims to heaven; and towards the end of both plays, before the last battle, the hero irritably keeps changing his mind.

More surprisingly there are a number of echoes from 2 *Henry VI*.[2] Both plays have witch scenes and equivocating prophecies; both mention 'Kerns and gallowglasses'; Suffolk counterfeits surprise after the murder of Gloucester, as Macbeth does after the murder of Duncan; the Cardinal on his death-bed behaves like Macbeth confronted by the ghost of Banquo; and, it has been suggested, both the Duchess of Gloucester and Queen Margaret have some resemblance to Lady Macbeth. Several images are repeated from the earlier play, and there is one striking verbal parallel:

[1] Cf. K. Muir, ed. *Macbeth*, pp. 195–6.
[2] Cf. G. Wilson Knight, *The New Adelphi* (1927).

He calles the King
And whispers to his pillow, as to him,
The secrets of his ouer-charged soule.

(III. ii. 374–6)

Foule whisp'rings are abroad: vnnaturall deeds
Do breed vnnaturall troubles: infected mindes
To their deafe pillowes will discharge their Secrets.

(V. i. 68–70)

Perhaps the theme of witchcraft called up the other associations.

The echoes from *Lucrece* are much more significant.[1] Murder, Shakespeare thought, was akin to lust and regicide to rape. *Lucrece* was his first serious attempt to analyse the psychology of crime. Tarquin's meditation before the deed, in which he exhibits a full consciousness of its wickedness and futility, resembles Macbeth's horror-struck realization of what he is about to do:

Those that much couet are with gaine so fond,
For what they haue not, that which they possesse
They scatter and vnloose it from their bond,
And so by hoping more they have but lesse,
Or gaining more, the profite of excesse
  Is but to surfet, and such griefes sustaine,
  That they proue banckrout in this poore-rich gain.

The ayme of all is but to nourse the life,
With honor, wealth, and ease, in wainyng age:
And in this ayme there is such thwarting strife,
That one for all, or all for one we gage:
As life for honour in fell battails rage,
  Honor for wealth, and oft that wealth doth cost
  The death of all, and altogether lost.

So that in ventring ill, we leaue to be
The things we are, for that which we expect:
And this ambitious foule infirmitie,
In hauing much torments vs with defect
Of that we haue; so then we doe neglect
  The thing we haue: and all for want of wit,
  Make something nothing, by augmenting it.

[1] Cf. M. C. Bradbrook, *Shakespeare Survey 4*, pp. 35–48.

What win I if I gaine the thing I seeke?
A dreame, a breath, a froth of fleeting ioy.
Who buies a minutes mirth to waile a weeke?
Or sels eternitie to get a toy? . . .
     Or what fond begger, but to touch the crowne,
     Would with the scepter straight be stroken down?

So Macbeth before the murder wishes not to lose the golden opinions he has earned and not to incur deep damnation at the prompting of ambition. At the end of the play he lacks the things which should accompany old age, 'Honor, Loue, Obedience, Troopes of Friends'.

Several critics have compared the setting of Duncan's murder with that of Lucrece's rape, so that we are not surprised when Macbeth himself compares his act to Tarquin's. The time of the rape is thus described:

Now stole vppon the time the dead of night,
When heauie sleep had closd vp mortall eyes:
No comfortable starre did lend his light,
No noise but Owles and Wolues death-boding cries;
Now serues the season that they may surprise
     The sillie Lambes: pure thoughts are dead and still,
     While Lust and Murder wake to staine and kill.

In *Macbeth* we have the owl shrieking, Murder alarumed by the wolf, and a night without stars. The couplet—

Who feares a sentence or an old mans saw
Shall by a painted cloth be kept in awe.

looks forward to Lady Macbeth's

     'Tis the Eye of Child-hood,
That feares a painted Deuill.

Tarquin's disputation between 'frozen conscience and hot-burning will' has been thought to resemble Lady Macbeth's temptation of her husband:

Vrging the worser sence for vantage still;
Which in a moment doth confound and kill
     All pure effects, and doth so farre proceede,
     That what is vile, shewes like a vertuous deede.

One of the recurrent images in *Macbeth*,[1] of winking at things too terrible for the eye, appears three times in *Lucrece*. Tarquin proposes to slay a groom to conceal his own crime, as Macbeth, following Holinshed's Donwald, murders the chamberlains. Lucrece speaks of 'the ocean of thy blood', and Macbeth fears that his bloodstained hand will incarnadine the multitudinous seas. The calling on darkness to conceal a crime is repeated by Lady Macbeth in her invocation of Night. Wolf, lamb, and treason are associated in the lines—

> Tis thou that execut'st the traytors treason:
> Thou sets the wolfe where he the lambe may get.

And the association is repeated in the scene between Malcolm and Macduff. Lucrece prays to Time to punish Tarquin:

> Let gastly shadowes his lewd eyes affright:
>> And the dire thought of his committed euill,
>> Shape euery bush a hideous shapelesse deuill.
> Disturbe his howres of rest with restlesse trances,
> Afflict him in his bed with bedred grones.

Here we get a forerunner of the terrible dreams that nightly shake Macbeth.

The richness of *Macbeth* depends partly on the fact that Shakespeare was making use of deeply rooted ideas and images—recalling his earliest experiments as a poet and dramatist, his school reading, and his long familiarity with the Bible. All these combined with the programme of reading he carried out for the specific purpose of writing the play. He may have read some of James I's works in order to study his patron's tastes, but his instinct led him to borrow only what he needed for his play. Not the least remarkable thing about Shakespeare's method is that one can always find a good poetic or dramatic reason for the inclusion of material apparently suggested by the demands of patronage.

[1] Cf. C. F. E. Spurgeon, *Shakespeare's Imagery*, p. 331.

❦ VII ❧

THE ROMAN PLAYS

(15) *Julius Caesar*

S HAKESPEARE'S use of North's translation of Plutarch has been studied many times, and there is little new to be said on the subject. He had read part, at least, of North as early as 1595, for there is a verbal echo of the first of the lives in his account of the amours of Theseus.[1] He had read the Life of Caesar, and may even have been considering a play on the subject by the time he wrote *Henry V*.[2] In 1599 he utilized the lives of Caesar, Antonius, and Brutus for the main incidents in *Julius Caesar*, but it is possible that the structure of the play owes something to a lost play. The quoting of 'Et tu, Brute' in the bad quarto of *3 Henry VI* (i.e. *The True Tragedie*) suggests that the words had already been used in a play about Caesar, for they have not been found in a non-dramatic source and bad quartos often incorporate lines and phrases from other plays.[3] In *The Massacre at Paris*, also a bad quarto, there is an allusion to Caesar's words before his assassination:[4]

> Yet *Caesar* shall goe forth.
> Let mean consaits, and baser men feare death,
> But they are pesants, I am Duke of *Guise*.

Nevertheless there are enough verbal echoes of Plutarch's three lives to make it reasonably certain that Shakespeare was mainly indebted to North. The first three acts draw upon all three lives, and the last two acts are chiefly based on the life of Brutus. Shakespeare follows North even in his mistakes (*Decius* Brutus, *Caius* Ligarius), but he omits, amplifies, and alters. It has often been pointed out that he takes considerable liberties with historical fact. There was a gap of four months between the triumph

[1] *M.N.D.* II. i. 77–80.   [2] *Henry V.* V. 26: IV. vii. 43.
[3] The words are not used in the authentic text.
[4] Marlowe, ed. Tucker Brooke, p. 474.

mentioned in the first scene and the feast of the Lupercal; and the disrobing of Caesar's images by the Tribunes took place later at the time of his projected Coronation. In the play these widely-scattered events take place on the same day. According to Plutarch, Brutus made two speeches after the assassination, one in the Capitol and one in the market-place, and Antony did not make his speech until the following day, after the reading of the will. Shakespeare telescopes Brutus's two speeches into one, and makes it more successful with his audience, so that Antony's triumph shall be the greater. Antony's speech, moreover, is delivered immediately after Brutus's, and the reading of the will becomes part of the speech. Octavius did not, in fact, arrive in Rome until some weeks later. Shakespeare omits his prolonged quarrels with Antony before the setting up of the Triumvirate.

The quarrel scene is a typical example of Shakespeare's method of manipulating the sources for dramatic effect. According to Plutarch, Brutus 'did condemne and noted Lucius Pella' on the day *after* the quarrel with Cassius; and Cassius was annoyed, not because he knew the man, or had pleaded for him, but because he had let off with a caution two of his friends attainted and convicted of similar offences, that is, of 'robbery and pilfery'. Shakespeare makes the offence bribery and opens the scene with a reference to it. The interference of Phaonius, the counterfeit cynic philosopher, which brings the first quarrel to an end, is utilized by Shakespeare; but whereas Phaonius merely quotes Homer—

> My lords, I pray you hearken both to me,
> For I haue seen moe yeares than suchie three—

Shakespeare's intruder is made a poet who rhymes vilely:

> Loue, and be Friends, as two such men should bee.
> For I haue seene more yeeres, I'me sure, than yee.

But the quarrel is over by the time he comes on the scene. Later in the scene Shakespeare twice mentions Portia's death—though the first account was probably meant to supersede the second—and this information, taken from the very end of the life of Brutus, is an effective conclusion to the quarrel. At the end of the scene Shakespeare introduces the episode of the ghost; he transfers the appearance from Abydos to Sardis; he makes the apparition Caesar's ghost, and not merely Brutus's evil spirit; and whereas in the source Brutus is 'thinking of weighty matters', in the play he has been listening to Lucius's song. The two battles in which Cassius and Brutus lost their lives are telescoped into one.

Equally significant are the changes made by Shakespeare in the characters of the source. He emphasizes Caesar's physical weaknesses and his *hubris*, but at the same time he makes him more noble than he is in Plutarch's life. For example, Caesar's reason for refusing to read Artemidorus's schedule, 'What touches vs our selfe, shall be last serued', is Shakespeare's invention. According to Plutarch,

> *Caesar* tooke it of him, but coulde neuer read it, though he many times attempted it, for the number of people that did salute him.

Brutus is given some humanizing touches—his care for Lucius, for example,—but he is made self-righteous, self-deluded, and overbearing. Casca's character, on which depends much of the effectiveness of the report of the scene in which Caesar is offered a crown, is largely Shakespeare's invention—the historical Casca was not ignorant of Greek.

Although Shakespeare borrows numerous phrases and ideas from North's prose he followed it less closely than he was to do in *Antony and Cleopatra* and *Coriolanus*. The most sustained borrowing is the scene between Brutus and Portia

> I being, O *Brutus* (says she) the daughter of *Cato*, was maried vnto thee, not to be thy bedfellow and companion in bed and at borde onelie, like a harlot, but to be partaker also with thee, of thy good and euill fortune. Now for thy selfe, I can finde no cause of fault in thee touching our matche; but for my part, how may I shewe my duetie towardes thee, and how much I would do for thy sake, if I cannot constantlie beare a secret mischaunce or griefe with thee, which requireth secrecie and fidelity? I confesse, that a womans wit commonly is too weake to keepe a secret safely: but yet, *Brutus*, good education, and the companie of vertuous men, haue some power to reforme the defect of nature. And for my selfe, I haue this benefit moreouer: that I am the daughter of *Cato*, and wife of *Brutus*. This notwithstanding, I did not trust to any of these things before: vntill that now I haue found by experience, that no paine nor griefe whatsoeuer can ouercome me. With these wordes she shewed him her wounde on her thigh, and told him what she had done to proue her self.

Shakespeare even here borrows few of North's actual words. He introduces the fine touch of making Cato the climax of Portia's appeal, he cuts out the sentence about the effects of education—the Senecan dramatist, Sir William Alexander, characteristically used it in his version of the scene—he inserts the image 'suburbs of your good pleasure' with its allusion to contemporary London, and he reveals Portia's wound only at the end.

> *Por.:* . . . Within the Bond of Marriage, tell me *Brutus*,
>   Is it excepted, I should know no Secrets
>   That appertaine to you? Am I your Selfe,
>   But as it were in sort, or limitation?
>   To keepe with you at Meales, comfort your Bed,
>   And talke to you sometimes? Dwell I but in the Suburbs
>   Of your good pleasure? If it be no more,
>   *Portia* is *Brutus*' Harlot, not his Wife.
> *Bru.:* You are my true and honourable Wife,
>   As deere to me, as are the ruddy droppes
>   That visit my sad heart.
> *Por.:* If this were true, then should I know this secret.
>   I graunt I am a Woman; but withall,
>   A Woman that Lord *Brutus* tooke to Wife:
>   I graunt I am a Woman; but withall,
>   A Woman well reputed: *Cato*'s Daughter.
>   Thinke you, I am no stronger then my Sex
>   Being so Father'd, and so Husbanded?
>   Tell me your Counsels, I will not disclose 'em:
>   I haue made strong proofe of my Constancie,
>   Giuing my selfe a voluntary wound
>   Heere, in the Thigh: Can I beare that with patience,
>   And not my Husbands Secrets?

That Shakespeare read Appian's *Auncient Historie and exquisite Chronicle of the Romanes warres, both Ciuile and Foren*, a translation of which was published in 1578, is not generally admitted; but there are several details he seems to have derived from this source. There is a reference to Caesar's falling sickness immediately after his refusal of the crown.[1] Appian tells us that the conspirators killed Caesar 'eyther for enuie . . . or as they said, for the loue of their countreys libertie'; and that Brutus acted 'either as an ingrate man . . . or very desirous of his countrys libertie, preferring

[1] *Shakespeare's Appian* (1956), ed. E. Schanzer, p. 14.

it before all other things, or that he was descended of the auntient Brutus'.[1] Plutarch, however, suggests that the conspirators other than Brutus were motivated by 'some private malice or envy' and Shakespeare refers more than once to this motive.

Appian uses the phrase that on the day of his assassination 'Caesar came forth', and Shakespeare uses it several times in the corresponding scenes.[2] Kittredge calls attention to Brutus's words:

> I suppose verye *Romaines* indeede wyll rather choose certaine death, as they haue oft done, than by an othe to abyde willing seruitude.

But there is little evidence that these influenced Shakespeare.[3] Antony's speech at Caesar's funeral has no great resemblance to the one given in the play, but, as Mr Schanzer has pointed out,[4] Shakespeare may have derived hints from Appian's account of Antony's theatrical delivery of his oration. Indeed, Shakespeare's character has little relation to Plutarch's 'plaine man, without subtilty' and considerable resemblance to Appian's character, loyal, histrionic, emotional, ruthless, and cunning. Appian's description of Antony's uncovering of Caesar's body seems to have suggested Shakespeare's account:[5]

> Then falling into moste vehement affections, vncouered *Caesars* body, holding vp his vesture with a speare, cut with the woundes, and redde with the bloude of the chiefe Ruler.

Shakespeare similarly makes Antony say:

> Kinde Soules, what weepe you when you but behold
> Our *Caesars* Vesture wounded?

It is striking that Appian and Shakespeare both use the word *vesture* and speak of its being wounded or cut with wounds. Plutarch describes the same incident but without the verbal parallel. Antony took 'Caesar's gown all bloody in his hand . . . shewing what a number of cuts and holes it had upon it'. He 'vnfolded before the whole assembly the bloody garments of the dead, thrust through in many places with their swords'.

---

[1] *Shakespeare's Appian* (1956), ed. E. Schanzer, pp. 15–16.
[2] p. 19. Cf. II. i. 194; II. ii. 10, 28, 48, 50.
[3] p. 37. It has been suggested (not very plausibly) that Brutus's oration at Caesar's funeral was influenced by Hamlet's defence of his assassination of the King in *The Hystorie of Hamblet*. As far as we know this translation was published after *Julius Caesar*, though Shakespeare may have read Belleforest in the original.
[4] ibid., p. xx.   [5] p. 44.

The people carry the litter[1]

> as an holye thing, to be buried in an holy place . . . they brought
> hym againe into the common place . . . and there . . . they
> buryed the body, and abode al night about the fyre.

Plutarch mentions that the mob burnt Caesar's body 'in the midst
of the most holy places'. In the play one of the citizens cries,
'Wee'l burne his body in the holy place'—a line which seems to
combine hints from the two sources.

Antony's prophecy of civil strife may have been suggested[2] by
an earlier passage in which, as the marginal gloss puts it, '*Antonie*
prophecieth'. When he is commanded to leave the Senate, before
the crossing of the Rubicon, he

> lept out as a man by inspiration, forespeaking warres, murders,
> attendures, banishments, spoyles, and all other mischiefe to
> come vpon them, protesting greate execrations to them that
> were the cause of it.

Finally it may be worth mentioning that Appian and Shakespeare
agree on the spelling of Calphurnia's name: North usually spells it
'Calpurnia'.

Two plays have recently been put forward as possible sources
of *Julius Caesar*. *Caesar's Revenge* was acted by students at Oxford
before it was published in 1606 or 1607. Mr E. Schanzer has suggested[3] that it was one of the sources of *Julius Caesar*. Certainly
from its style it would seem to have been written between 1587
and 1595, but it is not unknown for Oxford poets to write in a
style belonging to a previous decade, and we cannot therefore be
certain that Shakespeare was the debtor. If an Oxford author had
seen a performance of *Julius Caesar* soon after it was written he
might on the model of earlier plays and with the help of Appian
have composed his own tragedy. In that case his memories of
Shakespeare's play would account for the resemblances pointed
out by Mr Schanzer, though it does seem more probable that
Caesar's Revenge was written first.

As Mr Schanzer says, the play, like *Julius Caesar*, contains three
tragedies—the tragedy of Caesar's *hubris* that ends with the assassination, the Elizabethan revenge tragedy, and the psychological
tragedy of Brutus. In *Caesar's Revenge* the revenge tragedy predominates; in *Julius Caesar* the tragedy of Brutus predominates,

---

[1] pp. 45-6.   [2] Sig. N2ᵛ.   [3] *N.Q.* (1954), pp. 196-7.

though the other themes are both present. The hubristic tragedy of Caesar's fall is itself an inheritance from the plays of Muret, Grévin, and Garnier, though the author of *Caesar's Revenge* and Shakespeare himself may well have been influenced by one or other of the lost English and Latin Caesar plays. The treatment of Brutus's tragedy in *Caesar's Revenge* resembles Shakespeare's

in being psychological, consisting in Brutus's mental torments which the memories of his ingratitude to Caesar make him suffer. Just before the first appearance to him of Caesar's ghost Brutus exclaims in soliloquy:

> Caesar upbraves my sad ingratitude.
> He saved my life in sad Pharsalian fields,
> That I in Senate house might work his death.
> O this remembrance now doth wound my soul
> More than my poniard did his bleeding heart.

And upon the ghost's appearance Brutus expresses his longing for death. . . . Caesar's ghost . . . foretells Brutus: 'Thine own right hand shall work my wish'd revenge', which may have suggested the words that Shakespeare puts into the mouth of his Brutus at the discovery of Cassius's suicide:

> O Julius Caesar, thou art mighty yet!
> Thy spirit walks abroad, and turns our swords
> In our own proper entrails.

At the end of the play Brutus appears, still pursued by the ghost, and kills himself in despair.

Mr Schanzer suggests that Brutus's remorse, the identification of the evil spirit with Caesar's ghost, the linking of the suicide of the conspirators with the ghost's personal presence on the battlefield, and Brutus's melancholy may all have influenced Shakespeare's treatment. Finally he argues that since Antony's prophecy over the body of Caesar, with its grim picture of the horrors of civil war, is not borne out by what actually happens—the battle is not marked by excessive slaughter—the prophecy may have been influenced by similar speeches in *Caesar's Revenge*. Discord, from hell, and Caesar's ghost appear at the end of the play to express their satisfaction at the slaughter:

> I, now my longing hopes haue their desire,
> The world is nothing but a massie heape
> Of bodies slayne, the Sea a lake of blood.

So Antony refers to

> *Caesars* Spirit ranging for Reuenge,
> With *Ate* by his side, come hot from Hell;

and he concludes

> That this foule deede, shall smell aboue the earth
> With Carrion men, groaning for Buriall.

Shakespeare probably knew Kyd's *Cornelia,* translated from the French Senecan tragedy of Garnier. Here, too, he would have found descriptions of the horrors of civil war, with particular emphasis on unburied bodies. In the first chorus Kyd speaks of 'bloody warre (of other woes the worst)'; Emonye is said to be great 'with Souldiers bodies that were buried there'; and

> in the flowred Meades dead men were found;
> Falling as thick (through warlike crueltie)
> As eares of Corne for want of husbandry.

In Act II Cicero, describing the wars of Marius and Sulla, says they

> Spilt such store of blood in euery streete,
> As there were none but dead-men to be seene.

In Act IV Cassius complains of Rome:

> Thy chyldren 'gainst thy children thou hast arm'd . . .
> Now o're our bodies (tumbled vp on heapes,
> Lyke cocks of Hay when Iuly sheares the field)
> Thou build'st thy kingdom . . .

Italy and other countries

> Are full of dead mens bones by *Caesar* slayne.

In Act V Discord and Bellona urge on the slaughter. There is a stench of blood, dismembered bodies,

> And wretched heapes lie mourning of theyr maimes;
> Here horse and man (o'erturnd) for mercy cryde,
> With hands extended to the merciles,
> That stopt their eares, and would not heare a word,
> But put them all (remorceles) to the sword.

This same description uses the words *ranging* and *confines*, both to be found in Antony's prophecy.

It is also worth mentioning that Kyd's Caesar displays the same bombastic characteristics as in *Caesar's Revenge*, and he refers to himself in the third person. His remark about the desirability of

sudden death, though recorded by Plutarch, leads on to a sentiment
to be found also in Shakespeare's play.

> That death that comes vnsent for or vnseene,
> And suddainly doth take vs at vnware,
> Mee thinks is sweetest; And if heauen were pleas'd,
> I could desire that I might die so well.
> The feare of euill doth afflict vs more,
> Then th' euill it selfe, though it be nere so sore.

So Shakespeare's Caesar says:

> Cowards dye many times before their deaths,
> The valiant neuer taste of death but once.

Finally, there would seem to be some resemblances between
Cassius's sounding of Decius Brutus and his temptation of Marcus
Brutus and of Casca in *Julius Caesar*.

Cassius in both plays contrasts the degeneracy of the Romans of
his day with those of the past, and says he would rather die than
see Rome enslaved; Decius says that although he loves Caesar
dearly he would be avenged on him if he were determined to reign,
but he declares that Caesar is not yet a king and that he is not
bloody. So Marcus confesses that he loves Caesar well and that he
knows 'no personal cause to spurn at him'. Miss Joan Rees thinks[1]
that the inconsistency of Kyd's Caesar, both boastful and heroic,
may have stimulated Shakespeare to explore the deeper implica-
tions of the character.

Another minor source has recently been pointed out by Dr
Harold Brooks.[2] He has shown that for the warning of Artemi-

---

[1] *M.L.R.* (1955), pp. 135–41.
[2] Cf. *Julius Caesar* ed. T. S. Dorsch. Douglas Bush *M.L.N.* (1937), pp. 407–8,
suggests 'What touches vs our selfe, shall be last seru'd' might be a development of
Elyot's attribution of Caesar's failure to read the paper to his being 'radicate in
pride' (*The Gouernour*, II, v). J. C. Maxwell points out, *N.Q.* (1956), p. 147, that in
Elyot's chapter on flattery (II. xiv) we have a detailed account of how

> he which entendeth to take the fierse and mighty lyon pytcheth his haye or
> nette in the woode, among great trees and thornes, where as is the most
> haunte of the lyon, that beinge blynded with the thickenes of the couerte, or
> he be ware, he may sodainely tumble into the nette.

This method is compared to that employed by 'Subtyll flaterers', who achieve their
ends by a 'fayned seueritie' and entrap their victims 'the rather by cause this maner
of flatery is mooste vnlyke to that which is communely used'. So Decius Brutus, in
describing how Caesar is flattered by being told he hates flatterers (II. i. 203–8)
mentions that he

> loues to heare
> That Vnicornes may be betray'd with Trees,
> And Beares with Glasses, Elephants with Holes,
> Lyons with Toyles, and men with Flatterers.

dorus, containing the names of the conspirators, and for Caesar's reply to the Soothsayer, Shakespeare was probably indebted to Caesar's complaint in *The Mirror for Magistrates*:

> There met mee by the way a *Romayne* good,
> Presenting mee a scrole of euery name:
> And all their whole deuise that sought my bloud,
> That presently would execute the same.
> But I supposde that for some suit hee came,
> I heedelesse bare this scrole in my left hand,
> And others more, till leasure, left vnscand,
> Which in my pocket afterwards they fand.
>
> *Spurina* as I came at sacrifizes was,
> Nere to the place where I was after slayne:
> Of whose diuinings I did litle passe,
> Though hee to warne mee oft before was fayne.
> My hauty hart these warnings all disdayne.
> (Quod I) the Ides of Marche bee come, yet harme is none.
> (Quod hee) the Ides of Marche be come, yet th'ar not gone.

In Plutarch's account the corresponding words are:

> The Ides of Marche be come: So be they, softly aunswered the Soothsayer, but yet are they not past.

The Soothsayer's reply in *Julius Caesar*, 'but not gone', is closer to *The Mirror for Magistrates*, though Appian has 'but they be not yet gone'.

Shakespeare certainly drew on a number of different sources for his account of the portents accompanying Caesar's assassination. It will be convenient to begin with the corresponding passage in *Hamlet*.[1]

> The graues stood tenantlesse, and the sheeted dead
> Did squeake and gibber in the Roman streets;
> As starres with traines of fier, and dewes of blood,
> Disasters in the sunne; and the moist starre
> Vpon whose influence *Neptunes* Empier stands,
> Was sicke almost to doomesday with eclipse.

Here we have five portents mentioned—ghosts in the streets of Rome, stars with trains of fire, dews of blood, disasters in the sun,

---

[1] Cf. K. Muir, *N.Q.* (1948), pp. 54–5.

and an eclipse of the moon. In *Julius Caesar* itself we have thunder and lightning, an earthquake, a tempest dropping fire, a slave with a burning hand, a lion in the Capitol, 'Men, all in fire' walking the streets, an owl hooting at noonday in the market-place, 'exhalations, whizzing in the ayre', Calpurnia's dream, a lioness whelping in the streets, ghosts, a war in the heavens 'Which drizl'd blood vpon the Capitoll', comets, a beast without a heart, and the warning of the Soothsayer.

Altogether there are sixteen or seventeen portents and it is interesting to compare Plutarch's account:

For, touching the fires in the element, and spirites running vp and downe in the night, and also the solitarie birds to be seene at noone dayes sitting in the great market place: are not all these signes perhaps worth the noting, in such a wonderfull chaunce as happened? But *Strabo* the *Philosopher* writeth, that diuers men were seene going vp and downe in fire: and furthermore, that there was a slaue of the souldiers, that did cast a maruellous burning flame out of his hande, insomuch as they that saw it, thought he had bene burnt, but when the fire was out, it was found he had no hurt. *Caesar* selfe also doing sacrifice vnto the Gods, found that one of the beastes which was sacrificed had no hart: and that was a straunge thing in nature, how a beast could liue without a hart.

Plutarch proceeds to describe the warning of the Soothsayer and Calpurnia's dreams of Caesar being slain and the falling of the pinnacle on his house. At the end of his life of Caesar, Plutarch mentions other portents:

Againe, of signes in the element, the great comet which seuen nightes together was seene very bright after *Caesars* death, the eight night after was neuer seene more. Also the brightnes of the sunne was darkened, the which all that yeare through rose very pale, and shined not out, whereby it gaue but small heate: therefore the ayer being very clowdy and darke, by the weaknes of the heate could not come forth, did cause the earth to bring forth but raw and vnrype fruit, which rotted before it could rype.

Of the seventeen portents Plutarch thus mentions only nine and he does not state that the bird in the Capitol was an owl. For the remaining portents Shakespeare had recourse to other sources. In

o   197

Ovid's *Metamorphoses* (XV) there is a long account of the portents accompanying Caesar's murder, thus translated by Golding:

For battels fighting in the clouds with crasshing armour flew,
And dreadfull trumpets sounded in the aire, and hornes eeke
  blew,
As warning men before hand of the mischiefe that did brew.
And *Phoebus* also looking dim did cast a drowzie light
Upon the earth, which seem'd likewise to be in sorie plight:
From vnderneath amid the starres, brands oft seemd burning
  bright
It often rained drops of blood. The morning starre lookd blew,
And was besotted heere and there with speckes of rustie
  hew.
The moone had also spots of bloud. The screechowle sent from
  hell
Did with hir tune vnfortunate in euerie corner yel.
Salt teares from iuorie images in sundrie places fell,
And in the chappels of the gods was singing heard, and words
Of threatning. Not a sacrifice one signe of good affoords,
But great turmoile to be at hand hir hartstrings doo declare,
And when the beast is ripped vp, the inwards headlesse are.
About the Court, and euerie house, and churches in the nights
The dogs did howle, and euerie where appeered ghastlie sprights,
And with an earthquake shaken was the towne.

Ovid thus mentions several of the portents to be found also in Plutarch and several of the Shakespearian portents which are not in Plutarch—the war in heaven causing dews of blood, the earthquake, the owl—and his sentence about the moon may have suggested the lunar eclipse to Shakespeare.

Virgil in the first book of the *Georgics* likewise lists a number of portents at the time of Caesar's murder:

Quum caput obscura nitidum ferrugine texit
Impiaque aeternam timuerunt saecula noctem . . .
Armorum sonitum toto Germania coelo
Audiit; insolitis tremuerunt motibus Alpes.
Vox quoque per lucos vulgo exaudita silentes
Ingens; et simulacra modis pallentia miris
Visa sub obscurum noctis; pecudesque locutae;

198

Infandum! sistunt amnes, terraeque dehiscunt,
Et maestum illacrimat templis ebur, aeraque sudant . . .
Per noctem resonare lupis ululantibus urbes.
Non alias coelo ceciderunt plura sereno
Fulgura; nec diri toties arsere cometae.

Here we have an eclipse of the sun, earthquake, ghosts, wolves howling in towns, thunder and lightning, and comets. The thunder and lightning may have been suggested to Shakespeare by this passage, and the wolves may have suggested the lion. It is probable, however, that Shakespeare was indebted to yet another passage: Lucan's description of the portents which preceded the march on Rome after Caesar had crossed the Rubicon. Marlowe's translation probably appeared too late for Shakespeare to have made use of it, but it will be convenient to quote from it:

> Strange sights appear'd, the angry threatning gods
> Fill'd both the earth and seas with prodegies;
> Great store of strange and vnknown stars were seene
> Wandering about the North, and rings of fire
> Flie in the ayre, and dreadfull bearded stars,
> And Commets that presage the fal of kingdoms.
> The flattering skie gliter'd in often flames,
> And sundry fiery meteors blaz'd in heauen:
> Now spearlike, long; now like a spreading torch
> Lightning in silence stole forth without clouds,
> And from the northren climat snatching fier
> Blasted the Capitoll: The lesser stars
> Which wont to run their course through empty night
> At noone day mustered; *Phoebe* having fild
> Her meeting hornes to match her brothers light,
> Strooke with th' earths suddaine shadow waxed pale,
> *Titan* himselfe throand in the midst of heauen,
> His burning chariot plung'd in sable cloudes,
> And whelm'd the world in darknesse, making men
> Dispaire of day . . .
> Crownes fell from holy statues, ominous birds
> Defil'd the day, and wilde beastes were seene,
> Leauing the woods, lodge in the streetes of Rome . . .
> Soules quiet and appeas'd sight from their graues,
> Clashing of armes was heard in vntrod woods,
> Shrill voices schright and ghoasts incounter men.

Lucan describes other portents, including prodigious births and a sacrificial beast with strange entrails. It will be seen that he has the most striking lunar eclipse, and his lines are perhaps closest to the phrase 'stars with trains of fire'. He also provides in the reference to wild beasts in the streets of Rome the closest parallel to the lion in the Capitol. It should be mentioned, however, that Plutarch describes how Cassius's lions were let loose at the siege of Megara.[1]

[1] It should be added that Appian describes Calphurnia's dream in which she saw Caesar 'all to be goared with bloude, and therefore stopped hys going forth. In making sacrifices, manye fearefull tokens appeared, wherfore he determined to haue sent *Antony* to dissolue the Senate.' Decimus persuades Caesar to go in person to dissolve it; and when he arrives there and makes the customary sacrifices 'there was no harte, or as some say, no head of the entrailes'. The Diviner warns Caesar that this betokens death: 'he smiled and sayde, so it was in Spaine, when I ouerthrewe *Pompey*'. Caesar asks the Diviner to sacrifice again, with no better result. *Caesar's Revenge* seems to display a direct knowledge of Appian, though the portents mentioned in III. vi. comprise not merely Calphurnia's dream and a beast without a heart, but also the conjunction of Mars and Saturn, and ghosts:

> Which fill the silent woods, with groning cries:
> The hoarse Night-rauen tunes the chearles voyce,
> And calls the bale-full Owle and howling Dog
> To make a consort.

J. Dover Wilson refers to the portents mentioned by Nashe in *Christs Tears* (ed. McKerrow, ii. 60–2) preceding the Fall of Jerusalem; and T. S. Dorsch refers to Dekker, *Canaan's Calamitie* (ed. Grosart, i. 13 ff.); but I can find no evidence that Shakespeare made use of either.

A. Boecker, *A Probable Italian Source of Shakespeare's 'Julius Caesar'* (1913), argued that Shakespeare was influenced by Orlando Pescetti's *Il Cesare* (1594), but his arguments (and those of Sarrazin, *Eng. Stud.* xlvi, pp. 347 ff.) have been dismissed or ignored by later scholars. It is, of course, possible that Pescetti's influence was indirect, through a lost English play, but some of the parallels are striking. Calpurnia fears, as Shakespeare's Brutus hopes, that the death of Caesar will be performed in a theatre:

> Ahi pur, ch'anzi a gli Euripidi non porga
> Materia, onde risuonino i teatri
> Ne'secoli avvenir le sue sventure.

As in Shakespeare's play it is Cassius who urges that Antony should be killed, Brutus arguing that this deed would take away their reputation for disinterestedness and make them murderers, and that in any case Antony, a mere limb, would be powerless after Caesar's death:

> S'ad altri, oltre al Tiranno, darem morte,
> Si stimerà dal volgo, che le cose
> Sempre stravolge, e falsamente espone,
> Che non disio di liberar la patria,
> Ma privato odio, e brama di vendetta
> A ciò sospinti n'abbia, e di quell'opra,
> Onde da noi s'attende eterna fama,
> N'acquisterem vergogna, e biasmo eterno . .
> Col troncar della testa all'altre membra
> Troncasi ogni vigore, ogni possanza.

After the assassination Brutus addresses the conspirators:

> Ma scorriam per la terra,
> O voi, che fidelissimi compagni,

start

(16) *Antony and Cleopatra*

The main source of *Antony and Cleopatra* is, of course, Plutarch's Life of Antonius. Shakespeare's portrait of his hero is very close to Plutarch's, much closer, indeed, than his Antony in the earlier play. He made use of almost every incident in the later years of Antony's life, except the long, absorbing, but irrelevant, account of the Parthian campaign. One passage, contrasting Antony's present luxuriousness with his former powers of endurance, is taken from Plutarch's account of an earlier campaign. Another passage used by Shakespeare, describing the first meeting of the two lovers, refers to events before the opening of the play. Both these flash-backs are exceptionally full of verbal reminiscences, as a comparison will show:

. . . and moreouer sent *Hircius* and *Pansa*, then Consuls, to driue *Antonius* out of Italy. These two Consuls together with *Caesar*, who also had an armye, went against *Antonius* that beseeged the citie of *Modena*, and there ouerthrew him in battell: but both the Consuls were slaine there. *Antonius* flying vpon this overthrowe, fell into great miserie all at once: but the chiefest want of all other, and that pinched him most, was famine. Howbeit he was of such a strong nature, that by pacience he would ouercome any adversitie, and the heauier fortune lay vpon him, the more constant shewed he himself. . . . It was a wonderful example to the souldiers, to see *Antonius* that was brought vp in all fine-nesse and superfluity, so easily to drinke puddle water, and to eate wild fruites and rootes: and moreouer it is reported, that euen as they passed the Alpes, they did eate the barkes of trees, and such beasts, as neuer man tasted of their flesh before.

Mi siete stati all'onarata impresa
Con le coltella in mano,
Del Tirannico sangue ancor stillanti
E co' pilei su l'aste
E'l popolo di Marte
Chiamiamo a libertade.

The conspirators cry:

Libertà, libertà, morto è il Tiranno,
Libera è Roma, e rotto è il giogo indegno.

(cf. *J.C.* III. i. 78–80, 106–11.)

Anthony,

Leaue thy lasciuious Vassailes. When thou once
Was beaten from *Modena*, where thou slew'st
Hirsius, and *Pansa* Consuls, at thy heele
Did Famine follow, whom thou fought'st against,
(Though daintily brought vp) with patience more
Than Sauages could suffer. Thou did'st drinke
The stale of Horses, and the gilded Puddle
Which Beasts would cough at. Thy pallat then did daine
The roughest Berry, on the rudest Hedge.
Yea, like the Stagge, when Snow the Pasture sheets,
The barkes of Trees thou brows'd. On the Alpes,
It is reported thou did'st eate strange flesh,
Which some did dye to looke on: And all this
(It wounds thine Honor that I speake it now)
Was borne so like a Soldiour, that thy cheeke
So much as lank'd not.

The Cydnus passage is put into the mouth of Enobarbus at the
moment in the play when Antony is to marry Octavia and apparently to leave Cleopatra for ever. The tribute of the unromantic
soldier to the Queen's enchantment, driving him to conceits not
to be found in the source, is a masterly dramatic stroke.

Therefore when she was sent vnto by diuers letters, both from
Antonius him selfe, and also from his frendes, she made so light
of it and mocked *Antonius* so much, that she disdained to set
forward otherwise, but to take her barge in the riuer of *Cydnus*,
the poop whereof was of gold, the sailes of purple, and the
owers of siluer, which kept stroke in rowing after the sounde
of the musicke of flutes, howboyes, cithernes, violls, and such
other instruments as they played vpon in the barge. And now
for the person of her selfe: she was layed vnder a pauillion of
cloth of gold of tissue, apparelled and attired like the goddesse
Venus, commonly drawne in picture: and hard by her, on either
hand of her, pretie faire boyes apparelled as painters doe set
forth god *Cupide*, with litle fannes in their hands, with the which
they fanned wind vpon her. Her ladies and gentlewomen also,
the fairest of them were apparelled like the nymphes *Nereides*
(which are the mermaides of the waters) and like the *Graces*,
some stearing the helme, others tending the tackle and ropes of
the barge, out of the which there came a wonderfull passing

sweete sauor of perfumes, that perfumed the wharfes side, pes-
tered with innumerable multitudes of people. Some of them
followed the barge all alongest the riuers side: others also ranne
out of the citie to see her comming in. So that in th' end, there
ranne such multitudes of people one after an other to see her,
that *Antonius* was left post alone in the market place, in his
Imperiall seate to geue audience: and there went a rumor in the
peoples mouthes, that the goddesse *Venus* was come to play
with the god *Bacchus*, for the generall good of all *Asia*.

Eno.:   I will tell you.
        The Barge she sat in, like a burnisht Throne
        Burnt on the water: the Poope was beaten Gold,
        Purple the Sailes: and so perfumed that
        The Windes were Loue-sicke with them. The Owers
            were Siluer,
        Which to the tune of Flutes kept stroke, and made
        The water which they beate to follow faster;
        As amorous of their strokes. For her owne person,
        It beggerd all discription, she did lye
        In her Pauillion, cloth of Gold, of Tissue,
        O're-picturing that Venus, where we see
        The fancie out-worke Nature. On each side her,
        Stood pretty Dimpled Boyes, like smiling Cupids,
        With diuers coulour'd Fannes whose winde did seeme,
        To glowe the delicate cheekes which they did coole,
        And what they vndid did.
Agrip.:   Oh rare for *Anthony*.
Eno.:   Her Gentlewomen, like the Nereides,
        So many Mer-maides tended her i' th' eyes,
        And made their bends adornings. At the Helme
        A seeming Mer-maide steeres: the Silken Tackle,
        Swell with the touches of those Flower-soft hands,
        That yarely frame the office. From the Barge
        A strange inuisible perfume hits the sense
        Of the adiacent Wharfes. The Citty cast
        Her people out vpon her: and *Anthony*
        Enthron'd i' th' Market-place, did sit alone
        Whistling to th' ayre: which but for vacancie,
        Had gone to gaze on *Cleopatra* too.
        And made a gap in Nature.

The vivid opening lines are an addition of the poet, and it has been said that it 'gathers the vision into one whole which puts it imperishably before the mind's eye'.[1] The second addition describes the sails, and the third, the oars. As Mr W. A. Edwards remarks:[2]

Two things strike us at once about them: that Shakespeare is indulging in hyperboles so fantastic that we think of Donne; and that the additions contrive to diffuse a tone of luxury and sensuousness throughout the passage—love-sick winds, amorous water, the dimpled boys smiling, delicate cheeks, and a few lines later, 'flower-soft' hands.

Mr Middleton Murry suggests[3] that in these additions and in the last three lines of the passage

the successive elements—the winds, the water, the air—are represented all as succumbing to the enchantment of love which breathes from the great Queen and her burning barge; and by this varied return on a single motive North's inconsequential panorama is given an organic unity.

It will be noted that Shakespeare omits all the musical instruments except the flutes,[4] lest the more masculine howboys and viols should break the atmosphere of love and sensuousness. The fantastic hyperboles have the effect of showing that Cleopatra beggars all description. It should be added that the passage gains enormously from its position in the play. It is designed to remind the audience of Cleopatra's powers of enchantment at the moment when Antony is apparently leaving her for good.

The character of Enobarbus is virtually Shakespeare's creation. Plutarch tells us little about him except that

he being sicke of an agewe when he went and took a litle boate to go to *Caesars* campe, *Antonius* was very sory for it, but yet he sent after him all his caryage, trayne, and men: and the same *Domitius*, as though he gaue him to vnderstand that he repented his open treason, he died immediatly after.

This was before the Battle of Actium. In the play Enobarbus refuses to desert even after this battle. It is not until the end of Act 3 that he decides to leave his master. He is still present when Antony says farewell to his servants (IV. 2), and Antony's commendation

---

[1] J. M. Murry, *Countries of the Mind*, ii. p. 11.   [2] *Plagiarism* (1933), p. 110.
[3] op. cit., p. 12.   [4] W. A. Edwards, op. cit., p. 112.

of their loyalty has therefore a note of unconscious irony. Shakespeare makes Enobarbus die, not of an ague, but of a broken heart.

Plutarch mentions that Antonius was reputed to be descended from Hercules, that there was a rumour after his meeting with Cleopatra that Venus was come to play with Bacchus 'for the general good of all Asia', and that Cleopatra wore the apparel of the goddess Isis. Shakespeare makes use of these points indirectly. Antony refers to the death of Hercules (IV. xii. 43) when he is himself meditating suicide, the mysterious music is said to signify the departure of Hercules, Cleopatra is termed 'our terrene moon' (though Dr Hotson believes[1] this refers to the Egyptian fleet), and in the last scene she repudiates 'the fleeting moon'.

One scene in the play, where Seleucus accuses Cleopatra of lying about the amount of her treasure, is sometimes misinterpreted by commentators. Plutarch makes it perfectly clear—and this was certainly Shakespeare's intention also—that Cleopatra is acting a part:

> Then she sodainly altered her speache, and prayed him to pardon her, as though she were affrayed to dye, and desirous to liue . . . and so he tooke his leaue of her, supposing he had deceiued her, but in deede he was deceiued him selfe.

This is reinforced by the marginal gloss: 'Cleopatra finely deceiueth Octauius Caesar, as though she desired to liue'. In other words Cleopatra had fully determined on suicide: she pretended about the treasure to make Caesar believe she wished to live. There is no justification for assuming that she wavers in her resolution till the last moment. It has been argued[2] that in his treatment of Cleopatra's death Shakespeare was influenced by one of Horace's *Odes* (I. 37). There the courage and nobility of Cleopatra are stressed and her desire to avoid taking part in a Roman triumph:

> Quae generosius
> perire quaerens nec muliebriter
>   expavit ensem nec latentis
>   classe cita reparavit oras;
> ausa et iacentem visere regiam
> voltu sereno, fortis et asperas
>   tractare serpentes, ut atrum
>   corpore combiberet venenum,

---

[1] J. L. Hotson, *Shakespeare's Sonnets Dated* (1949), p. 10.
[2] P. D. Westbrook, *P.M.L.A.* (1947), pp. 392–8.

> deliberata morte ferocior;
> saevis Liburnis scilicet invidens
> privata deduci superbo
> non humilis mulier triumpho.

But although it is reasonable to assume that Shakespeare knew this poem, he could have developed from Plutarch's account the portrait of Cleopatra in her last days.

The fifth book of Appian's history deals with events up to the death of Sextus Pompeius. The passages relating to Antony's brother, Lucius, in *Antony and Cleopatra* can hardly be based on Plutarch alone, for he does not make clear, as Shakespeare and Appian both do, that Lucius had republican sympathies. Antony asks Octavius:[1]

> Did he not rather
> Discredit my authority with yours,
> And make the warres alike against my stomacke
> Hauing alike your cause?

Appian, but neither Goulard nor Plutarch, shows that Lucius was fighting against the triumvirate, and for the restoration of the republic: he never claimed to be fighting in Antony's name, and Antony is justified in claiming that he had the same cause as that of Octavius. But Fulvia, on the other hand, as Appian makes clear, used Antony's grievances as her justification for her wars, though her real motive was the desire to get him to return to Italy and so detach him from Cleopatra. The different war-aims of Lucius and Fulvia are thus reflected in the play, and Antony rightly claims that

> my Brother neuer
> Did vrge me in his Act . . .

and that

> *Fuluia*
> To haue me out of Egypt made Warres heere.

The last point, however, is made by Goulard in his life of Octavius, as well as by Appian.

The borrowings from Appian, relating to Sextus Pompeius, are equally significant, and they are fully discussed by MacCallum.[2]

---

[1] II. ii. 52–5. Cf. E. Schanzer, *Shakespeare's Appian* (1956), pp. 72 ff.
[2] *Shakespeare's Roman Plays* (1910), pp. 648–52.

Plutarch mentions very briefly Sextus Pompeius's inroads on Italy. Appian gives an account of his followers:

> Out of *Italy* all things were not quiet, for *Pompey*, by resorte of condemned Citizens, and auntient possessioners, was greatly increased, both in mighte, and estimation: for they that feared their life, or were spoyled of their goodes, or lyked not the present state, fledde all to hym . . . beside a repayre of yong men, desirous of gayne and seruice, not caring vnder whome they went, bycause they were all *Romanes*, sought vnto him.

This appears to be the source of two passages[1] in *Antony and Cleopatra*:

> The condemn'd *Pompey*,
> Rich in his Fathers Honor, creepes apace
> Into the hearts of such, as haue not thriued
> Vpon the present state, whose Numbers threaten,
> And quietnesse, growne sicke of rest, would purge
> By any desperate change . . .

and 'flush youth reuolt'. The verbal parallel ('present state') and the absence of any such account in Plutarch are fairly conclusive.

Antony expresses indignation at Pompey's murder (III. v. 19). Plutarch does not mention the murder; Goulard states that it was carried out by Antony's commandment; Appian, however, tells us:

> There bee that saye, that *Plancus* and not *Antony*, dyd commaunde hym to dye, whyche beeyng president of *Syria*, had *Antonyes* signet, and in great causes wrote letters in hys name. Some thynke it was done with *Antonyes* knowledge, he fearyng the name of *Pompey*, or for *Cleopatra*, who fauoured *Pompey* the great.

Appian at least allows the possibility of Antony's innocence.

There is some evidence that Shakespeare consulted the Countess of Pembroke's translation of Garnier's *Marc Antoine*.[2] The clearest

---

[1] I. iii. 48–51; I. iv. 52. Cf. E. Schanzer, *Shakespeare's Appian* (1956), pp. 76–7.

[2] Cf. E. Schanzer, *N.Q.* (1956), pp. 152–4. Apart from the parallels mentioned in the text, Schanzer also compares the passage in *Antonius* where Cleopatra swoons on parting from her children with her swoon in Shakespeare's play upon the death of Antony—in both plays she is addressed as *Madam* or *Madame*—and he compares the lines—

> now streight will I die,
> And streight with thee a wandering shade will be,
> Vnder the *Cypres* trees thou haunt'st alone—

parallel has been pointed out by Professor J. Dover Wilson.[1] In the Argument, Antony's marriage is described in these terms:

> who for knitting a straiter bond of amitie betweene them, had taken to wife *Octauia*.

Agrippa in Shakespeare's play uses a similar phrase in proposing that Antony should marry Octavia:

> To hold you in perpetuall amitie,
> To make you Brothers, and to knit your hearts
> With an vn-slipping knot, take *Anthony*,
> *Octauia* to his wife.

In a later scene Enobarbus prophecies:

> You shall finde the bande that seemes to tye their friendship together, will be the very strangler of their Amity.

The links between the two writers are substantial: knitting–knit, bond–band, amitie, taken to wife *Octauia*—take *Octauia* to his wife.

In the first scene of *Antonius*, the hero speaks of breaking from Cleopatra:

> Thou breakest at length from thence, as one encharm'd
> Breakes from th' enchaunter—

lines which, as Mr E. Schanzer has shown,[2] may well have suggested the line:

> I must from this enchanting Queene breake off.

One chorus in *Antonius* describes the operations of the Nile and mentions '*Nilus*' mire', the 'fatt slime' left behind, and the resulting rich harvest:

> Making therby greatest growe
> Busie reapers ioyfull paine,
> When his flouds do highest flowe.

Shakespeare likewise speaks of '*Nilus*' slime' and '*Nilus*' mud', and mentions also that the greater the flood the greater is the harvest:

---

with Antony's lines (IV. xiv. 61 ff.):
> Where Soules do couch on Flowers, wee'l hand in hand,
> And with our sprightly Port make the Ghostes gaze:
> *Dido* and her *Aeneas* shall want Troopes,
> And all the haunt be ours.

[1] ed. *A. C.* p. x.   [2] op. cit., p. 154.

> The higher Nilus swels
> The more it promises: as it ebbes, the Seedsman
> Vpon the slime and Ooze scatters his graine,
> And shortly comes to Haruest.

Cleopatra's lines (as Mr Schanzer has again pointed out):[1]

> Thy eies, two Sunnes, the lodging place of loue,
> Which yet for tents to warlike *Mars* did serue . . .

and the line describing Cleopatra:

> Her beamie eies, two Sunnes of this our world

may have suggested Shakespeare's opening speech:

> those his goodly eyes
> That o're the Files and Musters of the Warre,
> Haue glow'd like plated Mars: now bend, now turne
> The Office and Deuotion of their view
> Vpon a Tawny Front . . .

and also the description of Antony in the last scene:

> His face was as the Heau'ns, and therein stucke
> A Sunne and Moone . . .
> his rear'd arme
> Crested the World.

Finally, as MacCallum noted,[2] the lines at the very end of *Antonius*—

> A thousand kisses, thousand thousand more
> Let you my mouth for honors farewell giue—

spoken by Cleopatra about the dead Antonius, resemble the words spoken by the dying Antony in Shakespeare's play:

> vntill
> Of many thousand kisses, the poore last
> I lay vpon thy lippes.

There is stronger evidence that Shakespeare made use of Daniel's *Cleopatra* and his *Letter from Octavia*. The latter poem, which first appeared in 1599, has an Argument prefixed containing an account of Antony's marriage to Octavia:[3]

[1] op. cit., p. 153. J. Dover Wilson, however, draws attention to part of this parallel.
[2] He quotes the French as well as the translation, op. cit., pp. 44, 47, 58.
[3] Cf. R. C. Bald, *T.L.S.* (1924), p. 776; Willard Farnham, *Shakespeare's Tragic Frontier* (1950), pp. 172–3; H. Norgaard, *N.Q.* (1955), pp. 56–7.

For *Antonie* hauing yet vpon him the fetters of *Ægypt*, layd on by the power of a most incomparable beauty, could admit no new Lawes into the state of his affection, or dispose of himselfe, being not himselfe, but as hauing his heart turned Eastward, whither the poynt of his desires were directed, toucht with the strongest allurements that ambition, and a licentious soueraignty could draw a man vnto: could not truly descend to the priuate loue of a ciuill nurtred Matron, whose entertainment bounded with modesty, and the nature of her education, knew not to clothe her affections in any other colours, then the plaine habit of truth.

So, in the play, Antony exclaims (I. ii. 113):

> These strong Egyptian Fetters I must breake,
> Or loose my selfe in dotage.

Later on, when the marriage with Octavia has been arranged, Antony says (II. iii. 40):

> though I make this marriage for my peace,
> I' th' East my pleasure lies.

Maecenas refers to Octavia's modesty (II. ii. 241) and Enobarbus points out that since she 'is of a holy cold, and still conversation' (II. vi. 119) Antony 'will to his Egyptian dish again'.

Octavia in Daniel's poem (st. 2) imagines how her letter will reach Antony:

> Although perhaps, these my complaints may come
> Whilst thou in th' armes of that incestuous Queene,
> The staine of Ægypt, and the shame of Rome
> Shalt dallying sit, and blush to haue them seene:
> Whilst proud disdainfull she, gessing from whome
> The message came, and what the cause hath beene,
> Will scorning say, Faith this comes from your Deere,
> Now Sir you must be shent for staying here.

This may have given a hint for Cleopatra's words about the messengers from Rome in the first scene of the play:

> Nay heare them, *Anthony*.
> *Fuluia* perchance is angry . . .
> Call in the Messengers: As I am Egypts Queene,

Thou blushest, *Anthony*, and that blood of thine
Is *Caesars* homager: else so thy cheeke payes shame,
When shrill-tongu'd *Fuluia* scolds.

In a later stanza (36) Octavia imagines Cleopatra's wiles:

She armes her teares, the ingins of deceit
And all her batterie, to oppose my loue,
And bring thy comming grace to a retreit,
The powre of all her subtilty to proue:
Now pale and faint she languishes, and strait
Seemes in a sound, vnable more to moue:
    Whilst her instructed fellowes ply thine eares
    With forged passions, mixt with fained teares.

This is a good description of the Cleopatra presented in I. iii., II. v., and in Act IV, and although Plutarch gives a similar account, Daniel's is closer to Shakespeare's.

It is probable that Shakespeare had read the earlier version of *Cleopatra*.[1] There are a number of details common to both plays, which are not to be found in Plutarch. Daniel in his first act stresses Cleopatra's determination to hoodwink Caesar by committing suicide. She is particularly concerned at the thought of Octavia watching her disgrace:

I that liu'd and raign'd a Queene,
Do scorne to buy my life at such a rate,
That I should vnderneath my selfe be seene,
Basely induring to suruive my state:
That Rome should see my scepter-bearing hands
Behind me bound, and glory in my teares;
That I should passe whereas *Octauia* stands,
To view my misery, that purchas'd hers.

(63–70)

So in Shakespeare's play Cleopatra tells Antony (IV. xv. 27):

Your Wife *Octauia*, with her modest eyes,
And still Conclusion, shall acquire no Honour
Demuring vpon me.

---

[1] The best account is by Willard Farnham, op. cit., pp. 158–73. He calls attention to several parallels between the two plays, most of which I had noted independently. Daniel's Cleopatra has mixed motives for her actions—she wishes to avoid being led in triumph, to safeguard her children, and to be loyal to Antony. Shakespeare's Cleopatra has the same mixture of motives. Both Cleopatras refer to Antony as Atlas, and they both allude to their own wrinkles.

Later on (V. ii. 52) she tells Proculeius:

> Know sir, that I
> Will not waite pinnion'd at your Masters Court,
> Nor once be chastis'd with the sober eye
> Of dull *Octauia*.

Daniel makes Cleopatra say that Caesar (50–4):

> seekes to entertaine my life with wiles.
> But *Caesar*, it is more then thou canst do,
> Promise, flatter, threaten extreamity,
> Imploy thy wits and all thy force thereto,
> I have both hands, and will, and I can die.

The last line combined with several references to resolution—'For who can stay a minde resolu'd to die' (1183); 'For what I will I am resolu'd' (1449–50); 'her resolution' (1592)—to make Shakespeare's line (IV. xv. 49):

> My Resolution, and my hands, Ile trust . . .

and the last lines of Act IV:

> we haue no Friend
> But Resolution, and the breefest end.

As Professor Farnham points out,[1] Shakespeare follows Daniel in making Proculeius advise Cleopatra to sue for Caesar's 'grace', in making her refer to the violation of her privilege of dying, and in having her send a message to Caesar, declaring that she wishes to die.

Cleopatra temporizes with Caesar and soothes his pleasure (89) for the sake of her children. This motive is obscured by Shakespeare. He makes Caesar threaten to kill her children if she commits suicide (V. ii. 131). The meeting of Caesar and Cleopatra and the incident of Seleucus and the treasure are closely based on Plutarch both in Daniel and Shakespeare. It is probable that here too Shakespeare was influenced by Daniel:

Alas, sayd she, O *Caesar*: is not this a great shame and reproche, that thou hauing vouchesaued to take the paines to come vnto me, and has done me this honor, poore wretche, and caitife creature, brought into this pitiefull and miserable estate: and that mine owne seruants should come now to accuse me, though

---

[1] op. cit., p. 167.

it may be I have reserued some iuells and trifles meete for women, but not for me (poore soule) to set out my selfe withall, but meaning to giue some pretie presents and gifts vnto *Octauia* and *Liuia*, that they making meanes and intercession for me to thee, thou mightest yet extend thy fauor and mercy vpon me?

Daniel has the following version of the speech (684 ff.):

> Ah *Caesar*, what a great indignity
> Is this, that here my vassall subiect stands
> T' accuse me to my Lord of trechery?
> If I reseru'd some certaine womens toyes,
> Alas it was not for my selfe (God knowes),
> Poore miserable soule, that little ioyes
> In trifling ornaments, in outward showes.
> But what I kept, I kept to make my way
> Vnto thy *Liuia* and *Octauias* grace,
> That thereby in compassion mooued, they
> Might mediate thy fauour in my case.

Shakespeare's lines are as follows:

> O *Caesar*, what a wounding shame is this,
> That thou vouchsafing heere to visit me,
> Doing the Honour of thy Lordlinesse
> To one so meeke, that mine owne Seruant should
> Parcell the summe of my disgraces, by
> Addition of his Enuy. Say (good *Caesar*)
> That I some Lady trifles haue reseru'd,
> Immoment toyes, things of such Dignitie
> As we greet moderne Friends withall, and say
> Some Nobler token I haue kept apart
> For *Liuia* and *Octauia*, to induce
> Their mediation, must I be vnfolded
> With one that I haue bred?

The use of *toyes* and *mediation* (cf. mediate) is a slight indication that Shakespeare knew the Daniel scene, as neither word is used by North.

Plutarch makes a good deal of the fact that Dolabella 'did beare no euil will vnto Cleopatra' and of his warning that she was to be sent to Rome within three days. Daniel's Dolabella expresses his admiration of Cleopatra to Octavius and sends her a love-letter with the information she wants. Shakespeare, more dramatically, makes Dolabella inform Cleopatra by word of mouth, but his love is not directly expressed. Daniel's treatment, however, left one impression on Shakespeare. Cleopatra says (1094):

> I thanke the man, both for his loue and letter;
> The one comes fit to warne me thus before,
> But for th' other I must die his debter.

So Shakespeare's Cleopatra tells Dolabella (V. ii. 204)

> I shall remaine your debter.

Daniel's Cleopatra complains of the difficulty of suicide (1174–83):

> But what haue I saue these bare hands to do it?
> And these weake fingers are not yron-poynted:
> They cannot pierce the flesh being put vnto it,
> And I of all meanes else am disappointed.
> But yet I must a way and meanes seeke, how
> To come vnto thee, whatsoere I do.
> O Death, art thou so hard to come by now,
> That we must pray, intreate, and seeke thee too?
> But I will finde thee wheresoere thou lie
> For who can stay a minde resolu'd to die?

There are similar passages in Shakespeare:

> My Resolution and my hands, Ile trust (IV. xv. 49)

> Quicke, quicke, good hands (V. ii. 39)

> Where art thou, Death?
> Come hither, come. (V. ii. 46)

> my Nailes
> Are stronger than mine eyes (V. ii. 222)

The Messenger describes how Cleopatra decks herself for death (1477):

> Euen as she was when on thy cristall streames,
> Cleare *Cydnos*, she did shew what earth could shew;
> Even as she went at first to meete her loue,
> So goes she now at last againe to finde him.
> But that first, did her greatnes onely proue,
> This last her loue, that could not liue behind him.

So Shakespeare's Cleopatra declares (V. ii. 227):

> I am againe for *Cydnus*
> To meete *Marke Anthony*.

Daniel's Cleopatra speaks several times of the easy death afforded by the asps—

That with one gentle touch canst free our breath (1518)

> thou best freest vs from our liues worst terror,
> In sweetly bringing soules to quiet rest. (1523)

That open canst with such an easie key
The doore of life; come gentle cunning thiefe . . . (1534)

But still in one same sweet vnaltered cheare (1617)

Shakespeare's Cleopatra describes her death 'As sweet as Balme, as soft as Ayre, as gentle'. (V. ii. 310).
Daniel describes how Honour leads forth (1579)

> Bright Immortalitie in shining armour:
> Thorow the rayes of whose cleare glory, she
> Might see lifes basenesse . . .

and Cleopatra speaks of 'That enemy, base Life' (1600). Shakespeare's Cleopatra likewise contrasts her 'immortall longings' (V. ii. 280) with her baseness in dying after Iras (V. ii. 299).

The touch of the asp proves that the gold of Cleopatra's love is pure (1612), as the death of Shakespeare's Cleopatra makes her Antony's wife. As Daniel's Cleopatra dies (1651)—

> in her sinking downe she wryes
> The Diademe which on her head she wore:
> Which *Charmion* . . . espies,
> And hastes to right it as it was before.

Charmian in Shakespeare's corresponding scene says:

> Your Crownes awry,
> Ile mend it, and then play.

The evidence that Daniel revised his play after seeing a performance of Shakespeare's is much less conclusive. The date of the latter is not known, and it may have been written after the 1607 edition of Daniel's play. Daniel in this revision presents the death of Cleopatra on the stage instead of describing it by messenger and he introduces Dircetus (as Garnier had done) to relate the death of Antony to Octavius. The account of the hoisting of his body into the monument may owe something to a stage performance[1] (244):

> Shee drawes him vp in rowles of taffaty
> T' a window at the top, which did allow
> A little light vnto her monument.
> There *Charmion*, and poore *Eras*, two weake maids
> Foretir'd with watching, and their mistresse care,
> Tug'd at the pulley, hauing n' other aydes,
> And vp they hoise the swounding body there
> Of pale *Antonius* showring out his blood
> On th' vnder-lookers, which there gazing stood.

There are two fairly close parallels. Cleopatra, tugging on the pulley, is said to be heavier by her grief:

> when shee a fresh renewes
> Her hold, and with reinforced power doth straine,
> And all the weight of her weake bodie laies,
> Whose surcharg'd heart more then her body wayes.

In the same circumstances Shakespeare's Cleopatra cries:

> How heauy weighes my Lord!
> Our strength is all gone into heauinesse,
> That makes the waight.

Later in the same scene Dircetus quotes Antony's warning (280):

> And none about *Octauius* trust, said hee,
> But *Proculeius*; he's an honest man.

Shakespeare's Antony likewise says:

> None about *Caesar* trust but *Proculeius*.

North's version is not so close:

> and that chiefly she should trust *Proculeius* aboue any man else about *Caesar*.

There would seem to be no way of proving which poet was indebted to the other, though the evidence suggests it was Shakespeare.[2]

---

[1] Cf. Joan Rees, *Shakespeare Survey 6*, pp. 91 ff.

[2] Ernest Schanzer has persuaded me by his forthcoming article that Shakespeare was in fact the debtor. I can discover no evidence that Shakespeare had read Brandon's *Virtuous Octavia*.

Finally it may be mentioned that Miss Ethel Seaton has pointed out some curious echoes of the book of *Revelation* in *Antony and Cleopatra*.[1] Some of these are in the scene in which Antony falls on his sword:[2]

> there fell a great starre from heauen . . .
> time should be no more.
> Woe, woe, woe to the inhabitants of the earth . . .
> Therefore in those dayes shall men seeke death, and shall not finde it, and shall desire to die, and death shall flee from them.

> 2: The Starre is falne.
> 1: And time is at his Period.
> *All:* Alas, and woe.
> *Ant.:* Let him that loues me, strike me dead.
> 1: Not I . . .
>   Woe, woe are we sir.

A second parallel is to be found in the image of the falling star:[3]

> I saw a starre fall from heauen vnto the earth, and to him was giuen the key of the bottomlesse pit.

> When my good Starres, that were my former guides
> Haue empty left their Orbes, and shot their Fires
> Into th' Abisme of hell.

One of Octavius's speeches seems to echo[4]

> I will shew thee the damnation of the great whore that sitteth vpon many waters, With whom haue committed fornication the kings of the earth . . .

> He hath giuen his Empire
> Vp to a Whore, who now are leuying
> The Kings o' th' earth for Warre.

Cleopatra's description of Antony in the last scene may likewise be based on another passage from *Revelation*:[5]

> And I saw another mightie Angel come down from heauen, clothed with a cloud, and the rainebowe vpon his head, and his

---

[1] Ethel Seaton, *R.E.S.* (1946), pp. 219–24. It has been argued that Shakespeare had read Dio Cassius. Cleopatra's threat to pour gold down the throat of the messenger has been compared with the account of Crassus's death given by Dio Cassius: 'Crassi interitus, aurumque in os eius infusum'. Shakespeare may have picked up this information from some other source.

[2] viii. 10; x. 6; viii. 13; ix. 6.

[3] ix. 1, 2.   [4] xvii. 1, 2.   [5] x. 1–6.

face was as the sunne, and his feete as pillars of fire, And hee had in his hand a little booke open, and hee put his right foot vpon the sea, and his left on the earth, And cryed with a loud voice, as when a lion roareth: and when hee had cryed, seuen thunders vttered their voices. And when the seuen thunders had vttered their voices, I was about to write. . . . And the Angel which I saw stand vpon the sea, and vpon the earth, lift vp his hand to heauen.

> His face was as the Heau'ns, and therein stucke
> A Sunne and Moone, which kept their course and lighted
> The little O the earth. . . .
> His legges bestrid the Ocean, his rear'd arme
> Crested the world: His voyce was propertied
> As all the tuned Spheres, and that to Friends:
> But when he meant to quaile, and shake the Orbe,
> He was as ratling Thunder.

The cosmic imagery in both passages has considerable resemblances. In the Bible, the Angel is clothed with a cloud, and his face is as the sun. Antony's face is as the Heavens with a sun and moon stuck in it. The Angel's feet stand on the sea and the earth. Antony's feet bestride the ocean. The angel lifts up his hand; Antony's arm is 'reared'. Both their voices are like thunder.

Finally, in *Revelation* xxi, St John

> saw a new heauen, and a newe earth, for the first heauen, and the first earth were passed away. . . . And I Iohn saw the holy citie . . . come down from God out of heauen, prepared as a bride trimmed for her husband.

In the first scene of the play Antony tells Cleopatra:

> Then must thou needes finde out new Heauen, new Earth.

He declares:

> I will bee
> A Bride-groome in my death;

and at the end of the play Cleopatra is decked as his bride, with Charmian (as Shakespeare would learn from Plutarch) 'trimming the diademe' of her mistress. These echoes may be due to some fortuitous and undiscoverable cause, and may therefore be irrelevant to an interpretation of the play; but it is possible that the apocalyptic imagery was designed to express the grandeur of the theme and to raise the stature of the protagonists.

stop

(17) Coriolanus

Shakespeare takes the main incidents of Coriolanus's story from Plutarch's *Life*, though he selects and rearranges. He omits the departure of the common people from Rome, which Plutarch gives as the occasion for Menenius Agrippa's fable. The people agree to return to Rome on condition that tribunes of the Plebs should be elected to safeguard their interests. In the play Brutus and Sicinius are already tribunes. Shakespeare minimizes the people's genuine grievances, probably to arouse more sympathy for his hero, though it has been suggested that he did it because the Warwickshire insurrection was a threat to him as a man of property.[1] On the other hand he makes the question of the consulship and not a later insurrection about corn the cause of Coriolanus's banishment and he invents Coriolanus's insufferable behaviour during his candidature. He also passes over two acts of trickery by the tribunes. He makes Coriolanus go alone into exile. Aufidius's enthusiastic welcome—

> Know thou first,
> I lou'd the Maid I married; neuer man
> Sigh'd truer breath. But that I see thee heere
> Thou Noble thing, more dances my rapt heart
> Than when I first my wedded Mistris saw
> Bestride my Threshold—

was perhaps suggested by the chivalric touch in North's words:

> bicause that many times in battells where they met, they were
> ever at the encounter one against another, like lustie coragious
> youthes, striving in all emulation of honour.

[1] Cf. E. C. Pettet, *Shakespeare Survey 3*, pp. 34 ff.

Shakespeare had used the last phrase in an earlier scene (I. x.) where Aufidius complains:

> Mine Emulation
> Hath not that Honor in't it had.

But it is arguable that the envious plotter there depicted, who is necessary for the final assassination, is inconsistent with the noble character revealed in the later scene.[1] Aufidius is not present when Coriolanus surrenders to his mother's pleadings, and Shakespeare by departing from his source in this respect prepares the way for Coriolanus's death. Plutarch describes three embassies to Coriolanus before that of the women. The first consisted of his 'familiar friends' who refuse his hard conditions of peace, the second is of an unspecified character, and the third is of priests and soothsayers. Shakespeare alludes in passing to the terms of peace offered by Coriolanus, but otherwise seems to imply that he is determined to burn Rome. The embassy of the women is suggested by Valeria, a point Shakespeare does not use.

Of more significance, however, is the development of the characters of Menenius and of Volumnia. In the source the sole function of the former is to pacify the plebeians with a fable, and Volumnia is hardly mentioned till she goes to plead with her son. In the play Menenius appears in thirteen scenes and his role and Volumnia's are prominent throughout the play. There is nothing in Plutarch to suggest the fatal relationship between mother and son on which Shakespeare based his play, and the emotional immaturity of Coriolanus is brought out by the description of his young son, who is an invention of Shakespeare's.

Coriolanus's attack on the distribution of free corn and on the tribunes (III. i.), his speech to Aufidius at Antium (IV. v.) and the appeal of Volumnia for Rome are all based closely on North's prose. The following comparison will indicate how closely:

If thou knowest me not yet, *Tullus*, and seeing me, dost not perhapps beleeue me to be the man I am in dede, I must of necessitie bewraye my selfe to be that I am. I am *Caius Martius*, who hath done to thy self particularly, and to all the *Volsces* generally, great hurte and mischief, which I cannot denie for my surname of *Coriolanus* that I beare. For I neuer had other benefit nor recompence, of all the true and paynefull seruice I haue done,

---

[1] Cf. J. M. Murry, *Discoveries* (1924), pp. 276–8.

and the extreme daungers I haue bene in, but this only surname:
a good memorie and witnes, of the malice and displeasure thou
showldest beare me. Indeede the name only remaineth with me:
for the rest, the enuie and crueltie of the people of *Rome* haue
taken from me, by the sufferance of the dastardly nobilitie and
magistrates, who haue forsaken me, and let me be banished by
the people. This extremitie hath now driuen me to come as a
poore suter, to take thy chimney harthe, not of any hope I haue
to saue my life thereby. For if I had feared death, I would not
haue come hither to haue put my life in hazard: but prickt forward with spite and desire I haue to be reuenged of them that thus
haue banished me, whom now I beginne to be auenged on, putting my persone betweene thy enemies. Wherefore, if thou hast
any harte to be wrecked of the iniuries thy enemies haue done
thee, spede thee now, and let my miserie serue thy turne, and so
vse it, as my seruice maye be a benefit to the *Volsces*: promising
thee, that I will fight with better good will for all of you, then
euer I dyd when I was against you, knowing that they fight more
valliantly, who knowe the force of their enemie, then such as
haue neuer proued it. And if it be so that thou dare not, and that
thou art wearye to proue fortune any more: then am I also weary
to liue any lenger. And it were no wisedome in thee, to saue the
life of him, who hath bene heretofore thy mortall enemie, and
whose seruice now can nothing helpe nor pleasure thee.

Cor.:   If *Tullus* not yet thou know'st me, and seeing me, dost
        not thinke me for the man I am, necessitie commands me
        name my selfe.
Auf.:   What is thy name?
Cor.:   A name vnmusicall to the Volcians eares,
        And harsh in sound to thine.
Auf.:   Say, what's thy name?
        Thou hast a Grim apparance, and thy Face
        Beares a Command in't: Though thy Tackles torne,
        Thou shew'st a Noble Vessell: What's thy name?
Cor.:   Prepare thy brow to frowne: knowst thou me yet?
Auf.:   I know thee not. Thy Name?
Cor.:   My name is *Caius Martius*, who hath done
        To thee particularly, and to all the Volces
        Great hurt and Mischiefe: thereto witnesse may
        My Surname *Coriolanus*. The painfull Seruice,

The extreme Dangers, and the droppes of Blood
Shed for my thanklesse Country, are requitted:
But with that Surname, a good memorie
And witnesse of the Malice and Displeasure
Which thou should'st beare me, only that name remains.
The Cruelty and Enuy of the people,
Permitted by our dastard Nobles, who
Haue all forsooke me, hath deuour'd the rest:
And suffer'd me by th' voyce of Slaues to be
Hoop'd out of Rome. Now this extremity,
Hath brought me to thy Harth, not out of Hope
(Mistake me not) to saue my life: for if
I had fear'd death, of all the Men i' th' World
I would haue voided thee. But in meere spight
To be full quit of those my Banishers,
Stand I before thee heere: Then if thou hast
A heart of wreake in thee, that wilt reuenge
Thine owne particular wrongs, and stop those maimes
Of shame seene through thy Country, speed thee straight
And make my misery serue thy turne: So vse it,
That my reuengefull Seruices may proue
As Benefits to thee. For I will fight
Against my Cankred Countrey, with the Spleene
Of all the vnder Fiends. But if so be,
Thou dar'st not this, and that to proue more Fortunes
Th' art tyr'd, then in a word, I also am
Longer to liue most wearie: and present
My throat to thee, and to thy Ancient Malice:
Which not to cut, would shew thee but a Foole,
Since I haue euer followed thee with hate,
Drawne Tunnes of Blood out of thy Countries brest,
And cannot liue but to thy shame, vnlesse
It be to do thee seruice.

Three short examples, all mentioned by George Wyndham,[1] will serve to indicate the closeness with which Shakespeare follows his source. In Act II, Scene 3, the Folio prints the meaningless lines:

> And Nobly nam'd, so twice being Censor,
> Was his great Ancestor.

[1] *Essays in Romantic Literature* (1919), pp. 117 ff.

The missing line can be supplied directly from North:

> And Censorinus that was so surnamed,
> And Nobly nam'd so, twice being Censor . . .

The second example shows how Shakespeare was led into ana-chronism by his slavish following of North, who writes of Corio-lanus that

> he was even such another, as Cato would have a souldier and a captaine to be: not only terrible and fierce to laye aboute him, but to make the enemie afeard with the sound of his voyce and grimness of his countenance.

This is the corresponding passage in the play:

> Thou was't a Souldier
> Euen to *Catoes* wish, not fierce and terrible
> Onely in strokes, but with thy grim lookes, and
> The Thunder-like percussion of thy sounds
> Thou mad'st thine enemies shake . . .

In this passage the Folio misprints *Calues* for *Catoes* or 'Cato's'.

The third example is even more interesting. North mentions that 'a goodly horse with a caparison' is offered to Coriolanus; and in the play Lartius hails Coriolanus with the words:

> Oh Generall:
> Here is the Steed, wee the Caparison:

There is some evidence that Shakespeare consulted several dif-ferent versions of Menenius's fable of the Belly and the Members of the Body.[1] Sidney's version in his *Defence of Poesy* begins, like Shakespeare's, with the words 'There was a time'; both use the word *mutinous*; both mention that the fable was well known; and Sidney immediately after his version of the fable speaks of 'prettie tales', the description given by Menenius to the fable. The version given in Camden's *Remaines* contains the phrase 'swallowing gulfe of all their labours', although 'swallowing gulf' appears in *Richard III* as well as in *Coriolanus*. Camden uses the word 'Steward' which is closer than other versions to Shakespeare's *Storehouse* and *Awdit*. As there is some slight evidence that Shakespeare had read Cam-den's book while he was writing *King Lear*, it is quite possible that he knew this version of the fable.

---

[1] Cf. K. Muir, *N.Q.* (1953), pp. 240–2. For the Averell reference I was indebted to E. Honigmann, though he is not responsible for my deductions from it.

He had also read Livy's version of the fable and he probably knew Holland's translation. Holland, like Shakespeare, refers to *blood* and *veins*, and the sentence in which these words appear is closer to Shakespeare than the corresponding passage in the other versions.

> Then was it wel seen, that even the very belly also did no smal service, but fed the other parts, as it received food it selfe: seeing that by working and concocting the meal throughlie it digesteth and distributeth by the veins into all parts that fresh and perfect blood whereby we live, we like, and have our full strength.

>   But, if you do remember,
>   I send it through the Riuers of your blood
>   Euen to the Court, the Heart, to th' seate o' th' Braine;
>   And through the Crankes and Offices of man,
>   The strongest Nerues, and small inferious Veines
>   From me receiue that Naturall competencie
>   Whereby they liue.

But the version from which Shakespeare borrowed most was William Averell's *Meruailous Combat of Contrarieties*. Apart from words common to two or more sources, Shakespeare uses a large number of words which are to be found only in Averell. They include *superfluity, crammed, malicious, viand, instruments, mutually, participate, cormorant, sink, rivers, dissentious*, and several others. Shakespeare elsewhere in *Coriolanus* uses two words from Averell's title-page (*contrariety* and *malignity*). This is the only time Shakespeare uses the latter, though he uses *malign* in the Fable scene. *Pantrey* may have suggested *cubboarding* and *store-house*. In Averell's interpretation of the fable the connection between head and prince, and between heart and counsellor, is brought out clearly.

Shakespeare, then, in addition to any version he read at school, seems to have made use of Sidney's, Livy's, Camden's, and Averell's as well as that given by Plutarch.

LAST PLAYS

(18) Pericles

VARIOUS theories have been held on the relationship between Wilkins's novel, *The Painfull Aduentures of Pericles*, and Shakespeare's play. Some critics have argued that the play was based on the novel; others have argued that the novel was based on the play; Dugdale Sykes argued[1] that Wilkins based a play on the novel he had himself written, and that the last three acts of the play were afterwards revised by Shakespeare; and Mr Philip Edwards has suggested that the Quarto of the play and Wilkins's novel were based on reports of a play entirely by Shakespeare, the difference between the first two acts and the last three being due to the differing skill of reporters.[2]

Whatever the relationship between the novel and the play it can easily be shown that the former was greatly indebted to Laurence Twine's *Patterne of Paineful Aduentures*. Wilkins relies most obviously on Twine in the opening chapter, which describes events before the beginning of the play; in the description of the statue, to which there is a bare reference in the play; in the description of the storm, described in the play in four lines; in the description of the wedding, not described at all in the play; in Marina's song, not given in the Quarto of the play; and in part of the speech of Marina just before she is recognized by her father.[3] All these passages, therefore, except the last, are absent from the play. From this it would seem to be certain that Wilkins followed a play where he could and that he fell back on Twine where the play was deficient. This conclusion is supported by the title-page of the novel, where we are told 'it was lately presented by the worthy and ancient Poet *John Gower*', and by the concluding sentence of the

---

[1] *Sidelights on Shakespeare* (1919), pp. 143 ff.
[2] *Shakespeare Survey 5*, pp. 25 ff.
[3] Cf. K. Muir, *English Studies* (1949), pp. 65–83.

Argument, which refers to a performance by Shakespeare's company. It cannot be argued that these references to performance were inserted to sell a novel which had been written quite independently of the play, for in the third chapter the famine at Tharsus is described by Cleon in conversation with Dyonysa, though she knows as much about it as he does; and in Chapter V we are told how Helicanus informed his 'graue and familiar friend, Lord *Eschines*' about the incestuous relations of Antiochus with his daughter. Both Dyonysa and Eschines are dragged in as confidants. There can be no doubt that Wilkins based his novel on a play, though not necessarily on the extant play.

If Wilkins had based his novel on Shakespeare's play, we should have to conclude either that those passages in the novel which are neither in Twine's novel nor in *Pericles* were omitted by accident from the printed text of the play and somehow preserved by Wilkins,[1] or else that such passages were the invention of Wilkins.

Some light is thrown on this question by a consideration of the brothel-scenes of the play in which there are thirteen close parallels with Wilkins's novel;[2] and it is significant that none of the verse fossils in the novel correspond to lines of verse in the play. Moreover Marina and Lysimachus are given long speeches more elaborate than any in the play, and these, though printed as prose, are clearly based on blank verse. Lysimachus drops suddenly from indirect into direct speech, because Wilkins in adapting his original carelessly neglected to alter his pronouns:[3]

> or *his* displeasure punish at his owne pleasure, which displeasure of *mine*, thy beauty shall not priuiledge thee from, nor my affection, which hath drawen me vnto this place abate, if thou with further lingering withstand me.

Another indication that Wilkins's speeches must have been written originally as verse is that two passages contain repetitions of a word merely to complete lines of verse:[4]

> which too too many feele such houses are . . .
> let me euen now, now in this minute die . . .

Although we may accept Mr Edwards's theory that the Quarto

[1] He may have had access to the prompt-copy, or have procured a reported version of the play. He wrote for Shakespeare's company.
[2] Cf. K. Muir, *English Studies* (1949), pp. 71–3.
[3] G. Wilkins, *The Painfull Aduentures of Pericles*, ed. Muir (1953), p. 89.
[4] Wilkins, op. cit., p. 90.

text was supplied by two reporters, the brothel-scenes were the work of the more accurate one. Yet Wilkins produces long speeches in thinly-disguised blank verse of which there is little trace in the play. It is safe to conclude that the novel is based on an earlier version of the play; and since the novel is much closer to the first two acts of the play than it is to the last three, it seems likely that the earlier part of the play underwent less revision than the later part. This, rather than the two reporters and three compositors ingeniously put forward by Mr Edwards would appear to account for the manifest differences between the two parts, though it is not necessary for my argument to deny that there were two reporters and three compositors. If, as Mr Edwards thinks, the first two acts were as Shakespearian as the last three, we should expect those passages where Wilkins and the Quarto correspond to contain verse which is plainly Shakespeare's own. Manifestly they do not.[1] Yet in the first two acts the novel keeps so close to the text of the play, and the Quarto is so inaccurate, that we can amend its text by reference to the novel. For example, *sauers* (I. iv. 39) is correctly given by Wilkins as *summers*; and *sau'd one* (II. *Prol.* 22) is correctly given as *sends word*.[2] There are many places, moreover—not merely in the first two acts—where Wilkins seems to have recorded passages accidentally omitted by the Quarto. The best known is the phrase 'Poore inch of Nature', which fits neatly into the context:

> Thou hast as chiding a natiuitie,
> As Fire, Ayre, Water, Earth, and Heauen can make
> To harould thee from the wombe: *poore inch of Nature*
> Euen at the first, thy losse is more then can
> Thy portage quit . . .

It seems probable that some of Shakespeare's intentions have been blurred. In Act II Scene V Simonides informs the three knights that Thaisa has vowed to Diana to remain unmarried for another year. In spite of this she marries Pericles forthwith. We hear nothing more of the vow, but it is possible that Shakespeare intended us to think that Thaisa's misfortunes were caused by the wrath of the goddess. Pericles prays to her as Lucina, and his prayer is rejected. When Thaisa is restored to life, her first words are addressed to the goddess, and she decides to serve as priestess

---

[1] I owe this point to J. C. Maxwell.
[2] Cf. S. Lee, Introduction to facsimile of *Pericles*, p. 28.

in Diana's temple at Ephesus. Meanwhile Pericles has vowed 'by bright Diana' to keep his 'heyre' 'All vnsisterd' (if this is the correct reading) until his daughter marries. Marina prays to Diana in the brothel, and the goddess appears to Pericles in a vision. When Thaisa is restored to him he vows to offer nightly oblations to Diana. As Diana's temple is mentioned in several versions of the Apollonius story, the role of the goddess may well have been suggested to Shakespeare by the dénouement, but neither Gower, nor Twine, nor indeed Wilkins, mentions the vow.[1]

Shakespeare's play, as we have suggested, was based on an earlier play, perhaps by Heywood and Wilkins, perhaps by an unknown dramatist, conceivably by Shakespeare himself. In revising it in 1608 he rewrote the last three acts, substituting prose for verse in the brothel-scene, for example, but he revised the first two acts much less extensively. If the above argument is sound, we can roughly estimate the nature of Shakespeare's alterations by comparing Wilkins's novel with the text of the play; but since the text is bad and Wilkins introduces passages from Twine into the novel, it is impossible to be precise. One example may be given. Wilkins has the following passage in Chapter VI:

> the king . . . tolde him, that like a traitour, hee lyed. Traytour, quoth *Pericles*? I, traytour, quoth the king, that thus disguised, art stolne into my Court, with the witchcraft of thy actions to bewitch, the yeelding spirit of my tender Childe. *Pericles* . . . boldely replyed, That were it any in his Court, except himselfe, durst call him traytor, euen in his bosome he would write the lie: affirming, that he came into his Court in search of honour, and not to be a rebell to his State, his bloud was yet vntainted, but with the heate, got by the wrong the king had offered him, and that he boldly durst, and did defie, himselfe, his subiectes, and the prowdest danger, that eyther tyranny or treason could inflict vpon him.

We may suppose that the dialogue in Shakespeare's source ran somewhat as follows:

Sim.: Traitor, thou liest.
Per.:   Traitor!
Sim.:   Ay, traitor;
          That thus disguised art stol'n into my Court,

---

[1] Cf. K. Muir, *N.Q.* (1948), p. 362.

With the witchcraft of thy actions to bewitch
The yielding spirit of my tender child.

Per.: If any in thy Court, except thyself,   (5)
Durst call me traitor,
Even in his bosom I would write the lie.

Sim.: Now by the Gods, I do applaud his courage.

Per.: My actions are as noble as my thoughts,
That never relish'd of a base discent.   (10)
I came into thy Court in search of honour,
And not to be a rebel to thy state;
My blood is yet untainted but with heat,
Got by the wrong that thou hast offered me,
I boldly dare, and do, defy thyself,   (15)
Thy subjects and . . . the proudest danger
That tyranny or treason can inflict.

I have inserted three lines from the Quarto, the first of them im-
plied by Wilkins's words 'which noblenesse of his, the king in-
wardly commending'. Wilkins may have omitted something in
l. 6 and the last two lines are imperfect. Apart from these points
Wilkins appears to have reproduced the blank verse very accur-
ately.

The Quarto version runs as follows:

King: Traytor, thou lyest.
Per.: Traytor?
King: I, Traytor.
Per.: Euen in his throat, vnlesse it be the King,
That cals me Traytor, I returne the lye.
King: Now by the Gods, I do applaude his courage.
Per.: My actions are as noble as my thoughts,
That neuer relisht of a base discent:
I came vnto your Court for Honours cause,
And not to be a Rebell to her state:
And he that otherwise accountes of mee,
This Sword shall prooue, hee's Honours enemie.

It is difficult to be sure how far Shakespeare was responsible for
the alterations in this passage. The last couplet, one hopes, was the
responsibility of the reporter. It is possible that the earlier lines—

Thou hast bewitcht my daughter,
And thou art a villaine.—

are a version of the three lines (2–4) omitted from the passage given above. If it was Shakespeare who omitted them, presumably he did so to make Pericles react more immediately to the word 'traitor'.

The matter is complicated by the fact that the compositors of the Quarto appear to have occasionally used the novel to correct the reported text. This seems to be the only way to explain such parallels as the following:

> hee was a Gentleman of *Tyre*, his name *Pericles*, his education beene in Artes and Armes, who looking for aduentures in the world, was by the rough and vnconstant Seas, most vnfortunately bereft of shippes and men, and after shipwrecke, throwen vpon that shoare.

> A Gentleman of *Tyre*, my name *Pericles*,
> My education beene in Artes and Armes:
> Who looking for aduentures in the world,
> Was by the rough Seas reft of Ships and men;
> And after shipwracke, driuen vpon this shore.

The verse in the play reads as though it were clumsily converted from the prose of the novel, although this prose manifestly contains verse fossils. It may be worth mentioning that 'Gentleman', 'Artes', 'Armes', and 'Seas' are all given capitals in both versions; and that 'education', 'aduentures', 'world', 'shipwracke', and 'shore' are all without capitals. ('Ships' is the one word where the Quarto deviates from the novel in this respect.)

If Shakespeare's chief source was a lost play we cannot be sure what other sources he used. But the use of Gower as chorus makes it highly probable that he consulted the version of the story in the *Confessio Amantis*. This is supported by one or two verbal echoes:[1]

> mi lorde, I am a Maide
> And if ye wiste what I am
> And out of what lignage I cam
> Ye wolde not be so salvage.

> I am a maid, my Lorde . . . if you did know my parentage, you would not do me violence.

There are no verbal echoes of Twine's novel; and even if there were any, they might have come indirectly through the source-

---

[1] Gower, op. cit., (1889), p. 427.

play. There is only one scene which appears to be slightly closer to Twine's version than to that of Wilkins—Thaliard is relieved that owing to the disappearance of Pericles he does not have to murder him—but Wilkins may have deviated from the source-play at this point. It is only because of Shakespeare's usual habits of composition that we may suspect that he did consult Twine too. In some ways the play is reminiscent of *The Comedy of Errors*, as we have seen,[1] and there is good reason to believe that Shakespeare had read Twine's novel before writing the earlier play.

It would appear from a comparison of Wilkins's novel with the play, that Shakespeare made numerous alterations. He made the brothel-scenes more realistic and sordid. But, on the other hand, he whitewashed the character of Lysimachus. In the play he declares that he came to the brothel 'with no ill intent', and as soon as Marina appeals to him he desists from his wooing. In the novel he comes to the brothel with 'thoughtes intemperate, foule and deformed', and he threatens Marina, believing her pleading is a trick to raise her price. Shakespeare was anxious to make Lysimachus a less intolerable husband for the pure Marina, but we are left wondering why Lysimachus visited the brothel at all. One other alteration may be mentioned. In Twine's novel, Apollonius kicks Tharsia on the face; in Wilkins's novel Pericles strikes Marina on the face, and she swoons; in the play he pushes her roughly back. Such alterations show that in converting the 'mouldy tale' of *Pericles* into the first of the Romances, Shakespeare, although willing to borrow a great deal from the source-play, knew what to exclude.

(19) *Cymbeline*

Samuel Johnson dismissed *Cymbeline* in a sentence.[2]

To remark the folly of the fiction, the absurdity of the conduct, the confusion of the names and manners of different times, and the impossibility of the events in any system of life, were to waste criticism upon unresisting imbecillity, upon faults too evident for detection, and too gross for aggravation.

[1] Cf. p. 18 *ante*.
[2] *Johnson on Shakespeare* ed. W. Raleigh (1925), p. 183.

Harley Granville-Barker does not go as far as Johnson's 'unresisting imbecillity', yet even he speaks of Shakespeare as a 'wearied artist'.[1]

A study of the poet's manipulation of his sources shows, however, that he was not too wearied to take infinite pains. He was looking, we may suppose, for a plot through which he could express the theme of forgiveness and reconciliation. Realizing the weakness of *Pericles*, in which the hero and his daughter suffer undeserved trials at the hands of fortune, he wanted a story in which the disasters were caused by human agency. Perhaps the popularity of *Mucedorus*, an old play revived in 1607, led Shakespeare's company to search for similar old romantic plays worth revival or adaptation or for similar 'mouldy' plots which could be dramatized. Shakespeare had been reading Plutarch's *Lives* while he was writing the Graeco-Roman plays, and in the last of these, *Timon of Athens*, the hero, after his self-imposed banishment, lives in a cave. A cave also figures in *The Rare Triumphs of Love and Fortune*, then nearly thirty years old, written and published while the poet was still at school.[2] In this play, which opens with a debate between Jupiter and the other gods and goddesses, the Princess Fidelia is in love with the supposed orphan Hermione who had been brought up at the Court by her father, King Phizantius. Fidelia's rash and boorish brother, Armenio, discovering their love, fights a duel with Hermione. This is interrupted by the King, and Hermione is banished. The Princess's name suggested that assumed by Imogen in her disguise; and Hermione gave Shakespeare a name for the heroine of his next play. Posthumus Leonatus, like Hermione, is an orphan, brought up at Court, and in love with the Princess; and Cloten resembles Armenio in certain respects. This old play, therefore, was certainly one of Shakespeare's sources.

In the third act we meet the exiled lord, Bomelio—the long-lost father of Hermione—living as a hermit. Hermione sends a servant to ask Fidelia to meet him at a cave, and the servant betrays the plan to Armenio, who follows Fidelia and abducts her. But at the end of the play, by the intervention of Jupiter, the lovers are reunited, and the King is reconciled with Hermione's father. Armenio's pursuit of Fidelia may be compared with Cloten's pursuit of Imogen, and the exiled Bomelio resembles not only Belarius, but also Prospero, for he is a magician plotting revenge.

---

[1] *Prefaces*, ii (1930), p. 247.
[2] Cf. R. W. Boodle, *N.Q.* (1887), p. 405; J. M. Nosworthy ed. *Cymb.*, p. xxiv.

The vision scene in *Cymbeline* resembles the intervention of the gods in *Love and Fortune*, and there are several verbal parallels.

Of course, as Mr Nosworthy says,

It would be unwise to attach too much weight to such parallel features as a banished lover, a banished duke, a cave, and a sleeping potion, for these are part of the stock-in-trade of every writer of romance.

What is more significant is that

both plays present the banished lover as a pauper brought up at Court, both include a boorish brother, and both introduce Jupiter and use him, flagrantly, as a *deus ex machina*. Just as Belarius recognizes Cloten though he has not seen him for many years, so Bomelio recognizes Armenio, and just as Imogen offers her breast for the mortal stroke, so does Fidelia.

The old play, therefore, provided Shakespeare with hints for his initial situation, for his pastoral scenes, and for his last act. But clearly it would not do as it stood. The plot was inorganic and arbitrary, with too little complication, and not enough dramatic tension. It lacked also solidity of background. This Shakespeare provided by setting his scene in the early legendary period of British history, known to Elizabethans from Holinshed's *Chronicles*, the catalogue in *The Faerie Queene*, *Albion's England*, *The Mirror for Magistrates*, and from numerous plays which ranged from *Locrine* to *King Leir*, and included the highly popular and recently revived *Mucedorus*. Shakespeare had consulted some of these works a few years before, while he was writing *King Lear*.[1]

There were considerable differences between the versions of the Cymbeline story. In *The Mirror for Magistrates* there is a patriotic account of how Guiderius defeated a Roman army, thirty thousand strong, and of his challenge to meet Claudius Caesar in single combat. Holinshed tells how Cymbeline became king in 33 B.C. and that he reigned for thirty-five years. As he had been brought up in Rome he was excused by Augustus from paying tribute. At some later date the tribute was demanded and refused; but Holinshed, after some hesitation, ascribes this refusal to Cymbeline's eldest son, Guiderius. Holinshed admits that though the British chroniclers claimed that the Romans were twice defeated, the Romans, according to Latin historians, were ultimately victorious.

[1] Cf. pp. 141–66 *ante*.

Spenser makes Arviragus the brother to Cymbeline. Shakespeare follows Holinshed in making Cymbeline the father of Guiderius and Arviragus, though he makes him, and not Guiderius, refuse to pay the tribute.

Dr Harold F. Brooks has shown conclusively[1] that Shakespeare made use of *The Mirror for Magistrates* in his dramatization of this refusal to pay the tribute—not merely of Blenerhasset's 'Guidericus', but also of four tragedies by Higgins in the 1587 edition. The lines (III. i. 49–50)

> Till the iniurious Romans *did extort*
> This *Tribute* from vs, we were *free*.

echo Higgins's Guiderius:

> I sayd I would not pay them *tribute*, I,
> They *did extort* the same by force, perdy.
> Hee should not beare our *freedom* so away.

Earlier in the same scene (ll. 22–27) the Queen speaks of Britain, fenced

> With Sands that will not beare your Enemies Boates,
> . . . A kinde of Conquest
> *Caesar* made heere, but made not heere his bragge
> Of Came, and Saw, and Ouer-came: with shame
> (The first that euer touch'd him) he was carried
> From off our Coast, twice beaten: and his Shipping
> (Poore ignorant Baubles) on our terrible Seas
> Like Egge-shels mou'd vpon their Surges, crack'd
> As easily 'gainst our Rockes.

Higgins's Caesar speaks of 'our shatter'd ships' . . . 'that else had bulg'd themselues in *sand*'; and he admits:

> I haue no cause of Britayne conquest for to *boast*
> Of all the regions *first* and last with whome I wer'd.

Nennius speaks of

> Proud Caesar he for all his *bragges* and *boste*:
> Flew back to *shippes*. . . .
> The Monarche Caesar might have bene *ashamde*
> From such an Islande with his shippes *recoyle*. . . .

---

[1] In an appendix to Nosworthy's edition.

Irenglas makes the same point:

> When Caesar so, with *shameful* flight *recoylde*
> And left our Britayne land *vnconquerde first*.

Spenser, writing of the same incident, says:

> Yet twise they were repulsed backe againe,
> And twise renforst, backe to their ships to fly.

The debt to Blenerhasset in this scene is slight, if any, but Dr Brooks is probably right to suggest that Posthumus's description of Guiderius and Arviragus as

> Lads more like to run
> The Country base, than to commit such slaughter

was suggested by Blenerhasset's Guidericus who proposes to fall on the Romans—

> To byd the Bace, and fetch them from their denne.

The killing of Cloten and Posthumus's fighting in disguise against the Roman army were probably both suggested by Higgins's story of Hamo, a Roman who puts on British garments so as to have the chance of killing Guiderius. He is afterwards slain, according to Fabyan and Geoffrey, by Arviragus, beside a haven, as Cloten is slain near Milford Haven. He is

> hewde in pieces small:
> Which downe the cleeues they did into the waters cast.

Cloten's head is thrown into 'the creek behind our rock'. Holinshed omits the hewing in pieces, though this detail is mentioned by Fabyan and Grafton. Possibly, as Dr Brooks suggests, Cloten's intention to cut Posthumus's garments to pieces 'may have originated partly in Shakespeare's linking of the two'.

For the battle Shakespeare went to the Scottish section of Holinshed's *Chronicles*, to the story of how a peasant named Hay with his two sons helped to defeat the Danes at the Battle of Luncarty in A.D. 976. This story Shakespeare would have read at the time he was collecting materials for *Macbeth*, as it is to be found sandwiched between the account of Donwald and the story of the murder of Duncan.

Shakespeare still wanted a plot to combine with those he had already, one which would dramatically postpone the reunion of the lovers and make it a reconciliation as well as a reunion. The obvious resource was a story of jealousy, and he looked for one like *Othello* in which the husband is made to believe that his wife has been false by the slander of an Italian villain.[1] One of the best-known collections of Italian stories was Boccaccio's *Decameron* which would be available to Shakespeare in a French translation as well as in the original. Here in the 9th tale of the Second Day Shakespeare found the popular tale of a wager on a wife's chastity; it is thus conveniently summarized by Professor T. M. Parrott:[2]

At an inn in Paris some Italian merchants are mocking the idea of wifely virtue. Bernabo of Genoa, however, firmly maintains the chastity of his wife, Ginevra. One of the company, Ambrogiuolo, declares that he would win her as he has won others, and provokes Bernabo into a wager on her virtue. The tempter goes to Genoa and at once discovers that he has undertaken a hopeless task. Unwilling, however, to lose the wager, he gains admittance to the lady's bed-chamber concealed in a chest. While she sleeps he creeps out, notes the furniture and pictures of the room, steals a ring, a purse, and a girdle, and remarks on her breast a mole with a group of golden hairs. He returns to Paris and convinces Bernabo that he has won the wager. The husband then returns to Italy, sends a servant to bid Ginevra meet him outside the city and orders him to kill her on the way. Overcome by her tears and protestations of innocence the servant spares her, takes her dress to show his master as proof of her death, and leaves her his hat and doublet. Disguised as a man Ginevra becomes at last the trusted servant of the Soldan. One day she sees on a stall in the market-place her own purse and girdle exposed for sale. She hears from the owner, Ambrogiuolo, that they have been given him by his mistress, the wife of Bernabo. Using her influence with the Soldan she brings the two merchants together, and forces the slanderer to confess his trick and the husband to admit the murder of his wife. Ginevra then reveals herself and pardons her husband. Ambrogiuolo is impaled and stung to death by wasps and flies.

The resemblances to Shakespeare's play are sufficiently apparent —the wager, the realization of the seducer that he has undertaken

---

[1] An Italian plot may have been suggested to Shakespeare by the fact that Spenser refers to Brute's wife and Locrine's mother as 'fayre Inogene of Italy'. Several other names used by Shakespeare in the play are to be found in Holinshed and in *The Mirror for Magistrates*.

[2] *Shakespearian Comedy* (1949), p. 376. There is a slight indication, by no means conclusive, that Shakespeare read Boccaccio in a French translation.

a hopeless task, the concealment in a chest, the description of the pictures and furniture, the mole on Ginevra's left breast, the stealing of a jewel (a ring in Boccaccio, a bracelet in Shakespeare), the convincing of the husband that he has lost the wager, the plot to kill Ginevra, the relenting of the servant, the disguise of Ginevra as a man, and the final exposure of the slanderer are to be found both in Boccaccio and Shakespeare. The torture and death of the villain were used not in *Cymbeline* but in *The Winter's Tale* where Autolycus tells the Clown:[1]

> Hee ha's a Sonne: who shall be flayd aliue, then 'noynted ouer with Honey, set on the head of a Waspes Nest, then stand till he be three quarters and a dram dead: then recouer'd againe with Aquavite, or some other hot Infusion: then, raw as he is (and in the hotest day Prognostication proclaymes) shall be set against a Brick-wall, (the Sunne looking with a South-ward eye vpon him; where hee is to behold him, with Flyes blown to death.)

It is certain, therefore, that Shakespeare had read Boccaccio's version of the wager story. But, as we have been forced to recognize in studying his sources, it was his usual custom to consult more than one version of the stories he dramatized. Just as he went to Blenerhasset, Higgins, Spenser, and Holinshed for the pseudo-historical material in Cymbeline, so it is now known that he went to an English version of the wager story. This was entitled *Frederyke of Jennen*,[2] published originally in 1518, but reprinted in 1560. This story is in its essentials the same as Boccaccio's, but it differs in a number of details. In the *Decameron* all the merchants present at the wager are Italian. In *Frederyke of Jennen* there are four rich merchants from divers countries—Spain, France, Florence, and Genoa. This explains why in the corresponding scene in *Cymbeline* there is a Frenchman, an Italian, a Dutchman, and a Spaniard —the last two being mute. There is no reason to suppose that there was a source-play in which the Dutchman and the Spaniard were given lines to speak. In *Frederyke of Jennen*, as in *Cymbeline*, the wager is first suggested by the villain, and the odds are even instead of five to one as they are in Boccaccio. The villain of the tale declares that he has lost the wager as soon as he sees the heroine;

---

[1] Cf. *W.T.* IV. iv. 772 ff.
[2] J. M. Nosworthy in his Arden *Cymbeline* has an excellent discussion of Shakespeare's use of this story.

she is told that the chest contains jewels and plate, and agrees to keep it in her own chamber; the villain, on seeing the mark on her body, realizes that this 'privy token' will be convincing evidence; on his return he claims to have won the bet in the presence only of the holder of the stakes; the servant sends a bloody cloth soaked in the blood of a lamb to show that he has killed Ambrose's wife; and Ambrose repents the murder of his wife before he knows she is innocent. In all these details, nine in all, which are all absent from the *Decameron*, Shakespeare follows the English tale. It is certain, therefore, that unless there is some intermediate source, combining the two versions, Shakespeare must have made use of both.

The joining of the wager story with *The Rare Triumphs of Love and Fortune*, in which the heroine is a Princess, and the linking of play and novel with Holinshed, meant that the atmosphere of the story is completely changed. In place of a middle-class story of a merchant's wife we have a story of a Princess.

In Shakespeare's manipulation of these heterogeneous materials there is no sign of the wearied artist of Granville-Barker's imagination. One might, indeed, complain of the dramatist's sheer virtuosity. He displays extraordinary ingenuity throughout the play, as for example in the way in which Imogen is made to awaken beside the body of the headless corpse in her husband's garments, or in the scene of the wager, where Posthumus is driven to make his fatal bet in such a way that it is difficult to imagine him doing anything else, or in the extraordinary final scene where no less than twenty-four knots are untied.

The theatrical virtuosity has been ascribed to the influence of Beaumont and Fletcher's work. Certainly, as Thorndike pointed out long ago,[1] there are many resemblances between *Philaster* and *Cymbeline*. In both plays there is a Princess who is destined by her father to marry a boorish suitor. Posthumus is contrasted with Cloten, as Philaster is contrasted with Pharamond. Both heroes are driven from Court and both denounce the female sex. Imogen and Arethusa both are lost in the wilds. Imogen, like Bellario, dresses as a page. Arethusa is wounded by Philaster, and Imogen is struck by Posthumus. In both plays the villains are forgiven. Bellario resembles Bellarius in name, and Imogen in character, though it should be mentioned that the heroine of *Pandosto*, the source of *The Winter's Tale*, is named Bellaria. Both wander in masculine

---

[1] A. H. Thorndike, *The Influence of Beaumont and Fletcher on Shakespeare* (1901); but see H. S. Wilson, *English Institute Essays* (1951/1952).

attire, suffer from fatigue, beg for food, and wish for death. Both plays contain pastoral scenes; and both were performed by the same company. The resemblance between the two plays extends to individual speeches: passages in praise of the pastoral life in the fourth act of *Philaster* resemble those in the third act of *Cymbeline*, and Philaster's self-accusation resembles that of Posthumus. There is also a striking verbal parallel between a passage in *Philaster* and one in *The Winter's Tale*.

But it is by no means certain that *Philaster* preceded *Cymbeline*. Shakespeare had already turned his back on tragedy in *Pericles*, and though *Philaster* may have been written as early as 1608 it may have been as late as 1610. As Shakespeare is generally thought to have written in collaboration with Fletcher it is unreasonable to deny that one dramatist influenced the other; and it is quite possible that they saw each other's work in manuscript. On the whole it seems probable that the young Fletcher was influenced by the older poet who had already turned from tragedy to romance and that he was quick to exploit the popularity of the new *genre*.

It may be said, however, that even if the technique of *Cymbeline* was not influenced by that of Fletcher there are signs that Shakespeare was exhausted as a poet. The play is full of echoes of his own earlier work, and the echo is always feebler than the original. But, as I have suggested elsewhere,[1] this characteristic of *Cymbeline* was not due to poetic exhaustion, but rather to Shakespeare's desire to gather up the strands of his past work and weave them into the pattern of his new vision. Iachimo recalls Iago in name and function, and Imogen's bed-chamber, with the sepulchral imagery used in the scene, recalls Desdemona's. Posthumus's bet recalls Collatine's boast of his wife's chastity, and there are other echoes of *Lucrece*, *Troilus and Cressida*, and *Julius Caesar*. Cleopatra is depicted on the walls of Imogen's bed-chamber, and her sultry and adulterous charms are contrasted with the chastity of the British heroine.[2] The pastoral scenes recall *As You Like It*. It looks almost as though Shakespeare were treating afresh several of the themes he had dealt with at different stages of his career, and considering them again in the light of his new intuitions on reconciliation and forgiveness. Posthumus, for example, forgives an Imogen he believes to be guilty.

Of course the play is an odd mixture. The material taken from

---

[1] K. Muir & Sean O'Loughlin, *The Voyage to Illyria* (1937), p. 216.
[2] II. ii. 12; II. iv. 70, 100–4.

British legendary history is vastly different in kind from the wager-story in the *Decameron* and *Frederyke of Jennen*; the masque-like Vision violently contrasts with the scenes in which the Roman legionaries appear; classical Rome is mingled with Renaissance Italy; and there are other extraordinary disparities. The play is, in one sense, a bridge between the English Histories and the Roman plays; in another sense it is a link between pastoral romance and tragedy. Shakespeare's task was rendered easier by the calculated anachronism in Renaissance art and Elizabethan literature as well as by a certain historical innocence. But it seems probable that the confusion of *genres* was deliberately designed to assist the creation of an imaginary world in which the poet's new symbolic method could have unrestricted scope. The interpenetration of opposites gave a moral significance to the romantic material and set free the wager-scenes from the restrictions of realism.[1]

(20) The Winter's Tale

The source material of *The Winter's Tale* forms a great contrast to that of *Cymbeline*. Instead of going to six different works, Shakespeare relied almost entirely on Greene's romance, *Pandosto*, published in 1588. There is evidence that he used this edition rather than that of 1607. Greene devotes some pages to an explanation of how Pandosto came to be jealous. Bellaria (Hermione) often went into Egistus's bed-chamber

> to see that nothing should be amis to mislike him. This honest familiarity increased dayly more and more betwixt them: for *Bellaria*, noting in *Egistus* a princely and bountifull minde, adorned with sundrie and excellent qualities, and *Egistus* finding in her a vertuous and curteous disposition, there grew such a secret vniting of their affections, that the one could not well be without the company of the other.

Not unnaturally Pandosto becomes jealous. Shakespeare gives Leontes no such excuse. Partly to save time, and partly to leave no doubt in the minds of the audience of Hermione's innocence, he begins the play with Leontes already jealous; and he makes Her-

[1] Cf. K. Muir, 'The Dramatic Function of Anachronism' in *Proc. Leeds Phil. and Lit. Soc.* (1951), pp. 529–33.

mione press Polixenes to stay in order to test his suspicions. This, at least, seems to be the most satisfactory way of playing the first scene.

Shakespeare follows the earlier part of the source fairly closely. Greene described how the guard was sent to arrest Bellaria:

comming to the Queenes lodging they found her playing with her yong sonne.

On this hint Shakespeare constructed the scene (II. i.) in which Mamillius begins his interrupted tale. But Leontes himself, not merely the guard, comes in to order Hermione's arrest.

In the novel it is Bellaria who appeals to the oracle. The contents, already known to the reader, are read out at the trial; Pandosto immediately recognizes its truth and forthwith repents. Word is brought that his son is dead, and Bellaria is killed by the news. This order of events is quite satisfactory in a prose narrative, but it lacks dramatic tension. Shakespeare realized that he would spoil Hermione's speech at the trial, in which she appeals to the oracle, if he allowed her to appeal to the oracle in a previous scene; so he made Leontes himself decide to send a deputation to Apollo's temple at Delphos in order to satisfy other people. The substance of the oracle is not known till it is read out at the trial, and the King immediately declares that there is no truth in it. News is brought that Mamillius has died, and we assume, as Leontes himself does, that this is a judgement from Apollo on account of his blasphemy. Hermione faints, and Pauline brings word that she is dead. Bellaria is indeed dead; but Hermione recovers, unknown to Leontes.

The only substantial passage in the novel which Shakespeare borrows with comparatively little alteration is Bellaria's speech at the trial:

If the deuine powers bee priuy to humane actions (as no doubt they are) I hope my patience shall make fortune blushe, and my vnspotted life shall staine spightful discredit. For although lying Report hath sought to appeach mine honor, and Suspition hath intended to soyle my credit with infamie: yet where Vertue keepeth the Forte, Report and suspition may assayle, but neuer sacke: how I haue led my life before *Egistus* comming, I appeale to the Gods and to thy conscience. What hath past betwixt him and me, the Gods only know, and I hope will presently reueale: that I loued *Egistus* I can not denie: that I

honored him I shame not to confesse: to the one I was forced
by his vertues, to the other for his dignities. But as touching
lasciuious lust, I say *Egistus* is honest, and hope my selfe to be
found without spot: for *Franion*, I can neither accuse him nor
excuse him, for I was not priuie to his departure, and that this is
true which I haue heere rehearsed, I referre myself to the deuine
Oracle.

Shakespeare uses nearly all this speech, though he expands it,
and breaks it up by inserting interruptions by Leontes:

> If Powres Diuine
> Behold our humane Actions (as they do)
> I doubt not then, but Innocence shall make
> False Accusation blush, and Tyrannie
> Tremble at Patience. You (my Lord) best know
> (Who least will seeme to doe so) my past life
> Hath beene as continent, as chaste, as true,
> As I am now vnhappy; which is more
> Than Historie can patterne, though deuis'd
> And play'd, to take Spectators. For behold me,
> A Fellow of the Royall Bed, which owe
> A Moitie of the Throne: a great Kings Daughter,
> The Mother to a hopefull Prince, here standing
> To prate and talke for Life, and Honor, fore
> Who please to come, and heare. For Life, I prize it
> As I weigh Grief (which I would spare:) For Honor,
> 'Tis a deriuatiue from me to mine,
> And onely that I stand for. I appeale
> To your own Conscience (Sir) before *Polixenes*
> Came to your Court, how I was in your grace,
> How merited to be so: Since he came,
> With what encounter so vncurrant, I
> Have strayn'd t'appeare thus; if one iot beyond
> The bound of Honor, or in act, or will
> That way enclining, hardned be the hearts
> Of all that heare me, and my neer'st of Kin
> Cry fie vpon my Graue.
>
> For *Polixenes*,
> (With whom I am accus'd) I doe confesse
> I lou'd him, as in Honor he requir'd:

With such a kind of Loue, as might become
A Lady like me; with a Loue, euen such,
So, and no other, as your selfe commanded:
Which, not to haue done, I thinke had been in me
Both Disobedience, and Ingratitude
To you, and toward your Friend, whose Loue had spoke,
Euen since it could speake, from an Infant, freely,
That it was yours. Now for Conspiracie,
I know not how it tastes, though it be dish'd
For me to try how: All I know of it,
Is, that *Camillo* was an honest man;
And why he left your Court, the Gods themselues,
(Wotting no more than I) are ignorant.
     Your Honors all,
I doe referre me to the Oracle:
Apollo be my Iudge.

In Greene's story the baby, Fawnia, is turned adrift in a boat; and this seems to have suggested the story of Miranda to Shakespeare:

He caused a little cock-boat to be prouided, wherein he meant to put the babe, and then send it to the mercies of the Seas and the destenies. . . . The guard . . . carried the child to the King, who, quite deuoide of pity, commanded that without delay it should bee put in the boat, hauing neither saile nor rudder to guid it, and so to bee carried into the midst of the sea, and there left to the wind and waue as the destinies pleased to appoint.

The baby is carried alone to the coast of Sicily. Shakespeare makes Leontes King of Sicilia instead of Bohemia; and Perdita is deposited by Antigonus on the coast of Bohemia, where Polixenes is King. Possibly the first version of *The Tempest* had been written before *The Winter's Tale*, so that Shakespeare could not easily repeat the incident of the babe adrift in a boat. But in any case he must have felt that it would be hard for the audience to believe that a newly-born infant would survive under such circumstances, and it was stretching coincidence very far to make the winds and currents carry the bark to the precise spot the plot required her to be. Not that Shakespeare was unaware of the absurdities of the story; but he prepared the audience for them by laughing at them himself. The disposal of Antigonus, devoured by a bear, is described in absurd terms by the clown. As Mr Bethell points out,[1] Shakespeare was deliberately using an antiquated technique. The antiquity of the story is 'pressed home by the employment of out-moded technique'. By the use of exaggerated conventions and by continual reminders that the play is a play—'like an old tale', as we are told more than once—Shakespeare 'forbids absorption in the action', so that we can 'observe the subtle interplay of a whole world of interrelated ideas'. Mr Bethell also suggests that the antiquated technique is 'not only a means of commanding a special sort of attention, but is also in itself a statement about the nature of reality'. We are not meant, therefore, to be particularly perturbed by the exit of Antigonus, pursued by a bear. 'Gentlemen usually dine upon animals', says Mr Bethell, 'but now the bear will dine upon the gentleman.'[2]

Mr Bethell also suggests that Shakespeare was aware that Bohemia lacked a coastline, since there are contemporary jokes on the subject, and that he followed Greene's mistake deliberately, in order to indicate that the action of the play was taking place not in the actual Bohemia, but in a kind of Arcadia. Sterne's famous chapter in *Tristram Shandy* should prevent us from considering the matter too curiously.[3] But it may be worth mentioning that in Emmanual Ford's *Famous and pleasant History of Parismus, the valiant and renowned Prince of Bohemia* (1597) there is also a coast of Bohemia. In this novel a child is abandoned to the mercy of a nurse, who flies with it into the wilderness, and is eventually devoured by a lion. It has been suggested, too, that Shakespeare may have located the first part of the play in Sicily because Hermione, like Ceres, was Queen of Sicily, and because he wished to reinforce the Perdita–Persephone parallel implicit throughout the play.[4]

Greene describes the finding of Fawnia in words closely echoed by Shakespeare:

It fortuned a poore mercenary Sheepheard . . . missed one of his sheepe, and thinking it had strayed into the couert, that was hard by, sought very diligently to find that which he could not see, fearing either that the Wolues, or Eagles had vndone him . . . wandered downe toward the Sea cliffes, to see if perchaunce the sheepe was browsing on the sea Iuy, whereon they greatly doe feede.

[1] S. L. Bethell, *The Winter's Tale* (1947), pp. 47 ff.
[2] Bethell, op. cit., p. 65.   [3] *Tristram Shandy*, VIII. xix.
[4] Cf. E. Honigmann, *P.Q.* (1955), pp. 27–38.

So the Shepherd in *The Winter's Tale* complains that the hunters

> haue scar'd away two of my best Sheepe, which I feare the
> Wolfe will sooner finde than the Maister: if anywhere I haue
> them, 'tis by the sea-side, brouzing of Iuy.

Greene mentions a proposal to wed Dorastus (Florizel) to the daughter of the King of Denmark, and Shakespeare omits this as irrelevant to his purpose.

The sheep-shearing feast, of which Fawnia is the mistress, is mentioned in *Pandosto*, but it takes place before her meeting with Dorastus. By presenting the lovers at the feast, by introducing Polixenes and Camillo in disguise, and by confronting Florizel with his father, Shakespeare greatly increases the dramatic effectiveness of the story. In *Pandosto*, the original cupbearer who had helped Egistus to escape has faded from the story, and Dorastus and Fawnia have to reach Bohemia by another accident. In the play, Camillo's desire to return to his native land provides a reasonable motive for his help of the two lovers. In *Pandosto*, the old shepherd, going to the palace to inform the King of the circumstances of his discovery of Fawnia, is kidnapped and taken to Bohemia with the lovers. In the play, the shepherd and his son are lured to the ship by Autolycus, and Camillo tells the King of the lovers' escape.

In the novel, the fugitives are arrested as spies; and Pandosto, falling in love with his own daughter, promises to free Dorastus if she will yield to him. In the play Leontes receives the lovers with courtesy and affection, and promises to be their advocate with Polixenes. Shakespeare would probably have avoided the incest motive in any case; but nothing could better show his obsession with the themes of forgiveness and restoration than the way in which he transforms the ending of the story. Pandosto kills himself; but Hermione is restored and Leontes forgiven.

It has been suggested that Hermione's resurrection may have been derived from the Alcestis story, or from that of Pygmalion. Both are given in Pettie's *Palace of Pleasure*; Marston had told the Pygmalion story in verse; and it is also to be found in Ovid's *Metamorphoses*.[1] Most probably the 'resurrection' is a blending of

[1] There are, however, no verbal echoes of Ovid in the resurrection scene. E. Honigmann suggests (*op. cit.*) that the statue scene may have been influenced by *Amadis de Gaule*, ix, from which Shakespeare may well have taken the names of Florisel and Perdita. (It may be mentioned here that the name of Autolycus is to be found in Ovid and Homer; Antigonus is in Plutarch. These characters, as well as Paulina and the Shepherd's Son, were added by Shakespeare.)

the Pygmalion story with some folk-tale in which a lover's kiss revives a sleeping beauty. It may be mentioned that in *The Tryall of Chevalry* (1605) Ferdinand, supposed dead, poses as his own statue.

A number of critics have pointed out how Shakespeare greatly improved the loose structure of Greene's novel. By his alterations he was able to bring together all the main characters in the last scene of the play. Polixenes's pursuit of the lovers enables him to be reconciled to Leontes, and Leontes to Hermione, and Perdita reunited to her parents; whereas in the novel, after Pandosto's recognition of Fawnia they all have to embark together to pay Egistus a visit.

Several passages in *Pandosto* were closely echoed in the play. Some of these echoes are in the corresponding context, as when Dorastus soliloquizes:

> And yet *Dorastus*, shame not at thy shepheard's weede. The heauenly Gods have sometime earthly thoughtes. *Neptune* became a Ram, *Iupiter* a Bul, *Apollo* a shepheard: they Gods, and yet in loue: and thou a man appointed to loue.

Shakespeare, anxious to avoid the insipidities of pastoral, inserts in the corresponding speech, spoken not in soliloquy but to Perdita, a few touches of rather grotesque realism:

> The Goddes themselues
> (Humbling their Deities to loue) haue taken
> The shapes of Beasts vpon them: Iupiter
> Became a Bull, and bellow'd: the greene Neptune
> A Ram, and bleated: and the Fire-roab'd God,
> Golden Apollo, a poore humble Swaine,
> As I seeme now.

This speech, as Mr Honigmann has pointed out,[1] also echoes a passage in Francis Sabie's blank verse poem derived from *Pandosto*, *The Fisshermans Tale* (1595):

> Loue conquers all things: it hath conquered
> *Apollo* once, it made him be a swaine.
> Yea mightie *Mars* in armes inuincible,
> It forced hath to lay aside his speare,

[1] IV. iv. 27. Honigmann thinks, too, that Antigonus's dream of Hermione and the storm in the same scene (III. iii.) may owe something to Sabie (B2ʳB3ʳD4ʳE1ʳE2ʳ) and that two passages in IV. iii. (109–10, 55–6) may be derived from Sabie too (C3ʳD2ʳ).

> Loue made the sea-god take a Wesils shape,
> Yea mightie *Ioue*, whose rage makes earth to shake,
> Loue made to take the snow-white shape of Bull.

In two or three respects, though not in most, Shakespeare is closer to Sabie than he is to Greene.

The most interesting echoes from *Pandosto* are those which appear in a different context in the play. When Paulina attacks Leontes's courtiers for their spineless time-serving:[1]

> 'Tis such as you,
> That creepe like shadowes by him, and do sighe
> At each his needlesse heauings: such as you
> Nourish the cause of his awaking—

Shakespeare borrowed a phrase from a description of the effect of the Queen's death on the common people—'they went like shadowes, not men'. And when Leontes decides that it is impossible to keep wives chaste[2]—

> Be it concluded,
> No Barricado for a Belly. Know't;
> It will let in and out the Enemy,
> With bag and baggage.

he borrows a phrase describing the sudden flight of Egistus—

> For *Egistus*, fearing that delay might breede danger . . . taking bagge and baggage, by the helpe of *Franion* conueied himselfe and his men out at a posterne gate of the Cittie.

There are more verbal echoes from *Pandosto* than from any other novel used by Shakespeare as a source.

As mentioned above, Mr Honigmann has shown that Shakespeare was slightly indebted to *The Fisshermans Tale* and its continuation, *Flora's Fortune*. His title, and the remark of Mamillius 'A sad Tale's best for Winter', may be derived from Sabie's confession that he wrote his book to expel 'the acoustomed tediousnes of colde winters nightes'. Pandosto sends six messengers to Apollo's temple after Fawnia has been exposed; in *Flora's Fortune* and *The Winter's Tale* two are sent before Perdita (Flora) is born. Greene speaks of the 'loude voice' of the oracle; Sabie speaks of 'thundering voyces'; and Shakespeare mentions

> the eare-deaff'ning Voyce o' th' Oracle,
> Kin to Ioues Thunder.

[1] II. iii. 33 ff.   [2] I. ii. 203 ff.

247

Sabie uses the conventional image:

> And as a Turtle Doue, when she hath lost
> Her louing mate, so seem'd he to lament . . .

And Paulina at the end of the play uses the same image:

> I (an old *Turtle*)
> Will wing me to some wither'd bough, and there
> My Mate (that's neuer to be found againe)
> *Lament*, till I am *lost*.

It should be added that, though Flora is mentioned by Greene, the name of Sabie's heroine may have suggested Florizel's lines

> no Shepherdesse, but *Flora*
> Peering in Aprils front.

In the scenes in Bohemia Shakespeare recreates a lost world of innocence, which is prevented from being unreal or sentimental by the introduction of Autolycus, 'the snapper-vp of vnconsidered trifles', who might have stepped out of any of the pamphlets by Greene or Dekker, exposing the iniquities of the criminal underworld; and one of whose tricks does in fact come from one of Greene's coney-catching pamphlets written nearly twenty years previously. Greene mentions that the singing of ballads

> is nothing els but a sly fetch to draw many togeather, who listning vnto an harmelesse dittie, afterwarde walke home to their houses with heauie hearts.

He gives an example[1] of how two rogues

> got vpon a stal singing of balets which belike was some pretty toy, for very many gathered about to heare it, and diuers buying, as their affections serued, drew to their purses and paid the singers for them. . . . Counterfeit warning was sundrie times giuen by the rogue and his associate, to beware of the cut pursse, and looke to their pursses, which made them often feel where their pursses were, either in sleeue, hose, or at girdle, to know whether they were safe or no. Thus the craftie copesmates were acquainted with what they most desired, and as they were scattered, by shouldring, thrusting, feigning to let fall something, and other wilie tricks fit for their purpose: heere one lost his purse, there another had his pocket pickt.

[1] R. Greene, *Third Part of Conny-Catching* (1923), p. 27.

Another of the cony-catching pamphlets describes two more of Autolycus's tricks—the stealing of linen, and the robbing of the Shepherd's son; and Greene's account of the qualities necessary for the successful pick-pocket are echoed by Shakespeare's rogue.[1] It is curious that Shakespeare should be able to combine in a single play the two totally different kinds of work written by Greene—the romantic, unrealistic novel and the sordid documentaries of the seamy side of Elizabethan London.

The discussion about grafting, which introduces Perdita's flower catalogue is, as Mr Wilson Knight has shown,[2] a microcosm of the whole play. It is a discussion on 'great creating Nature'. The cultivated flowers are contrasted with the natural flowers of the countryside, just as Perdita's world is contrasted with the world of the court, and just as Sicily is contrasted with Bohemia. Polixenes, in arguing the case for grafting, is unconsciously justifying the marriage of his son to the country maiden:

> You see (sweet Maid) we marry
> A gentler scion to the wildest Stocke,
> And make conceyue a barke of baser kinde
> By bud of Nobler race. This is an Art
> Which do's mend Nature: change it rather, but
> The Art it selfe is Nature.

The discussion of the relative importance of art and nature is often found in Elizabethan literature. It has been argued that Shakespeare had a more profound conception than Bacon. But it is possible that he was echoing a discussion by Puttenham in *The Arte of English Poesie* about the relative importance of nature and art in poetry.[3] Puttenham argues that art in some cases is 'an ayde and coadiutor to nature' or

> a meane to supply her wants, by re-enforcing the causes wherein shee is impotent and defectiue.

He goes on to compare the artist or poet with the gardener:

> In another respect arte is not only an aide and coadiutor to nature in all her actions, but an alterer of them, and in some sort a surmounter of her skill, so as by meanes of it her owne effects

---

[1] Cf. *W.T.* ed. Q and J. D. Wilson, p. xxii and notes on IV. iii. 20, IV. iii. 23, IV. iv. 592, 665, 678.
[2] G. W. Knight, *The Crown of Life* (1947), pp. 104 ff.
[3] H. S. Wilson, *S.A.B.* (July 1943), pp. 114-20.

shall appear more beautifull or straunge and miraculous, as in both cases before remembred. . . . And the Gardiner by his arte will not onely make an herbe, or flowr, or fruite, come forth in his season without impediment, but also will embellish the same in vertue, shape, odour and taste, that nature of her selfe woulde neuer haue done: as to make single gillifloure, or marigold, or daisie, double: and the white rose, redde, yellow, or carnation, a bitter mellon sweete, a sweete apple, soure, a plumme or cherrie without a stone, a peare without core or kernell, a goord or coucumber like a horne, or any other figure he will: any of which things nature could not doe without mans help and arte. These actions also are most singular, when they be most artificiall.

Puttenham goes on to justify that which

A Poet makes by arte and precepts rather than by naturall instinct: and that which he doth by long meditation rather than by a suddaine inspiration.

It is not certain whether Shakespeare was recalling Puttenham in this scene; but there can be no doubt that in the reference to Proserpine he was echoing Golding's translation of Ovid.[1]

While in this garden *Proserpine* was taking her pastime,
In gathering eyther violets blew, or lillies white as lime . . .
Dis spide her: lou'd her: caught her vp . . .
The ladie with a wailing voyce afright did often call . . .
And as she from the vpper part her garment would haue rent,
By chance she let hir lap slip downe, and out the flowers went.

So Perdita, distributing flowers, invokes her:

O *Proserpina*,
For the Flowres now, that (frighted) thou let'st fall
From *Dysses* Waggon: Daffadils,
That come before the Swallow dares, and take
The windes of March with beauty: Violets (dim,
But sweeter than the lids of *Iuno's* eyes,
Or *Cytherea's* breath); pale Prime-roses,
That dye vnmarried, ere they can behold
Bright Phoebus in his strength (a Maladie
Most incident to Maids:) bold Oxlips, and

[1] V. 398 ff.

The Crowne Imperiall: Lillies of all kinds,
(The Flowre-de-Luce being one). O, these I lacke,
To make you Garlands of: and my sweet friend,
To strew him o're and o're.

One curious point is worth adding. There is some slight evidence that there was an earlier version of the play in which Hermione was not resurrected. Simon Forman, who saw the play on 15 May 1611, makes no mention of this incident, and, though he gives garbled versions of other plays, the omission of all reference to the climax of the play is somewhat strange. There is no instance in all Shakespeare's plays of a living person appearing in a vision, though Hermione appears to Antigonus at the end of Act III. Finally, it has been suggested[1] that Autolycus was intended to play some part in the discovery of Perdita's birth, but as the play stands his presence in Act V is unnecessary to the plot. These last two points could, however, be explained by the assumption that Shakespeare changed his mind in the course of composition.

[1] J. E. Bullard, W. M. Fox, *T.L.S.* (1952), p. 189.

❴ IX ❵

CONCLUSION

As the Histories remain to be discussed, it is possible at this stage to offer only provisional conclusions. It would be rash to make any large generalizations. It cannot be said, for example, that Shakespeare never invented a plot, as that of *Love's Labour's Lost*, at least, may have been his own invention. Nor can it be maintained that he invariably used an earlier play, though Mr G. A. Greer has tried to show[1] that for twenty-two of his plays Shakespeare made use of an earlier play, and that for two only of his plays has no source-play been suggested. Mr Greer plausibly argues that whenever possible Shakespeare used translations, and much less plausibly, that he may not have been able to read Italian, French, Greek, or Latin. This extreme view is, I believe, quite untenable. No one denies that Shakespeare did make use of translations, though there is no doubt that he could read Latin, French, and Italian, if not Greek. How else can we account for his reading of Buchanan, his use of apparently untranslated Italian works, the French scenes of *Henry V*? Professor Baldwin rightly disclaims any responsibility for the idea that Shakespeare was a learned man;[2] but readers of his several volumes will allow that the poet absorbed a fair amount of education.

No one disputes that for five of his plays (*Measure for Measure*, *Henry IV*, *Henry V*, and *King Lear*) Shakespeare made some use of an earlier play; but it is certain that even for these he used other sources as well. There is not a single play that can be shown to have merely a dramatic source, though it may be admitted that the loss of so many Elizabethan plays makes it possible to argue that all, or nearly all, Shakespeare's plays may have had a dramatic source.

It would be satisfying to be able to show that just as Shakespeare's work falls into several periods in respect of versification, characterization, and imagery, so in respect of sources it shows a

---

[1] *N.Q.* (1955), p. 479.
[2] T. W. Baldwin, 'On Atomizing Shakespeare', *Shakespeare Jahrbuch*, xci (1955), pp. 136–44.

characteristic development, from the simple to the complex, or from the complex to the simple. But there is nothing to support such a theory. Although *The Two Gentlemen of Verona* may be based solely on an earlier play, another comedy of Shakespeare's first period, *The Comedy of Errors*, combines several different sources in a way which, from the point of view of construction, would be worthy of his maturity. Some of his mature comedies—*The Merchant of Venice*, *Twelfth Night*, *Measure for Measure*—have a variety of sources; but *As You Like It* and *All's Well that Ends Well* appear to have only one. Of the great tragedies, two have many sources; but *Othello*, though it displays a wealth of background material, has only one source for its plot, and *Hamlet* may be based on the source-play alone. *Antony and Cleopatra* has five or six sources; *Coriolanus*, apart from Menenius's fable, has only one. In his last period Shakespeare uses many sources with *Cymbeline*, and few with *The Winter's Tale*.

It seems probable that more sources will eventually be discovered, though such discoveries are unlikely to lead to radical modifications of our knowledge of Shakespeare's methods of work. He naturally followed the methods of imitation which he had learnt at school, and his genius was displayed more in the imaginative fusion of details from different sources than in pure invention in the modern sense. How conscious the process of fusion was must remain a matter of opinion. He may conceivably have had several books before him as he wrote, or he may have relied on his unconscious mind to perform the act of fusion. At times, as when in *The Winter's Tale* he versifies Bellaria's defence or in *Henry VIII* the defence of Katherine, we may be fairly sure that *Pandosto* or Holinshed was actually before him. In those passages there is no fusion of sources, but the close imitation of a single one. More often, however, Shakespeare appears to rely on his memory. In the passage quoted in the last chapter (p. 246) the fusion of Greene and Sabie could hardly have been a conscious process. He is not likely to have been aware of his echoes of Nashe's *Pierce Penilesse* in the fourth scene of *Hamlet*. Still less can he have been aware of the biblical echoes in *Macbeth*, or of the echoes from Horace and Harsnett in *King Lear*. There are, nevertheless, some linked echoes from passages which were linked also in such compilations as Erasmus's *Adagia*, and it may be assumed that in such cases Shakespeare amplified his material by referring to such a work.

Professor T. W. Baldwin has given examples of the way in which Shakespeare organized his dramatic material so as to conform with Terentian five-act structure, but this aspect of his dramatic craftsmanship must be reserved for the second volume.

Meanwhile it should be emphasized that the study of Shakespeare's sources is no substitute for criticism. I have been asked more than once what use it is to know the raw materials from which Shakespeare constructed his plays. Does not such study lead us away from the plays as dramatic masterpieces? The answer must be, I think, that the sources throw relatively little light on the finished plays, though now and again, when the interpretation of a passage is disputable, the knowledge of a source may show us which interpretation is the more likely—e.g. with the incident of Cleopatra's treasure. There are other occasions when the knowledge that Shakespeare deviated from his known sources will cause us to ask questions which may lead us to a true interpretation of the play. But apart from such a limited use of source-study as an adjunct to criticism, it may be justified on wider grounds. Anything which throws light, however dim, on Shakespeare's craftsmanship or on his methods of composition is not without interest, and stands in no need of defence.

SUMMARY

Play	Main Source	Subsidiary Sources	Discussion
The Comedy of Errors	Menaechmi (Plautus)	Amphitruo (Plautus) Menaphon (Greene) Acts xix Supposes (Gascoigne) Patterne of Painefull Aduentures (Twine)	p. 18
The Two Gentlemen of Verona	Lost play?		p. 259
The Taming of the Shrew	Lost play?	Supposes (Gascoigne)?	p. 259
Titus Andronicus	Play by Peele?	Metamorphoses (Ovid)? Thyestes (Seneca)?	p. 258
Love's Labour's Lost	Not known		p. 258
Romeo and Juliet	Romeus and Juliet (Brooke)	Lost play? La Hadriana (Groto)? The Palace of Pleasure (Painter) Giulietta e Romeo (da Porto)?	p. 21
A Midsummer-Night's Dream	Not known	'The Knight's Tale' 'The Merchant's Tale' The Legend of Good Women Plutarch's Lives (North) Diana (Montemayor) Metamorphoses (Ovid) Apuleius' Golden Ass (tr. Adlington) A Gorgious Gallery of Gallant Inventions A Handful of Pleasant Delites Of the Silkewormes, and their Flies (Mouffet)	p. 31
The Merchant of Venice	Il Pecorone	The Orator (Silvayn, tr. L. Piot) Zelauto (Munday) Gesta Romanorum (tr. Robinson) The Jew of Malta (Marlowe) Lost play?	p. 47
Much Ado about Nothing	Lost play?	Bandello? The Faerie Queene? The Courtier (Castiglione)? Orlando Furioso (Ariosto)? The Rocke of Regard (Whetstone)?	p. 52
As You Like It	Rosalynde (Lodge)		p. 55

Play	Main Source	Subsidiary Sources	Discussion
The Merry Wives of Windsor	Lost play?		p. 259
Julius Caesar	Plutarch's *Lives* (tr. North)	*Caesar's Revenge* *Cornelia* (Kyd) Appian's *Civil Wars* (tr. W.B.)	p. 187
Twelfth Night	Riche *His Farewell to Militarie Profession*	*Gl'Inganni* (Gonzaga)? *Gl'Inganni* (Secchi)? *L'Interesse* (Secchi)? *Gl'Ingannati*? Bandello?	p. 66
Troilus and Cressida	*Troilus and Criseyde* (Chaucer)	*The Testament of Cresseid* (Henryson) *Recuyell of the Historyes of Troy* (Caxton) *Troy Book* (Lydgate) *Euphues his Censure to Philautus* (Greene) *Iliad* (tr. Chapman)	p. 78
All's Well that Ends Well	*The Palace of Pleasure* (Painter)? *Decameron*?	*On Nobility* (Nenna)?	p. 97
Measure for Measure	*Promos and Cassandra* (Whetstone)	*Heptameron of Civil Discourses* (Whetstone) *Hecatommithi* (Giraldi) *Epitia* (Giraldi) *Siuquila* (Lupton)?	p. 101
Hamlet	Lost Play	*Histoires Tragiques* (Belleforest)? *A Treatise of Melancholy* (Bright) *Dido* (Marlowe) *Pierce Penilesse* (Nashe)	p. 110 p. 10
Othello	*Hecatommithi* (Giraldi)	Pliny's *Natural History* (tr. Holland) Contareno's *The Commonwealth and Gouernment of Venice* (tr. Lewkenor)	p. 122
King Lear	*King Leir*	*Chronicles* (Holinshed) *The Mirror for Magistrates* *The Faerie Queene* *Arcadia* (Sidney) *Declaration of Egregious Popishe Impostures* (Harsnett)	p. 141
Macbeth	*Chronicles* (Holinshed)	*Tres Sibyllae* (Gwinn)? Boece's *Chronicles* (tr. Bellenden)? *Rerum Scoticarum Historia* (Buchanan) *De Origine....* (Leslie) *Daemonologie* (James I) *Hercules Furens, Agamemnon* (Seneca)	p. 167

Play	Main Source	Subsidiary Sources	Dis-cussion
Timon of Athens	Lost play?	Plutarch's *Lives* (tr. North) *Timone* (Boiardo)? *Timon* (Lucian)?	p. 260
Antony and Cleo-patra	Plutarch's *Lives* (North)	*Antonius* (Garnier, tr. Countess of Pembroke) *Cleopatra* (Daniel) *Letter from Octavia* (Daniel) Appian's *Civil Wars* (tr. W.B.) *Revelation*	p. 201
Coriolanus	Plutarch's *Lives* (North)	*Defence of Poesie* (Sidney) Livy (tr. Holland) *Remaines* (Camden) *A Meruailous Combat of Contrarieties* (Averell)	p. 219
Pericles	Lost play?	*Patterne of Painefull Aduentures* (Twine) *Confessio Amantis* (Gower)	p. 225
Cymbeline	*Decameron* (Boccaccio)	*Frederyke of Jennen* *The Rare Triumphs of Love and For-tune* *The Faerie Queene* *The Mirror for Magistrates* *Chronicles* (Holinshed)	p. 231
The Winter's Tale	*Pandosto* (Greene)	*The Fisshermans Tale* (Sabie) *Coney-Catching* pamphlets (Greene)	p. 240
The Tempest	Not known	Accounts of Bermudas shipwreck *Metamorphoses* (Ovid) and Gold-ing's translation *The Rare Triumphs of Love and Fortune*	p. 260 p. 3

257

APPENDIX

SEVEN plays, of which the sources are not precisely known, remain to be discussed. Some readers may think that *Much Ado about Nothing*, *Hamlet*, and *Pericles* should have been relegated to this appendix, since the main sources of these plays are presumably lost; but the advantages of discussing them in their chronological position seemed to outweigh the disadvantages.

(1) *Titus Andronicus*

It is generally supposed that some scenes of the play are not Shakespeare's, or not wholly his. George Peele, for example, may have collaborated with Shakespeare, or have written a play which Shakespeare revised. An eighteenth century chapbook, entitled *The History of Titus Andronicus*, may be substantially the same as the source of the play. Ralph M. Sargent (*S.P.*, 1949, p. 167) thinks that the entry in S.R. (1594) refers to this rather than the play. As the play is not likely to have been written as late as this, we should have to assume it was based on an earlier version of the prose account. The ballad published with the prose is influenced by the play. The eighteenth-century title-page says that it is 'newly translated from the Italian', and, as J. C. Maxwell suggests, the original story may have come from Italy. There does not appear to be any Elizabethan phraseology in the chapbook version. Sargent compares it with the play and outlines the changes made by Shakespeare if this was his source. It is clear that the author or authors of the play also used Seneca's *Thyestes* and Ovid's *Metamorphoses*.

(2) *Love's Labour's Lost*

Although a number of vague analogues have been found, it seems likely that the rather tenuous plot of *Love's Labour's Lost* was substantially Shakespeare's invention. The play may be influenced by contemporary French history, by the *commedia dell'arte*, by the Gray's Inn Revels, and by Lyly's *Endimion* and *Gallathea*. The play appears to contain a great deal of topical satire, perhaps of Ralegh, Chapman, Florio, and Harvey, though the details are still a matter of controversy.

(3) *The Two Gentlemen of Verona*

The ultimate source of the play was Montemayor's *Diana* which Shakespeare could have read in a French translation (1578). In this Felix is sent to a foreign court, to prevent his marrying Felismena. She follows him, dressed as a man, and finds that he is wooing Celia. She becomes his page and is sent with a letter to Celia, who falls in love with the messenger. Celia dies, and Felix and Felismena eventually marry. A lost play, *Felix and Philiomena*, was performed in 1585, and this may have been Shakespeare's main or only source. It seems probable, though we cannot be sure, that it was Shakespeare who introduced into the story the rivalry between the two gentlemen; but as the exact contents of the lost play cannot be known it is impossible to discuss Shakespeare's use of his sources.

(4) *The Taming of the Shrew*

The Taming of the Shrew may be derived from *The Taming of a Shrew*: this, until recently, was the orthodox view. It has been argued, on the other hand, that *A Shrew* is a kind of 'bad quarto' of *The Shrew*. According to a third theory, which I incline to accept, both plays were derived from a common original. There are objections to all three theories. If Shakespeare's play was based on *A Shrew*, it is odd that there is so little verbal reminiscence of the source. *A Shrew*, moreover, has at least one characteristic of a bad quarto: it incorporates passages of Marlowe's plays. If, on the other hand, *A Shrew* is merely a piratical version of *The Shrew*, it is equally strange that there are not more verbal links between the two plays. Professor Peter Alexander thinks that it is superfluous to posit a third play, as the 'minor confusions in *The Shrew*' are 'not of a kind to warrant the creation of a completely unknown play to explain them'. It is not the place to support any of these theories here, and still less to propound a new one. Some critics, moreover, regard the Bianca scenes, based on Ariosto's *I Suppositi* or on Gascoigne's *Supposes*, as un-Shakespearian. The state of our knowledge is such that it would be unprofitable to discuss the question of sources.

(5) *The Merry Wives of Windsor*

Even if we discount the legend that the play was written in a fortnight in response to a royal command, it may nevertheless have been adapted from a lost play, by Porter or another. The lost play entitled *The Jealous Comedy* (1593) has been put forward as a possible source; and so have stories in Tarlton's *Newes out of Purgatory* (1590) and in *Il Pecorone* (1558), one of the sources of *The Merchant of Venice*. In the present state of our knowledge it is useless to pursue the matter further.

(6) *Timon of Athens*

Professor G. Bonnard has argued (*Études Anglaises*, 1954, pp. 59–69) that the academic play *Timon* and Shakespeare's play were both derived from an earlier play now lost. The use of 'banditti' and 'solidares' suggests that there may have been an Italian source, perhaps, as R. Warwick Bond believed, Boiardo's *Timone*. (Cf. *Studia Otiosa*, 1938, pp. 75 ff.) Bonnard has pointed to the indirect influence of the *Arabian Nights*, for Timon's banquet. Shakespeare certainly went directly to North's translation of Plutarch's lives of Antony and Alcibiades, and directly or indirectly to Lucian's *Timon*. He probably knew Painter's version of the story, and other sources have been suggested. Some scholars believe that Shakespeare had a collaborator, and others that he left the play unfinished. As I believe that there may have been a dramatic source, the detailed discussion of sources is hardly possible.

(7) *The Tempest*

Various analogues have been discovered for the plot of *The Tempest*, but none which can reasonably be regarded as a direct source. Warton recorded that William Collins informed him (erroneously) that the plot of the play was to be found in *Aurelia and Isabella*. It is possible that Collins really had read the source of *The Tempest* but had failed to remember the actual title. Neither Ayrer's *Die Schöne Sidea*, nor Eslava's *Noches de Invierno* (1609), nor even Calahorra's *Espejo de Principes y Caballeros* (1562; translated later) —though all three have points in common with *The Tempest*—is likely to have been its source. Some have thought that the play may be based on *scenari* of the *Commedia dell'Arte*, but, as Mr Kermode points out, the 'extant *scenari* post-date Shakespeare'.

Although the main source of *The Tempest* has not been discovered, some books known to Shakespeare have left their mark on the play. From *The Rare Triumphs of Love and Fortune* Shakespeare took a few minor details, as we have seen in discussing *Cymbeline* (p. 232 *ante*). He recalled some details of the *Æneid*, as Mr J. M. Nosworthy has shown (*R.E.S.*, 1948, pp. 281–4), and other details of the *Metamorphoses* (cf. p. 3 *ante*). He may have recalled one of Erasmus's *Colloquies*—the *Naufragium*—available in William Burton's translation. Gonzalo's ideal commonwealth is the one undisputed borrowing from Florio's translation of Montaigne's essays. But Shakespeare owed more to books of voyages. From Eden's *History of Travaille* (1577) he derived the name of the god Setebos, and possibly Alonso, Sebastian, Antonio, Ferdinand, and Gonzalo. More significant are the borrowings from pamphlets concerned with the Bermudas shipwreck. Jourdain's *Discovery of the Bermudas*, the Council of Virginia's *True Declaration* (1610), and William Strachey's *True Reportory*, all provided Shakespeare with background information. Strachey's letter was not published until 1625 in *Purchas His Pilgrimes*; but there is some evidence that Shakespeare knew Strachey personally, and as Sir Dudley Digges was the stepson of Thomas Russell, Shakespeare's executor, the poet could have obtained inside information about the shipwreck from this source. There were, therefore, a number of minor sources of *The Tempest*, but it is highly probable that there was a main source as yet unidentified.

INDEX

263